UNLIKELY WARRIOR

MEMOIRS OF A VIETNAM COMBAT MEDIC

C. Michael Dingman

xulon PRESS

DEDICATION

Dedicated to the American grunts, the boots on the ground, who have defended our nation's freedom since its inception, but especially to the men of 1st Platoon, Delta Co., 3rd Battalion, 506th Infantry 1970 and to all the Currahees who walked the jungle trails of Vietnam and Cambodia with me, who faced the fear of night and longed for the morning light. Welcome home, my brothers!

ACKNOWLEDGMENTS

My sincere thanks to my Platoon Leader, Richard Greig, for the many hours spent in conversation helping me recall events and details I had long ago forgotten, for giving me permission to use some of his pictures and for reading and editing my book; to John Nauman, Tom Landers, Ken Wydeven, and others too numerous to mention for sharing with me details I could never have known without them; to Tom Landers for allowing me to use some of his pictures; to my son-in-law and daughter, Christopher and Amy Rush, for editing my book and making many helpful suggestions; to Larry Keith, a retired Navy officer who also made editorial and technical suggestions, and to my pastor and colleague, Dr. Angus McDonald, who encouraged me to finish writing my story, a project I had begun many years before and might never have finished without his gentle prodding.

TABLE OF CONTENTS

INTRODUCTION

"Only be careful, and watch yourselves closely
so that you do not forget the things your eyes have seen
or let them slip from your heart as long as you live.
Teach them to your children and to your children after them."
Deuteronomy 4:9

Another hot, humid night in Vietnam. I can hardly believe I have been called back to serve another year in Vietnam with my old infantry unit, the famed 506th Infantry from which came the Band of Brothers in WWII. The triple canopy jungle is dense with foliage, the darkness so thick you can almost cut it with a knife. The Viet Cong, who have fought in these jungles for decades, would like nothing better than to score a major victory against the Americans tonight. Movement can be heard on our platoon's perimeter. Every man's senses are heightened, adrenalin flowing through their veins as they wait for the inevitable. "Pop! Swish," a trip flare is ignited, lighting up the jungle with blinding brilliance. Viet Cong seem to be everywhere! Claymore mines are set off, massive explosions thundering, "K-BOOM! K-BOOM!" and then again, "KABOOM!" A wall of steel pellets and shrapnel cut through the front line of the approaching enemy. Hot volleys of fire fill the air as more of the enemy move forward, AK-47s cracking with their high pitched "ak-ak-ak." M-16s and M-60 machine-guns answer back from our own positions, pouring hot led into the surrounding jungle. "Grenade!" someone yells, as a chicom flies through the air into our perimeter, bouncing on the ground twice before exploding with a massive bang, causing my ears to ring and my head to throb as shrapnel and dirt fly in all directions. "Medic! Medic!" someone cries off to my left, and then again, "Medic! Medic!" from yet another direction.

"What am I to do?" I think. "Who should I help first, and how can I reach them without getting myself killed?" My heart races as I grab my aid bag and begin to crawl through the thick darkness, interrupted by flashes of light from exploding grenades. Then it happens. A grenade lands not far from me and explodes with roaring thunder. Shrapnel tears through the flesh in my back, burning as it burrows deep into my body! "Ahhhhhhh!" I scream, writhing in pain.

"Wake up! Wake up!" I hear my wife say, as my mind struggles to pull itself from the dreadful nightmare. Sweat pours from my head and body. My pillow and the sheet beneath me are soaked. "You're having another nightmare!" my wife says. "Wake up!" Even after I wake up, it is difficult to separate reality from fantasy. "Where am I?" I wonder. Had I really gone back to Vietnam a second time, or was my mind simply playing tricks on me? The dream is so real I feel almost certain I had been there a second time. But, of course, I hadn't. I had only done one tour, yet, in some ways, I had never left Vietnam. It is still very much a part of me, even though many years have passed since I walked those jungle trails. The nightmare itself is not real, but the experiences that spawned it are, indelibly etched on the recesses of my soul, creating an incredible sense of reality even as I sleep. This is my story.

So, why write a book about Vietnam so many years after the fact, especially when so many other books have already been written? Perhaps it is because it is just that: *my* story. My story and no one else's. No matter who you talk to, each person has a unique story. If you listen, really listen, a person's story really is his or her own and no one else's. Each is different, though they may share similarities. Even those who go through the same battle, fighting side by side, see it differently, feel it differently within the context of their own uniqueness, their own identity. In that sense, each person's war is different, even when it is the same war. Therefore, if he could articulate it, he must have something to add to the larger story of war and its impact on people. Perhaps that is reason enough.

But there is also the value of passing stories down to those who follow, to one's children and grandchildren, a practice that unfortunately has become a lost art for most in our modern western culture. My parents and grandparents passed few stories down to my siblings and me. Family history seemed unimportant to them. I know my grandmother McCabe on my mother's side traveled west on a wagon train in the early 1900s. I asked her about it before she died, and she told me she was only four years old at the time, but she remembered clearly riding in the back of the wagon.

I once asked my mother where the McCabes originated from. My wife and I had discovered a shop in the British exhibit at Epcot Center in Orlando, Florida where you can look up your family name in a book. If it is listed, they can give you the early family history and, in some cases, the family crest. We purchased the history and crest for my wife's father's family, the Maggachs, who originated in Scotland. The history gave us some of the variations of the name and a little about some of the early characters back in the 1600s. My mother's maiden name was listed as well, but there were two families by that name, one from Scotland and the other from Ireland. When I called her, she had no idea which country her family had come from, and she didn't know if anyone else in her family would know. It was unimportant to them, and so the history of the McCabes is unknown, at least to me.

Some facts are like rare gems buried deep under heaps of genealogy. For example, someone on my dad's side of the family once traced our family roots back to Martha Washington by marriage. My wife's family actually goes back to the Mayflower through her mother's ancestors. I have the charts somewhere. My older daughter did a report on it in the eighth grade. I still do not know from which country my dad's family came or when they immigrated to the United States. Supposedly they emigrated from England to Canada and from Canada to Pennsylvania. Eventually they went by wagon train to Iowa and then to Colorado, but there are no written records of it as far as I know.

You find your story in the strangest places and when you least expect it. When I moved from the West Coast to Pennsylvania with my wife and two daughters in 1994, we discovered a small town on the Delaware River called Dingman Ferry. It was named after Andrew Dingman, who emigrated from Holland to New Amsterdam. He established a ferry service over the river in 1735. I have pictures of us in front of the Dingman Ferry Post Office, Dingman Creek, and Dingman Falls. Whether we are in some way related to this line of Dingmans I do not know, because no one in my family can tell me. Again, family history was not all that important to them, and so the stories are lost.

Perhaps the lack of passing down family histories today has in some way contributed to the lack of a sense of community this country once had. We have become a nation of individuals without a sense of the common heritage we share with our ancestors who immigrated to this country. We have lost our sense of history. Yet, it was our fathers, grandfathers, and great-grandfathers who fought this nation's wars, winning and protecting the freedoms we enjoy. It was they who fought the Revolutionary War, experienced the horrors of the Civil War, suffered the hardships of the Depression, fought in the trenches in World War I, and again in World War II, and Korea. I know I have ancestors who were there, who fought and lived to tell the stories of their experiences, but because they either were never told or never written down, they are lost forever.

For example, I know that my paternal grandfather served with Company E of the 168th Infantry in World War I because it is engraved on his tombstone. I asked my father what he knew about granddad's experience. He told me his dad had been wounded and talked about having marched through three countries in Europe, including Germany. He remembers his dad having nightmares and yelling in his sleep, "Get down Jim, or you're going to get shot!" But his dad didn't talk much about his experiences and so they are lost forever. His wounds were clearly visible, but his stories remained secrets known only to him.

My father served as a cook in the Merchant Marines in the Pacific during World War II. Writing this book motivated me to ask him about his own experience. I learned my father was on an oil tanker that refueled Navy ships at sea. To avoid being sunk by enemy submarines, they traveled across the ocean in zigzag patterns as they made their way to their destinations. Once, they picked up thirteen survivors of a sunken tanker. The rest of the crew, about twenty-three in number, had been lost. Another time their tanker was supposed to refuel an aircraft carrier, but the carrier was sunk, and so they had to continue zigzagging around for a couple of more weeks while they waited for another ship that needed their precious fuel. In April 1946, he was on a ship in the cold Alaskan waters, on its way to Dutch Harbor in the Aleutian Islands, when it was struck by a series of tidal waves from a deep-sea earthquake. Gigantic waves crashed over the sides of the ship and water seeped in everywhere. Dishes stored in trays designed to hold them even in heavy seas were tossed wildly about the galley. Tanker trucks strapped to the deck were ripped loose and tossed about like toys before being washed overboard. The ship's catwalk running from the officers' quarters and control room at the front of the ship to the seamen's quarters aft was torn away by the sheer force of the waves. The ship began to list to one side as it took on water, and the crew feared it would roll and all would perish. Fortunately, the ship remained upright, and, after the waves had passed, it managed to limp into Dutch harbor. Divers there repaired six torn hull plates, enabling the ship to make its way to Oakland, California for more extensive repairs.

If I had not asked, I would never have known these things about my father. His experiences reside deeply in his own memory, in part making him who he is. Concerning my other ancestors' experiences, I am aware of no records of them. Somehow their stories have been lost, like the trucks on my father's ship, washed away by the seas of time, because no one cared to write them down and pass them on. If they had, I would have enjoyed reading them, getting to know and understand my ancestors, my forefathers and -mothers. I would like to know what they saw and felt, not just who was born to whom, when and where. Genealogies can be so cold and barren, but life stories, the realities and experiences of what people saw and felt, are what make men and women who they are.

Whether anyone else will read this story, it is worth the telling, if for no other reason than to pass on to my children and their children after them who I was – what I saw, and what I felt. In some small way it may help them feel like they belong and give them a greater sense of history, knowing I was part of it. Hopefully, there will be lessons they can learn that will encourage them in life. Perhaps they will also be encouraged to tell their own stories, breaking the cycle of silence, and family history will once again be valued.

CHAPTER ONE

ANYTHING BUT BRAVE

"Better a patient man than a warrior,
a man who controls his temper
than one who takes a city."

Proverbs 16:32

As a child I was anything but brave. I was a fearful child, not confident at all; a follower, not a leader. I was small for my age, a fair-skinned tow-head; the third of four children born into a family of modest means.

My dad was a big man, over six feet tall and 200 pounds, who had dropped out of fourth grade as a child to help support his family in the hills of western Colorado during the post-Depression era. During World War II, he joined the Merchant Marines serving as a cook. Afterward, he continued his career as a baker working mostly nights. He was strong with bulging biceps, large hands, and thick fingers from lifting heavy bags of sugar and flour day after day. He emptied them into the big mixer at the bakery in the pre-dawn hours while everyone else slept warmly in their beds.

From the time I was small I think I feared him. He told me once even as a baby I didn't want to be held by him. I don't remember ever hugging him as a child, though I do remember playing on his lap and ducking from him many times as he swung one of those huge hands at me in a moment of discipline. I don't think he ever intended to harm me but rather to scare me just a little, which he did. He would swing and I would duck and laugh; he would warn me to settle down or next time I would really get it. It didn't take much to correct me. At heart I was a child who wanted to please: a peacemaker, not a warrior.

Even as a teen I did not see any sense in violence. I had always been able to avoid it by staying away from conflict. I had never been in a fight and never intended to be. Like any boy who grew up with two brothers and a sister, I had been in a few wrestling matches, but we never really hurt each other.

I went out for wrestling as a freshman in high school but missed a bunch of practices for some reason. Maybe it was a lack of confidence kicking in. At the urging of the coach and a friend, I turned out for the first wrestling meet of the season. I won my match but severely sprained an ankle in the process, which put me out of commission for several weeks. I never went back. I think I could have done well. I was small but fast and could easily outmaneuver my opponents, but my insecurity about competing and having to relate to my peers overcame my desire to belong. So, after that, instead of playing sports, I watched them.

It seemed every Friday night after the football game there would be fights somewhere. Kids got drunk and tried to prove their manhood by beating someone up or getting beat up. One Friday night I remember standing outside of the malt shop across the street from the high school, leaning up against the hood of a car talking to some girls and commenting about how stupid I thought it was to get into fights. Suddenly a boy standing nearby who overheard me came over, grabbed me by the shirt, lifted me off the ground, and barked, "Do you want to fight?"

My mind went blank. I heard myself saying, "No!"

"Then you had better shut your mouth!" he yelled, and, after putting me down, walked away, laughing. I gathered my senses, brushed myself off, and, though somewhat embarrassed, continued talking with the girls as if nothing had happened. True to form, I avoided the fight.

Another time, a friend from a neighboring county came to visit me one Saturday and asked me if I knew any girls. I think I must have been in the ninth or tenth grade at the time. I knew this pretty young blond, an eighth grader. I knew where she lived, because I had a newspaper route that took me by her home twice each week. I called her and asked if we could come over and say "hi," and she said yes. We hopped on our bikes and rode on over.

As it turned out, she was home alone, and my friend thought this would be a great time to make advances on her. I was stunned. He pinned her up against a wall with his body and tried to kiss her. She resisted. I told him to lay off. He was bigger than I was, but I could not let this pass. He tried to shrug me off, but I again insisted he leave her alone. After a third warning, he said we should take this outside, so we did. I could visually see myself getting beaten up by this kid who outweighed me by fifty pounds and was at least six inches taller than I was. But when we got outside and faced each other, he backed down. The episode over, we jumped on our bikes and headed back home.

I don't think I ever saw him after that, which suited me just fine. That was a milestone for me. I had to make a choice between peace and honor, and I had chosen honor. I had faced my fear of violence and overcome it.

The only other time I can remember being close to fighting was as a senior in High School. I had a locker partner, a junior who did not like me. We never really talked at all, but his disdain for me was clear. I would put my books on the top shelf of the locker. He would later put them in the bottom of the locker and put his books on the top shelf instead. Perhaps he figured since he was big and tall and I was short and small this made more sense, but to me I was the senior and he was the junior, so I should have the top shelf. For the most part, we tried to avoid each other, but this battle went on for months. One day we wound up at the locker at the same time, and I can't remember what, if any, words were spoken, but the tension was so great I wanted to lunge at the guy and tear him apart.

The halls were crowded, and I remember looking at him and he at me. We stood there in the center of the hallway like two growling dogs, teeth bared, ready to attack. For a moment I was ready to take him on like David against Goliath, but then my sense of survival kicked in. I knew if I took him on I would get my butt kicked right then and there in front of everyone, not to mention having to deal with the Principal afterwards. I could see the kids in the hallway staring in anticipation of what was going to happen. There was no way I could beat this kid who was twice my size, or so it seemed. So I caught my breath, sucked it in, turned, and walked away.

For the rest of the year I avoided him, abandoning the locker and taking my books home, carrying back and forth what I needed each day. Some might call it cowardice and others the better part of valor, but I just saw it as surviving at a time when life was already miserable. My parents had gotten divorced when I was a freshman; my older brother had been drafted into the Marines and was in Vietnam; my sister had dropped out of high school to get married without my mother's knowledge or permission; my younger brother was living with my dad, and I had stayed with mom who had recently remarried.

I had become a loner for the most part unable to relate to my peers. I even ate lunch every day at the malt shop across the street, sitting at the counter by myself, where I didn't have to talk to anyone. For seventy-five cents I could buy a cheeseburger, fries, and a root beer float. I was more comfortable talking to the owner of the shop than to my peers.

The performing arts became my outlet. Speech squad, drama club and choir, filled my extracurricular time. It was much easier to perform in front of people than to actually interact with them as an equal. I used words in ways other boys used their brawn. I attended football and basketball games and even went out on a few dates, attending the sock hops after the games, but I had only a few guys I could call my friends. I even started a chess club my junior year and through it met a fellow who became my best friend at the time. He was younger than me, but like me was a bit of an awkward loner, so we made a good pair.

My timidity was especially evident at one point when I was dating two girls at the same time. It wasn't so much that I liked them as much as I knew they both liked me, and I didn't have the heart to break up with either one of them. It was during basketball season, and somehow I wound up inviting both of them to the same home game one Friday night. When they both showed up, they sat one on either side of me but were as cold as a chilly night in the middle of January. Both insisted I make a choice, and I did. Perhaps that's why I had invited them both: unconsciously, I knew it would bring things to a head, and I would have to face the inevitable. It was something I did not have the courage to do otherwise.

Such is the way of an unlikely warrior. All young men are afraid to one degree or another when it comes to breaking up with girls. Most just aren't as afraid as I was. Most are smart enough not to wind up with two girls on the same date, unless of course they happen to be Fonzi from *Happy Days*, who always wound up with two girls on the same date, both quite happy to be there.

Fortunately, we outgrow those awkward teen years, or at least we mostly do, and we move on to more important things like carrying guns and killing people. Real guns and real people, not like when we were kids playing in the woods. The awkward boys of junior high and high school, the geeks as well as the jocks, the choirboys and actors, football players and wrestlers grow up into manhood and are called off to war to fight for their country. Some, it seems, are born for such adventure, but many, like me, are timid by nature, peacemakers who hate conflict and otherwise avoid it at all costs.

Some were successful at avoiding going to Vietnam by staying in college or getting deferments for other reasons. Some headed to Canada, while others, like me, answered the call when it came and went off to war, even though we knew we were not really cut out for it. As I would soon learn, there were many different reasons why some went and others did not, but in the end, each person dealt with his own reasons and faced his own fears. That's the way it has always been and the way it will always be as long as there are wars. It is the way of war and, for some, the passage from boyhood to manhood.

When it comes to war, no one can really know what it is like, unless they have been there. You can get a sense of war from the movies, with their graphic depictions of violence and death, and from books that describe in gruesome detail the experiences of those who have been there. The art of making movies today has reached the point that little is left to the imagination. What cannot be reenacted can be recreated by digital computers in such a way it looks real. Whole armies and armadas are created from just a few models digitally reproduced and knit together ingeniously on the screen with cannons firing, guns blazing, and people flying through the air in tumultuous explosions. The skilled writer can also write in such detail it makes you feel almost as if you are there when you read it. In your mind you can see the battle unfolding in vivid color, hear the cannons roaring, and smell the heavy aroma of sulfur in the air from expended ordnance.

But you are not there, and it is not real. You cannot smell or taste war in this way. You cannot feel the emotions only felt by those who were there, the adrenaline rush, the fear of death, and the horror of a night so dark you cannot see your hand in front of your face, not to mention the enemy who might sneak up on you and cut your throat should you happen to fall asleep.

The stench of war belongs only to the warrior who has seen it, tasted it, smelled it, and felt it deep within his own soul. The experience is so real and so deep some choose to bury it deep inside themselves, never to be talked about again. It is too personal, too painful. For others there is healing in telling the story, in writing about it, in sharing it with others, even though they know no one can really understand unless they have been there.

I am thankful I have been able to tell my story over the years. Perhaps that is why I have not suffered to the same degree others have. My faith and the ability to share my story with others who lovingly accept me as I am have kept it from eating away at me, from festering like an oozing sore full of poison ready to burst at any time.

Even though my experiences may not seem to me to have been as horrific as what many others have experienced, it does not take much to drive a person to despair and bitterness. Many who went through no more than I turned to alcohol or drugs in an effort to cover their pain, to dull their memories and silence their nightmares. Some turned to crime. Others chose isolation in the woods, away from people as much as possible. Marriages failed, children were alienated, crimes were committed, and some of my brothers rot away in prison, still fighting an unfinished war within their souls.

By the grace of God I have been spared much of the pain. But still, along with all of those who have faced the ravages of war, I carry within my soul scars that can never be healed, the guilt of wondering if I could have done something different to save someone's life, and the shame of having been afraid, even though I know *everyone* was afraid. In part these scars bind us together. This bond motivates warriors to gather year after year at reunions to recount their stories and comfort one another as they remember what it was like to have been a young man at war. This bond brings tears to their eyes as they salute the flag and visit the graves of those who did not come back alive. It is a bond like no other; a bond forged in the heat of battle.

Like many others my age, I was an unlikely warrior in an unpopular war. I had grown up playing with toy guns, pretending to be a warrior as a child. Growing up in farm country in Oregon, in the shadow of majestic Mt. Hood, there was plenty of room for such games. Many an hour was spent building forts and running through the lush, thick cover of sword ferns, rhododendrons, and giant fir trees, pretending to be a soldier on the prowl for the enemy in the jungle. But at heart, I was not a warrior. I was just a kid pretending to be one, pretending to be brave, pretending to kill or be killed. None of this was real. It was simply make-believe, a game to have fun, after which I would come home to dinner and a warm bed to sleep in.

But war is not fun, and it is not make-believe. People die and do not come home for dinner. Others suffer debilitating wounds, and everyone is changed in some way. It is said the soldier who goes off to war can never really come home, and that is true. For he is not the same person he was when he left, and those he left behind are also changed. Nothing is the same.

CHAPTER TWO

A NEW BEGINNING

"Therefore, if anyone is in Christ, he is a new creation;
the old has gone, the new has come!"
2 Corinthians 5:17

I did not grow up in a religious family. When my older siblings and I were young, my mom would send us to the little white country church just a few blocks down the street. I vaguely remember walking there holding the hands of my older brother and sister. I have a suspicion my mother only wanted to get us out of the house so dad could sleep in and she could clean, since the house always seemed cleaner when we came home. Dad worked the graveyard shift during the week, and weekends were his only chance to get a normal night's sleep. But we didn't keep going for very long.

When I was about ten years old, a neighbor invited my siblings and me to a series of evening meetings at the same Baptist church that now met in a nice new brick building across the street from the little white country church of old. They were having a contest to see who could bring the most guests, the oldest Bible, the biggest Bible (and who knows what else), and it sounded like fun, so we went.

The speaker was a chalk artist who drew beautiful drawings lit up by black lights to illustrate his messages. Suddenly it seemed as if the evangelist was speaking only to me. He explained Christ died for my sins and the only way to heaven was by asking Him to be my Savior. At the end of his message, he asked a question I knew I could not answer: "If you were to die tonight, are you sure you would be in Heaven tomorrow?"

I couldn't say I would, because, to my knowledge, I had never put my faith in Christ. This was the first time I had really even heard about sin and the need for salvation. So, when the evangelist gave an invitation to come forward, I responded. A voice inside my head tried to stop me: "Your family will laugh at you!" it said, but I thought to myself, "I don't care!" and went forward anyway.

If anyone else went forward that night it was unimportant to me, because in my mind I was answering God's call. A woman took me into a little room next to the podium where we knelt, and I was led in the sinner's prayer. Afterward I felt as if the whole world had been lifted off my shoulders. Surely Jesus had come into my heart, and now I would go to heaven! As the Bible says I had passed from death to life in that single moment. As I exited that little room, the evangelist was still picking up his things on the podium. He looked at me and said, "Are you saved?"

I responded excitedly, "Yes, I am!"

He then asked, "How do you know you're saved?"

I answered, "Because I feel so good!"

He then shook his finger at me and said sternly, "No, that's not right! You know you are saved because the Bible tells you so!" Though somewhat deflated at the moment, I have never forgotten those words and have been so thankful over the years. Feelings change, but God never changes.

I went to Sunday school for a while after that and received a Bible for attending seven weeks in a row. Some ladies picked me up each week, but without encouragement from home to keep going, I eventually stopped. Sleeping in and playing on Sunday mornings were much more appealing to a ten-year-old in the long run, and none of my friends went to church. We were all a bunch of country kids who enjoyed riding our bikes, playing war in the woods, swimming, fishing, and picking berries in the summer to make some spending money.

Just a few years later, the family I thought would laugh at me had disintegrated, and I had no real friends to speak of. The summer before I entered high school we moved away from the little farming community where I had spent my childhood years, away from the little house my dad had bought for just a few hundred dollars and added a couple of rooms to including an indoor bathroom with running water and a flushing toilet. We moved into a much larger house in town just five miles away. My dad hoped a bigger house and new location might save his marriage, but it was only a matter of time before he realized it was already too late for that.

Five miles might as well have been a thousand miles for me. Even though the kids I had grown up with went to the same high school, it just wasn't the same. We seldom saw each other except in the hallways and perhaps an occasional class. At the end of the day, we went home to our own houses in our own neighborhoods, and I was too timid to make new friends.

The upheaval in my family didn't help either. Within a year, my parents were separated and then divorced. My sister wanted to get married and got my dad to sign the papers as she was underage. We couldn't let Mom know, so my brothers and I went to the wedding without her, a small wedding performed in a home in secrecy. I hated deceiving my mom, but what was I to do? How could I make peace in this mess?

For a while, my brothers and I stayed with Mom, but my older brother got a job at the shipyard and moved into an apartment with a friend after he graduated from high school.

He was later drafted into the Marines and after training was sent off to Vietnam. My mom, little brother, and I couldn't afford to stay in the big house anymore, so we moved a little further out of town again, into a smaller house. Shortly after that my little brother decided to move in with Dad, who had remarried, and I was all alone except for Mom, who worked nights as a cocktail waitress.

During my junior year in high school, my life took a significant turn. I was reaching a point of despair due to an overwhelming sense of loneliness. Day after day, I would go to school and come home, watch T.V., do my homework, go to bed, and then repeat the process all over again. Speech competitions, drama, and choir helped, but I wound up going home after each event by myself and felt so desperately alone.

Then, in the summer of 1965, my mother remarried and my stepdad came to live with us along with his daughter, Lori, who was in middle school. Her dad was an avowed atheist, or at least an agnostic, but Lori went to church faithfully every Sunday with an aunt and uncle.

The arrival of a stepdad and stepsister couldn't fill the void I felt. There were times I would try to read the Bible in search of comfort, but the comfort wouldn't last long. Like many un-churched people, I knew there was something there, but I had no idea where to look or how to understand it. I can remember standing at my bedroom window one day and thinking maybe I should just kill myself. At the same time I thought, "Maybe if I went to church it would help, but what church should I go to?" There were so many, and I had no idea which one was the right one. I can remember crying out to God, promising to go if He would show me. I had no idea at the time He had already provided the answer in the form of a stepsister six years younger than I was.

Before long Lori began inviting me to go to church with her. At first I resisted her invitations, embarrassed perhaps to be seen tagging along with my new little sister. And yet, part of me knew this was exactly what I needed, so I went. The small church met in a house they were converting into a real church building with the addition of a sanctuary with a full basement with a kitchen, fellowship room, and classrooms. They had a good group of teens that went to different high schools than I did, and they took an interest in me. Suddenly I had a whole new set of friends, and I couldn't get enough of church or the Bible. As I attended meetings on Sundays including Youth Group on Sunday afternoons, and Bible Study on Wednesday nights, I began to understand what had happened to me at the age of ten. Jesus had never left me. He had always been there, and now I could see how He wanted to fill the emptiness in my heart with His love. As a result, my senior year was a big improvement over the first three years of high school.

After graduating, I attended a small one-year Bible school in Culver City, California. The school's motto was, "One Year for Life," but little did I know just how much that one year would impact me. It was there I met the girl who would one day become my wife, and a desire began to grow within me to be in full-time Christian ministry.

But first there would be other lessons to learn and battles to fight. In many ways I was still just a boy and had not yet passed into manhood. The days were not far ahead when I would again have to decide whether or not I was willing to fight. This is a question every young man must answer if he is to go to war. For some the answer is clear, but for unlikely warriors like me, it is much more complicated than that. War is real, and people die. If you are to go, you must decide if it is worth it, if you are willing to take the risk, to be wounded, or worse yet never to come home again at all. No, I was not there yet. Manhood is something that must be grown into and comes through struggle and hardship. In time I would get there, but the time was not yet.

CHAPTER THREE

DIFFICULT CHOICES

"Trust in the LORD *with all your heart*
and lean not on your own understanding;
in all your ways acknowledge him
and he will make your paths straight."

Proverbs 3:5-6

Gresham, Oregon, where I grew up, was a quaint town with a population of 3,000 located about 15 miles east of Portland. Mount Hood, Mount St. Helens, and the Cascade Range were all visible on sunny days. As a child I used to watch airplanes flying high overhead and thought flying was something only rich people did. I couldn't imagine as a child growing up in farm country I would ever fly in an airplane. In my small mind that was something far beyond anything I might experience. But after I graduated from high school in 1967, to my surprise, I found myself flying from Portland, Oregon to Los Angeles to attend a one-year Bible school in Culver City. Just a few months before that as I prepared for high school graduation, a young lady from my church asked me if I had ever considered going to Bible school. I didn't even know such schools existed. Now, here I was flying to Southern California, the home of Hollywood and Disneyland.

I had never been to California before. When we took vacations, it was always to Colorado, where my parents had grown up: the little towns of Hotchkiss, where my mom's parents lived, and Paonia, a few miles away, where my dad's father and stepmother lived in a log cabin.

My grandparents on my mom's side of the family, Dee and Lottie McCabe, were cobblers; their shop was right next door to their big two-story house. I loved visiting Grandpa and Grandma McCabe. It was always an adventure. They made chaps and repaired boots, shoes, and canvas works for the local ranchers. They sold saddles and harnesses as well. I loved the smell of the leather in their shop and the red freezer chest-like Coca-Cola machine. There I could get an ice cold Coke for a dime, lifting the lid up and sliding the glass bottle out along a steel track until it came out.

They had a Magpie by the name of Wilks that could talk, which they kept in a big outdoor cage in the side yard next to the house. They would let it out to fly sometimes, but it would always come back, until one day they let it out and never saw it again.

They were known as the King and Queen of the Grand Mesa, a big lake on a flat top mountain. It was there I caught my first rainbow trout using raw hamburger and cheese for bait. When Grandpa would catch one he would cry out at the top of his deep voice, "R – A – I – N – B – O – W!" and everyone knew Dee McCabe had caught another one as his cry echoed across the lake.

My grandparents had a black 1930s-era hearse they converted into their fishing wagon. They put a bed in the back where the coffins used to go. Because the side doors opened out in opposite directions, like French doors in a home, they attached canvas extensions to them so there was a room on each side to sit, sleep, or eat in. We fished from a small rowboat, and Grandpa always knew where the best spots were.

While I was at Bible school, my older brother, three years my senior, came home from Vietnam and was stationed at Camp Pendleton in San Diego. Since it was just a couple of hours' drive from L.A., he came up to see me one weekend.

He had been stationed in Vietnam up North near the DMZ (Demilitarized Zone), but he didn't want to talk much about what he had experienced. Whenever asked about it, he would simply say he didn't do much, just that he had kept watch over a generator at night to keep it running. Somehow, I thought he must have been hiding something. I had heard guys coming home from Vietnam often did not want to talk about what they had experienced. The TET (Chinese Lunar New Year) Offensive at the end of January of that year (1968) terribly embarrassed the Nixon administration, and as more and more G.I.s came home in flag-draped boxes, the anti-war sentiment grew. Those who did come home alive were often treated with disdain and called baby killers. No parades. No honor. Just ridicule and shame.

Years later I learned he was telling the truth, and the scars he carried were different from my own, but very real nonetheless. He never had to go out on patrol or face combat in the jungle, but he did have to attend the funerals of the Marines who died every day. They stuck rifles in the ground by their bayonets, hung helmets on the butts of the rifles, placed a pair of boots in front of each rifle, and the Chaplain said a few solemn words and offered a prayer before "Taps" was played. Day after day, he attended those funerals and struggled with the guilt it was not he who died. It took years for him to forgive himself, and finally accept he had served honorably, doing the job he was asked to do. Only then did we experience the bond of brotherhood that had somehow evaded us in our youth, an even greater bond than we could have ever known before: a bond of brothers who had gone to war and come home again.

Near the end of my year at Bible school, I worked part-time as a Recreation Director for a children's home in downtown Hollywood. This home, which had been the Los Angeles Orphan Home Society at the turn of the century, had moved out of downtown L.A. into the country in the early

1900s. The area was nothing but holly groves, so the home became known as Hollygrove Home for Children. In time the holly groves gave way to the kind of urban sprawl that affects every major city, and Hollywood grew up around it. Today it takes up a city block on the corner of Melrose and Vine Streets, and no longer serves as a residential home for children but instead places them in group homes in communities with real families. Marilyn Monroe even lived in this home for a while as a child. She did not speak very kindly of it in her autobiography, but today it is a wonderful place of help and healing for children; a haven in the midst of the glitz and glitter of Hollywood. Most people do not even know it is there since well-trimmed hedges and a chain link fence seclude it.

As school came to an end, the director of Hollygrove offered me a full-time job as the Recreation Director and Weekend Cottage Parent. I loved working with children. In high school I had considered pursuing a career in teaching or working in an orphanage, perhaps as a social worker. I had even applied to and been accepted at a teacher's college in Southern Oregon before I decided to go to Bible school. By living and working at the children's home, I could establish residency and attend college tuition free. I accepted the offer on the condition I could go home for two weeks to see my family.

Once I was back in Oregon with my family and my friends, I began to feel as if I were being unfaithful to the Lord. I had gone to Bible school because I wanted to grow in my Christian faith so I could be a better witness to my family. Now, here I was abandoning them so I could go off and play with children and go to school, doing what *I* wanted to do. Somehow, it just didn't seem right. I don't think it was homesickness, as I had not ever felt homesick while I was at Bible school. It was a deep down conviction that gnawed away at my stomach when I thought about it.

Not knowing what I should do, I sought the counsel of the elders of my church, only to be told they could not tell me what God's will was for my life. I called the director of the Children's Home to explain my dilemma, and she was sympathetic but also said the decision was up to me. I knew it wasn't fair to keep them in suspense right up until the last minute, so I set a date for my decision and prayed for God to give me wisdom. When the turmoil didn't subside, I knew I couldn't go, so I called the director and declined the job. Only at that point did the turmoil leave and a sense of inner peace return, giving me assurance I was doing the right thing.

Now I had to get a job. My dad told me they were hiring at the bakery where he worked, so I put in an application and went in to work a night shift. I had no idea what to expect but soon found out just how hard bakery work is. I was put at the end of a conveyer line where the hot bread pans came after passing through the oven and were emptied. My job was to take the hot pans off the line and stack them up. The person training me made it look easy, but no matter how hard I tried, I could not keep up, and pans would wind up going onto the floor. By the lunch break, I was hot and feeling sick. When I told the boss I didn't feel well, he sent me home, and I was never called back.

After that my mother told me the flower shop in town was looking for a delivery truck driver. That sounded simple enough, so I went down and talked to the owner and to my surprise he hired me. It didn't pay a lot, but it was a start, and I would be able to pay off what I still owed the Bible school. It was a job I enjoyed, and my employer seemed to be pleased with my work.

I became involved in my local church, and the girl I had met at Bible school, whom I had dated at the end of the school year, came up to visit me. We liked each other a lot, and I asked her to marry me even though I was not ready for such a serious commitment. It had taken me an hour sitting at the top of Multnomah Falls overlooking the Columbia River just to get up enough nerve to kiss her for the first time. I quickly realized I had jumped the gun and stopped communicating with her. I was afraid to tell her up front, so I left it up to her to figure out what was happening. I hurt her far more by my silence than if I had just come out and told her I wasn't ready for marriage. Later she told me she had never wanted to see or talk to me again after that.

As the year passed, I realized it would only be a matter of time before I would be drafted. As I contemplated that, I began to ask others and myself if it was right for a Christian to be involved in war. My church did not teach pacifism, nor did it teach it was every man's obligation to go to war in the service of his country. Once again, it was considered a matter of personal conscience. No one could tell me what God's will was for my life in such matters.

As I prayed for direction, someone told me there were two types of Conscientious Objectors or C.O.s as they were called. There were those who believed it was wrong to serve in the military at all, who performed alternative service instead, working as hospital orderlies or in some other public service job for two years. And there were others who were not against military service as long as they could serve in a non-combat role, which did not require them to take the life of another. In both cases the objection had to be on religious grounds and the draft board had to give its approval.

As I studied the Bible and saw God instructed His own people to go to war in the Old Testament and God used many military people throughout history, I could not say it was wrong to be in the military. In fact, when soldiers were baptized by John the Baptist and they asked him what they should do, he instructed them to continue to do their jobs but not to use their position to take advantage of other people. The New Testament also tells us God has given governments the power of the sword for the purpose of punishing evildoers. That must also include acts of war when its enemies attack a country or if an ally is attacked. At the same time, Jesus commanded His followers to love their enemies and to do good to those who spitefully used them. How was I to balance these conflicting truths?

After serious thought and prayer, I concluded I could do both. I believed God needed and wanted people of faith in the military, and it also seemed reasonable to me since the government provided a way to serve without having to kill anyone, I should take advantage of it. It was not that I believed it was wrong for anyone to kill in times of war, but rather that God was calling me to take a different path. I would serve, but as a non-combatant. I had no idea what that meant, but I was satisfied it was the right decision for me.

I wrote a letter to the draft board explaining my position and a couple of months later received a letter granting my request. Little did I know my decision would in no way keep me out of combat. In fact, it would have quite the opposite effect, almost guaranteeing I would go to Vietnam and be assigned to an infantry unit where I would face the same risks, rigors, and fears any combat soldier would face. Instead of becoming a non-combatant, I would become an unlikely warrior, a soldier with the right to refuse to carry a weapon, but a warrior nonetheless.

In May of 1969, I received the letter every nineteen-year-old dreaded and hoped would not come. It was sent at the directive of the President of the United States, including a greeting and one simple sentence: "You are hereby ordered for induction into the Armed Forces of the United States, and to report at **Armed Forces Examining & Entrance Station 425 S. W. Taylor Street Portland, Oregon 97204** on **25 June 1969** at **6:30 A.M.** for forwarding to an Armed Forces Induction Station."

This was followed by instructions about what to bring and a warning that any failure to report could result in a fine or imprisonment. No mention was made of my status as a conscientious objector. I could only assume it was a matter of record and would be honored.

The next few weeks were spent taking care of odds and ends. I had previously moved into my own small apartment. Now I gave notice to my employer, moved back home, and prepared to say my goodbyes before heading off to boot camp.

Early on the morning of June 25th, my mother drove me to the Armed Forces Entrance and Examination Station. I cannot remember what we talked about. What's a mother to say when her son is about to go into the military during a time of conflict? What's a son to say? Such times are filled with silence or small talk. The time came when the car pulled up to the curb, and I had to get out. I'm sure I must have given her a kiss and told her I loved her before saying goodbye.

The decision had been made. Once again I had chosen honor instead of peace. So, I went into the Station and did what all inductees did: answer questions, fill out paper work, take tests, stand in line in my skivvies to take a physical, and finally take an oath to defend the Constitution of the United States and obey the lawful orders of my superior officers. My status as a Conscientious Objector duly noted, I was inducted into the United States Army, the only branch willing to take us C.O.s. A half-dozen draftees were taken into the Marine Corps, their names read out loud. The rest of us were loaded on buses and taken to Fort Lewis, Washington, 180 miles or so north of Portland, where we began our journey to become soldiers. There I would soon learn the consequences of my decision to be a conscientious objector, an unlikely warrior.

CHAPTER FOUR

FROM SAN ANTONIO TO VIETNAM

"Whom have I in heaven but you?
And being with you, I desire nothing on earth.
My flesh and my heart may fail,
but God is the strength of my heart
and my portion forever."
Psalm 73:25-26

Induction and boot camp are about turning boys into men and men into soldiers. Inductees must first have their identities taken away from them: names are exchanged for numbers, their heads are shaved and uniforms issued so they all look alike; then they are humiliated to the point they are willing to follow any lawful order given to them. At the induction station, we were made to move in formation as if we were soldiers, but we were more like first graders on the first day of school, having not yet learned how to keep step. We were told when to eat, sleep, and go to the bathroom. Civilian clothing was traded for fatigues. We stood in long lines baring our arms for shots, and in the mess hall we were given ten minutes to eat. The sergeants were constantly yelling at us to hurry up and get a move on.

On about the third day my name was called along with three others, and we were told we were being sent to Fort Sam Houston in San Antonio, Texas. While there we went through the same basic training as any other soldier with the exception of weapons training. Following basic we went to

Advanced Individual Training (A.I.T.) to become medics. We were told this was the only position recognized by the Geneva Convention as noncombatant, and thus the only thing the Army could do with us. However, I later learned Presidential Executive Order 10028 issued on January 13, 1949 by President Eisenhower allowed far more latitude. Not many of us had ever actually read the order itself and only knew we had the right to serve as noncombatants. We just had no clue what that meant. At least one person from our Basic Training Unit was chosen to become a Chaplain's assistant, though I never learned how. Perhaps he had read the order and pressed to be allowed to serve in another capacity, or perhaps he had a family member with influence.

I suppose an argument can be made that in every area of service other than the medical field, a soldier should be required to carry a weapon for the protection of himself and others. In the Marine Corps for example, Chaplains are not allowed to carry a weapon, so their assistants have to. It seems to me, however, there should have been no reason why we could not have served as clerk typists or in some other capacity that did not require us to be placed in a combat situation.

At the same time there may be some truth to the Geneva Convention argument. According to the Geneva Convention, fixed medical units and those used to transport wounded personnel are considered protected from hostilities, even if they are armed for the purpose of self-defense or for the defense of the wounded. In wars prior to Vietnam, medics wore red crosses on armbands and on their helmets to signify their protected status, but this was often ignored by the enemy, so the practice was discontinued. Red crosses only made the medics easier targets. The enemy knew they could greatly disable our forces by targeting field officers, radio operators, and medics. All of these, of course, are facts I learned much later.

Travel vouchers and transfer orders in hand, we were taken to the Sea-Tac Airport, where we caught a commercial flight to San Antonio. We had a brief stopover in Portland, so I called home to let my family know what was happening. Then it was off to Texas. When we arrived, the heat almost knocked me off my feet as I exited the plane and walked down the stairs to the tarmac. Having grown up in western Oregon, I had never experienced that kind of heat before. We found the Military Liaison Desk and arranged transportation to our Basic Training Unit. Being raw recruits, we didn't know how to read our travel orders properly: we did not know we had been given several days to travel. But once we checked into our basic training unit, it was too late. We were stuck, even though it would be a week or two before the rest of our class arrived from various parts of the country and our training would begin. In the meantime, we were given K.P. and various other details around the fort, including garbage detail on the 4th of July. The first week we were there, someone from another class on the second floor of our barracks tried to kill himself by cutting his wrists. Fortunately, someone found him, and he was rushed to the hospital, but it made me wonder what lay ahead. Could basic training really be so horrific someone would want to kill himself? What could have possibly been going through his mind?

For me, basic training went pretty much without a hitch. We went through the usual grueling training, getting up at 4 AM for P.T. and running a mile before having breakfast. Then much of the day was spent in classes, including learning how to march in close order drills, and, of course, we had to double time everywhere we went. If we were caught walking, we had to do pushups to the satisfaction of the sergeant or officer who had caught us. Because it was summer, the heat and humidity occasionally reached dangerous levels, at which point they would forgo the P.T. We learned how to march, pitch tents, read a map and compass, cook and eat C-rations, evade the enemy, and even defend ourselves in hand-to-hand combat. They couldn't give us weapons training, but they were determined to teach us something about the art of war one way or another.

One of our classmates, who should have never been drafted, was a Jehovah's Witness and committed pacifist. He refused to salute the flag or take hand-to-hand combat. He was constantly being ridiculed and threatened with bodily harm, but I never saw him waiver from his commitment. To this day I don't know what they finally did with him, but I can only assume he was eventually discharged.

I found myself for the first time making friends with people very different from me. Where I grew up there were no African-Americans. My school mates were all white, with the exception of a few Japanese and Korean Americans who owned the berry-farms where we worked during the summer. In high school, we had a foreign exchange student from Africa one year, but that was as close as I had come to knowing someone of African heritage. Now, here I was living, eating, and training with people of all races.

Since all of us at basic training, as conscientious objectors, were people of faith to one degree or another, our faith provided a basis for friendship. Even though we didn't agree on all points of religion, most of us considered ourselves to be Christians. Having not been exposed to prejudice as a kid, I can honestly say I felt as free to be friends with a black person as a white or brown one and never sensed any conflict because of it, nor understood why there should be. On bivouac (an overnight field exercise), I shared my two-man tent with a black friend instead of one of my Caucasian friends.

The only time we were allowed to leave the basic training compound was to attend church on Sundays at the base chapel. As we walked to and from services, I had some interesting conversations with some of my black brothers who tended to be of the Pentecostal persuasion. Though they seemed to accept me as a Christian, when I asked them if I was going to Heaven even though I had not experienced what they called "the second blessing," they would just smile, shake their heads, and laugh. I don't think they really thought I was going to Hell, but at the same time they had a hard time seeing past their Pentecostal upbringing, which taught them that speaking in an unknown language was the only real proof of being born into the family of God.

Today I am saddened the racial conflicts of the '60s and '70s largely prevented those friendships from continuing beyond the experiences of Army training and combat in the jungles of Vietnam. In spite of whatever camaraderie we might have felt on the battlefield, racial tension was always just under the surface, and those friendships rarely survived once we were back in the States.

Part of every basic training program included going through the tear gas chamber and a live fire exercise pretending to assault a hill with loud explosions going off around you and low crawling for seventy-five meters over logs and under barbed wire with machine guns firing live ammunition three feet over your head. I remember one somewhat stocky fellow making the assault with us up the hill, and every time an explosion went off he would jump and scream at the top of his voice. We were surprised and perhaps a little suspicious of this response, and yet it seemed he was genuinely terrified. Later he explained he had always reacted this way to loud noises. I had to wonder how he had gotten this far and how he would handle a real combat situation if he ever wound up on the battlefield.

A.I.T. was ten weeks of emergency medical training and hospital procedures. I am sure it was far inferior to the training medics receive today, but at the time it was the best the Army had to offer. The instructors made it clear that we were NOT being trained to be corpsmen but as combat medics. Giving injections, inserting intravenous needles, diagnosing and treating illnesses, making a hospital bed properly, and maintaining a sterile environment were all part of the course. But we were also instructed how to properly treat combat wounds, including head wounds, traumatic amputations, massive abdominal wounds, and how to reach a wounded man under fire and carry him to safety for evacuation. Triage was an important aspect as well, making decisions about who to treat first in a given situation and who to leave untreated (if need be) in order to take care of those most likely to survive.

In spite of the instructors' reminders we were being trained as combat medics, we all held out hope somehow we would be assigned to some safe duty, perhaps in Germany, where we had lots of troops, or even stateside. During my fifth week of A.I.T., I wrote home with news very few of the classes graduating ahead of us were going to Vietnam: *"I've heard that for the next four months they're only sending volunteers, but I don't know the validity of the statement. From the looks of things I could even easily get stationed in the states for a-while."* That's the way it always was with scuttlebutt. You would hear a rumor but never knew how true it might be. Part of me always wanted to believe the best, so I would hang on to those rumors hoping they might prove right.

As graduation grew nearer we became acutely aware the odds were against us. The war in Vietnam had reached its peak with 300,000 troops committed to the cause. As soldiers were killed or wounded, or completed their tours of duty, more were needed to fill their ranks. On October 2nd, I wrote home that approximately 200 medics would be going to Vietnam, and I would get my assignment any day now. Still I wrote I thought I was pretty safe and could be assigned elsewhere. That was my last letter home from Fort Sam Houston. I told them I would call when I found out where I was going.

When I learned I was going to Vietnam, I was crushed. A few in our class received other assignments, including one to Hawaii, but a lot of us were chosen to fill those much-needed 200 slots to Vietnam. I had hoped against hope somehow God would keep me from having to go to war. I was angry and disappointed. I remember going for a long walk under the Texas stars that evening and thinking, "Lord, why should I even be a Christian if this is the way You are going to treat me?" Almost immediately a thought came to me as if it were not my thought at all but that of another. It was as if God Himself were speaking, asking one simple question: "If you could give Me up, what would you have left?" The answer was as clear as the Texas sky. I looked up at the stars and realized if I gave up my faith in Jesus Christ, I would have nothing left, for it was He who gave purpose and meaning to my life. It was He who had filled the emptiness and given me courage at a time when I had considered ending my life. Christ had given His life for me, and now my life belonged to Him. He WAS my life!

With this realization I knew I could go forward, trusting Christ to take care of me just as He had up to this point. No matter what happened, He would be there for me, and I need not be afraid. He could keep me safe just as easily on the battlefields of Vietnam as He could in San Antonio, Texas or Berlin, Germany. And even if I were to be wounded or killed, God had my life in His hands. I knew where I would go when I died, and I need not fear death. As His child, nothing could happen to me He did not allow, and His intentions toward me were good. I could trust in the words of the Bible: "In all things God works for the good of those who love him, who have been called according to his purpose." (Romans 8:28, NIV).

Graduation day was October 31st, 1969, one day after my 20th birthday. Four days later, November 4th, my orders were cut for Vietnam. Those headed to Vietnam had to go through an additional week of classes to prepare for what lay ahead. About the only thing I remember besides sitting in classrooms and watching films is marching in the torrential rain wearing ponchos. Having grown up in the northwest I was used to the rain but had never seen it rain like that week. Oregon can experience rain and drizzle for days on end, and it can pour hard, but in Texas rain came down in unforgiving torrents with loud claps of thunder as dark clouds filled the sky and cold fronts clashed against the hot Texas air. Perhaps this was God's way of preparing us for the torrential rains of Vietnam, where we would spend days trying to stay dry under our ponchos and nights sleeping on what little high ground we might be able to find.

We left Fort Sam Houston on November 6th, and I was to report to the U.S. Army Overseas Replacement Station in Oakland, California on December 2nd, with 23 days' delay en route. The fellow terrified by loud explosions in Basic Training also received orders for Vietnam. I remember him commenting there was no way he would go. If need be he would flee to Canada like so many others were doing to avoid the draft. Only now, instead of being a draft dodger, he would be a deserter. I have often wondered what happened to him.

On my way home I stopped off in Colorado to see my grandparents. I then flew to Oregon and spent Thanksgiving with my family. Leave went by all too quickly with time spent saying goodbye to family and friends.

The ride to the Portland Airport on December 1st was largely characterized by silence and small talk. Just five months earlier, I had been on my way to become a soldier, and now I was on my way to war. What's a mother to say when her son is going off to war? What's a son to say, except, "I love you, and please don't worry. I'll be all right."

At the airport, I was surprised to discover a group of friends from church had come to see me off. These were the young people from my youth group who had befriended me at a time when I had very few friends. Now, here I stood in my uniform, surrounded by friends as I prepared to leave for a country on the other side of the world. I was so overwhelmed they would care enough to come see me off that any sense of foreboding was gone for the time being. When it came time to board the plane, hugs were given and farewells said as cameras flashed.

Once on the plane and seated, I was surprised to see two of the guys had persuaded the attendants to let them take one last picture of me on the plane. Once again I broke out in a big smile of joy at their thoughtfulness and was truly happy to have such good friends. One of them looked at me and asked, "What are you smiling about?" He couldn't understand my being happy at a time like this. At that moment I realized my friends had come to see me off, not knowing if they would ever see me alive again. As brave as they were trying to be, they were in that moment more afraid than I was.

I flew to Oakland and that evening got together with some of my classmates from Bible school, staying overnight with the family of one of them. Even Barb, the girl I had broken up with a year earlier, who never wanted to speak to me again, came to see me off, albeit somewhat reluctantly.

The next day I got up at 8:30 AM and arrived at the Transfer Station at 12:30 PM. I didn't get to go to bed again until 10 PM the next night as they kept us up, going through lines, turning in our uniforms, getting combat boots, fatigues, and the rest of what we would need in the way of clothes and duffle bags. Once again the old Army adage "Hurry up and wait!" was proven true.

Thursday evening, December 4th, we were taken by bus to Travis Air Force Base northeast of Oakland, and somewhere between 2200 hours and 2400 hours I boarded a Saturn Airlines stretch jet with 237 other GIs headed to Vietnam. On either side of me sat two of my best friends from boot camp and A.I.T. In fact there were lots of guys on that plane I had gone through training with, guys I would never see again once we received our assignments and were scattered throughout Vietnam.

It was a long flight with refueling stops in Hawaii and the Philippines. We were allowed to get out at both stops to stretch our legs in the terminal. We crossed the International Date Line between Hawaii and the Philippines and lost almost a whole day. Soldiers walked up and down the aisles talking to the stewardesses, laughing and having fun. Some got too loud, creating a party atmosphere. They understood all too well this might be their last chance to have a good time for a long time. Undoubtedly there were some on that plane who would not return alive, making the trip home in flag-draped boxes, their lives taken from them on the battlefield. Others would return on stretchers with arms and legs missing or having sustained some other serious injury. And still others might never return at all, their remains scattered in some desolate jungle blown apart by a booby trap, grenade, or mortar round, with only bits and pieces left to be gathered and returned to loved ones.

None of us would ever come home the same as we had left. We would all be changed in one way or another as we came face-to-face with the stark realities of war and the fear of death. We would lose our innocence and our boyhood on the battlefield and become men, whether we liked it or not. Many would not like the men they had become, while others would look back with pride for having served and survived. But for now, we were still just boys, unlikely warriors on our way to war. We would run through the woods again, hiding behind trees and crawling through the underbrush as we had done many times before, pretending to be soldiers searching for the elusive enemy. But this time it would be real, with real guns and real death. All of this and more must have played through our minds as the plane descended from the sky and landed in Bien Hoa at Tan Son Nhut Airbase outside of Saigon. "Gentlemen, welcome to the Republic of Vietnam. We hope you had a pleasant flight."

Me in a Class A uniform in a picture taken in San Antonio on my first pass from AIT (Advanced Individual Training). Hawkers on the sidewalk would hand you a ticket for a "free" picture, and then after the sitting, a salesman would put the screws to you to buy a whole set of pictures.

Me in front of the barracks holding my Certificate of Completion from A.I.T. I now had a designation of MOS 91A10, the Army's classification for combat medics.

CHAPTER FIVE

IN COUNTRY

"There is a time for everything,
And a season for every
activity under the heaven:
a time to be born and a time to die,
... a time to love and a time to hate,
a time for war and a time for peace."

Ecclesiastes 3:1-2, 8

Walking off the plane was like walking into another world. For those of us entering Vietnam for the first time, we could not help but wonder how long it would be before we heard gunfire or the sound of mortars exploding. How safe would it be, and what would we do if suddenly something were to happen? All we knew was we were now in a war zone and would start earning the combat pay that came along with it.

It was a beautiful day, warm and humid, but not too hot. After getting our duffle bags, we were loaded onto buses for the short seven-mile ride through Bien Hoa to the Transient Detachment at Long Bien. The bus windows were covered with wire mesh to prevent grenades or other devices from being thrown at us in an attack. I was immediately taken aback by the poverty of the Vietnamese people as we drove past their dilapidated housing. Apart from a one-week mission trip to Mexico during my year at Bible school, I had never been to a third-world country.

At Long Bien I learned I was assigned to the famed 101ˢᵗ Airborne Division and was told I would ship out in the next day or two. It rained briefly that afternoon, and a rainbow of hope could be seen in the distance. I was assigned a bunk for the night, just in case I didn't get shipped out that day. In the meantime, I was able to walk around and relax a bit.

There was an "open mess" called the Jet Set Club with a stereo, television, pool tables, shuffleboard, and a lounge with free coffee. I bought a coke, sat down, and wrote home to let them know I had arrived safely: *"I've been assigned to a really great division known as the 101ˢᵗ Airborne Division, and presently operating in 1 Corp[s] of V.N. which is the northern most sector. The place I'm headed for is named Phu Bai where I'll be assigned to a company. I may still be put in a hospital or some other medical unit for this division, or I may be elsewhere."*

Obviously I had no clue where I would wind up, even though I always tried to think positively about the unknown possibilities. I Corp[s] was the same region where my brother had been stationed at a fire base just three years earlier, where he attended the daily funerals of his fellow Marines. I could only wonder what might lie ahead for me.

It was nice to be in the club writing home. There were Christmas lights and two Christmas trees, one inside the club and one out in front of it. Maybe I wouldn't miss Christmas altogether after all, I thought.

Even though the comfort of Christmas was all around me, the war wasn't far away. That evening I could see the lights from flares dropped from helicopters in the distance. I could also hear the sound of artillery fire. We were told sniper fire or a mortar round might occasionally hit the base, but otherwise it was relatively safe.

The next day, Sunday, Dec. 7ᵗʰ, I was told I would be going to Phu Bai that evening. I don't remember what time it was when I and some others were trucked down to the airstrip where we would catch our transport plane north, but as with most things in the Army, we spent a good deal of time just waiting. Light turned into darkness, and I grew tired as my body and mind had not yet adjusted to the time change.

The terminal was nothing more than a large open air tent with chairs in rows, just as they would be at an airport back home. At some point a small group of us were called out to the tarmac to put our duffle bags on a pallet that would be loaded onto the C-130 when it arrived. We then went back to the tent to wait for the announcement for us to board. By this point, it was getting very late. I sat down and pulled my hat down over my eyes to rest while we waited. Before long I was sound asleep.

I don't know why no one woke me up when it came time to board, but when I awoke my flight was long gone and my duffle bag with it. I hadn't heard the boarding announcement over the loudspeaker. As a result I had to catch another flight later that morning. I arrived at Camp Campbell near Phu Bai at 10 AM, where I joined the others at the Replacement Detachment Center for the 101st Airborne Division.

That evening I wrote another letter home informing my family of my arrival up north. I didn't tell them, however, that I had missed my flight and lost my duffle bag, which was an embarrassing way to start my tour of duty. My duffle bag was nowhere to be found. I filed a missing baggage report, but it did no good. For all I knew, my things had already made their way to the black market by means of some G.I. supporting a drug habit.

All I had were the clothes on my back, and after a couple of days I decided to go to the chaplain for help. He took me over to supply to get some more fatigues, underwear, and socks, as well as some toiletries at the commissary. I guess this was not all that unusual. I had gotten paid after processing in, so I did have some money, though most of it had been sent home.

After three days at Camp Campbell, on Dec. 11th, a bunch of us were sent off to Camp Haines, which was right next to Camp Evans, for five days of what was called SEARTS "In Country Training." SEARTS stood for Screaming Eagle Replacement Training School. This was the final preparation before being assigned to our units. Our stay there included firing range practice, tactical training, and going out on a patrol.

When it came time to go to the armory for weapons, a couple of other conscientious objectors and I informed the sergeant of our status. Shortly after that we were told to report to the company commander's office, where he tried to persuade us to change our minds. I imagine this was standard practice, the first test of a C.O.'s conviction. My assumption is that some, when they were actually in Vietnam facing combat, may have decided to carry a weapon. We, however, stood firm and were told we would be put on detail while everybody else was at the firing range.

We scraped and painted latrines and took turns pulling watch at the barracks to protect everybody's belongings while they were away. When the others returned from one of their exercises, one of the guys asked me how I could even think about going into combat without a weapon. He said he was Catholic and had attended seminary to become a priest. I tried to explain to him my trust was not in the weapons of man but in God. I shared that because I had a personal relationship with God through faith in Jesus Christ, I was His child and nothing could happen to me that was not in His will. If I were wounded, He had a purpose for it, and if I were killed, I would be in Heaven, which is far better. He just shook his head and said he couldn't do it, that his faith was not that strong.

During the off hours some of us went to the enlisted men's club. I believe it was here I first made the decision to allow myself to have some beers along with the rest of the guys and got slightly drunk. I am sure I must have tried to justify my actions by telling myself I would only have a couple, and that I was entitled to since I was in Vietnam and could die here. Perhaps I just felt it would help me bond with the others. Even as a Christian, there was still part of me that deeply longed to be accepted by other people.

The day came when we medics were issued the necessary medical packs to go on patrol with the platoons. We were each assigned to a different platoon, which in turn was sent out to different parts of the base perimeter to search for enemy activity. We knew we were in a relatively secure area, but we were also told there was always the possibility of enemy contact.

The platoon I was with hiked out about four miles from 1 PM to about 5 PM without incident. The terrain was somewhat hilly, covered mostly by fields of "elephant grass" about waist high. Two of the platoons received some sniper fire, which we heard from a distance, but no one was hurt, and no sniper was found. So, from that perspective, the patrols were relatively uneventful.

The whole point was to give us the feel of being on patrol in a relatively safe situation before being assigned to units in the field. It was important for us to learn how to space ourselves out while on the move, and how to move as quietly as possible. You never wanted to be too close to the guy in front of or behind you just in case a sniper hit them, or they stepped on a booby trap, or an ambush took place. If you clustered together you increased your chances of being wounded or killed. Of course, we had been taught these things in Basic Training and A.I.T., but it's not the same when you're there for real, knowing the smallest mistake could cost you or someone else his life. The division wanted to make sure incoming replacements were properly trained before going out to the field, and this refresher course was meant to accomplish that.

After our SEARTS Training, we had a little graduation and then most of the guys were off to their units. Twenty of us, however, were still without orders and had to play the waiting game. I wrote home to let my family know what was happening, and I also wrote to Barb. I couldn't receive mail yet, since I had not been assigned to a unit, but that didn't prevent me from writing.

A full week went by, and some of us still did not have orders, so they finally sent us back to Camp Campbell on Tuesday, Dec. 23rd, to track them down.

When I first arrived in Phu Bai the weather was cooler and rainier than it had been down south. It reminded me of the fall weather we had in Oregon, though not as cold. As the days went on, it seemed to get better with a little rain in the morning and clear skies or partial cloudiness the rest of the day. It was supposed to be monsoon season, but for some reason it wasn't all that bad.

Those of us waiting for orders were kept busy with details here and there, stringing barbed wire on the base perimeter, doing carpentry work, helping in the bakery, etc. Maybe six or seven hours were spent each day doing whatever odd jobs they had for us.

One good thing about Camp Evans and Camp Campbell was the food. I could never really complain about Army food. I had excellent food at my Basic Training Camp, and the food during A.I.T. wasn't all that bad either. We always had decent food with plenty of selection, including salads, meats, veggies, desserts, and beverages. Occasionally we would have steaks and even strawberry shortcake for dessert.

Movies were shown outdoors every night, weather permitting. The only Vietnam movie made during the war, *Green Berets,* starring John Wayne and David Jansen, was playing. For some reason, I never seemed to be able to get through a whole movie but instead caught bits and pieces of several while I was there.

A buddy and I spent a lot of time in the enlisted men's club drinking sodas and playing cards when we weren't working. I also spent time every morning and most evenings at the chapel reading and praying. I figured I might as well enjoy myself while I could, since I had no idea what lay ahead for me in the coming months. As long as I reported to formation once each day to see if my orders were in and did my work, everybody seemed happy. For now I was living high on the hog with a roof over my head, a cot to sleep in, three hot meals a day, and cold sodas at the E.M. Club. What more could a guy want?

On Christmas Eve, I wrote home I was still at Camp Campbell waiting for orders and quite happy to keep waiting. I thought if I really pushed I could probably track down my orders, but why hurry things? Life was good as long as I was doing what they told me to do, so why rush it? If I was headed to a field unit, I might as well enjoy the delay as long as I could!

Bob Hope's USO Show came to Camp Eagle on Christmas Day. I thought it would be nice to go, but since I was a new guy with no assignment yet and had no clue how to get there, I didn't even try. I knew it would likely be jammed with others far more deserving. I hadn't even been out to the field yet. With the exception of the one patrol in SEARTS training, I had done nothing but hang out and do odd jobs, drink cokes at the E.M. Club, watch movies, and write letters home. I was sure those who had been there a while and faced the hardships of combat would enjoy it far more than I. Besides, I probably wouldn't even be able to get in, so the other replacements and I decided to hang out at the Replacement Detachment Center.

A good thing can only last so long. On January 12th, I received my orders. Strangely enough, they had been cut on December 11th, the same day I had headed to Camp Haines for SEARTS Training. No one could tell me why they had taken so long to reach me, but I didn't care, since it had all been good time anyway.

The sergeant who handed me my orders said I had been assigned to a "crack unit," the 3rd Battalion, 506th Infantry Regiment. Many years later I would come to understand what the sergeant meant as I learned about the "Band of Brothers" who had parachuted behind enemy lines in France on D-Day during WW II. Eventually a book would be written about these heroic soldiers, followed by an award-winning HBO television mini-series. Now, in another war, the men of the 506th Infantry were once again proving they were a rare breed that could get the job done. Unlike the rest of the 101st, which was operating in I Corps, the 3/506 was detached and on loan (i.e., given OPCON or Operational Control) to any division in II Corps that needed extra assistance. During WW II, when the battalion was first formed and trained in Taccoa, Georgia, part of their daily training was running up and down Currahee Mountain, and so it was fitting they should also take that name as their motto: "Currahee," a Cherokee word meaning "Stand Alone."

Orders in hand, I caught a transport plane to Phan Thiet on the coast about 150 miles Northeast of Bien Hoa, where I had entered the country 34 days earlier. This was where the battalion had been headquartered since its arrival in Vietnam in October of 1967, in the southernmost part of II Corps. They had spent their first two years operating in the Binh Thuan, Lam Dong, and Ninh Thuan Provinces. On November 5, 1969, they moved north to the Ban Me Thout area in Darlac Province to secure a valuable supply link, Highway QL-21. Forty-eight days later, on December 23rd, they moved even further north to Binh Dinh Province, on the coast just below I Corps to support the 173rd Airborne Brigade. In just over a month, I had gone from one end of the country to the other twice and still had not yet reached my final destination. But the clock was ticking, and it was only a matter of days before I would find myself on the field of battle.

Phan Thiet was beautifully situated on the South China Sea. The weather was great, and I could see the beach below the base. Because the rest of the battalion was now up north, only a small contingent of Headquarters Company, to which the medics belonged, was still in Phan Thiet. I learned I would be assigned to an infantry platoon for six months and then spend the rest of my time at the Battalion Aid Station. At least that was the way the rotation was supposed to work due to the high risk field medics were exposed to, but it always depended on receiving enough new medics to replace those on the line.

While at Phan Thiet, I spent time helping out in the aid station, but since there were so few people at Phan Thiet, things were pretty slow. An occasional soldier would come in for shots or to get some medications, and that was about it. I had the chance to talk with some of the medics who had completed their six months in the field and was encouraged to learn it might not be as bad as one would imagine. There was always the possibility of seeing combat, but most of the time was spent performing mundane duties while caring for the daily needs of your soldiers. Pushing pills and handing out Band-Aids for minor cuts and scratches was much more common than having to deal with gunshot and shrapnel wounds.

Five days after arriving in Phan Thiet, Saturday, January 17th, I caught a transport back North to LZ Uplift. There I met our Battalion Surgeon, Capt. David H. Dail, who told me what my options were. I could go to a platoon in the 173rd for a while, as they were short medics, replacing one of our own medics who was filling in there but would be leaving to join a Recon Team, or I could go to a fire base for a while to work at the aid station there, or I could replace a medic in our own Delta company, who was having problems including falling asleep during his radio watch.

It didn't take much for me to decide I would prefer being with one of our battalions' platoons. I did not want to go to the 173rd, which would only be temporary, and I had no clue what it would be like to be on a fire base, so I chose Delta Co. I was anxious to finally settle into a unit for a while, hopefully for the duration of my field duty. It had been six weeks since I had arrived in country. I certainly wasn't looking to be a hero, but I had chosen the path of an unlikely warrior because I believed God wanted me to be a witness for Him. I had already had numerous opportunities to share my faith with others, but having a place to call home and build deeper relationships was important, too. I needed to find out if I could do what I was trained for. There was no more putting it off. In the meantime, I would continue to help out in the aid station while I also got the equipment and supplies together I needed to go into the field.

The following day, Sunday, January 18th, I performed my first real duties as a medic. One of the platoons from Delta Company had come in from the field for a break and was due for plague, cholera, and tetanus shots. It was nice finally to be on the other end of the needle and to begin using the skills I had learned.

What I didn't know was this was the company I would soon be assigned to. I would be the medic for First Platoon, which was still out in the field. Medics were part of Headquarters Company and were assigned by the Battalion Surgeon to the various platoons as needed. One medic was assigned for every platoon of 25 to 30 men. We were accountable to the Battalion Surgeon for our work instead of to the Platoon Leader. We were the medical "experts" in the field and were given the authority to make the decisions relative to the health of the troops we served. This gave us a measure of leverage with our troops and platoon leaders, which I would later use to my advantage.

After the shots were given, I attended church services at the chapel and then returned to the aid station to begin the process of getting ready for the field. I received a brand new aid bag and filled it with compresses of various sizes, surgical clamps, scalpels, scissors, intravenous kits, I.V. fluid, morphine, tourniquets, alcohol swabs, and so on. I also filled a box with sick call supplies, including a variety of pills, ointments, solutions, and Band-Aids. One of the experienced medics helped make sure I got what I needed. That afternoon I went to battalion supply and received my field equipment, including a back pack, five canteens, flak jacket, mess kit, poncho, poncho liner, gas mask, steel pot, utility belt, and an empty metal ammo can to put my sick call supplies in so they would stay dry.

Our battalion was going to be moving in a couple of days by truck to LZ English, where I would catch a re-supply chopper to the field. I wrote home, filling them in on all of the details. Unlike a lot of guys who didn't want to tell their families what was going on, I held very little back. I saw it as an opportunity to share with them how God was working in my life and watching over me. I wrote, *"I'm really not worried at all. I've been reading the Scriptures a lot and keeping in touch with the Lord and He's given me a calm heart (Psalm 23). The Lord is all powerful and merciful!"*

Looking back it seems strange that just a year and a half earlier I had made the decision to stay home to be a witness to my family instead of moving to Los Angeles to work in the children's home and attend college. If I had gone to college, I would have been given a deferment and could have avoided the draft for at least four more years. By then the war would have been over for all but a few Americans. Now, here I was over eight thousand miles away and through my letters I was able to share more about my faith than I had ever been able to in person. In addition, I really believed I was on a mission for God. I wrote to Barbara again telling her I would be going out to the field in just a couple of days and added, *"I'm a combat medic, but most of all I'm a Servant of Christ with an urgent message to be taken to the farthest ends of the earth, and praise the Lord, He is allowing me to do just that!"*

That night about 9:00 PM there was an alert and the sirens went off. Supposedly "Charlie" was trying to penetrate our perimeter. The lights went out, and everyone took up defensive positions. I grabbed my aid bag and was ready to rush to anyone's aid who might need it. Those on the perimeter put out some firepower, what was called a "mad minute," and then there was silence. After about an hour, the all clear signal was given, and the lights came back on. Apparently it was a false alarm, as there was no sign of "Charlie," so we caught our breath, calmed down, and went to bed.

Tomorrow would be another day, and I would learn soon enough what it meant to run into the enemy and hear the *ak-ak-ak* of AK-47s raining down fire on us. Soon enough I would be called on to use the skills I had acquired to save the lives of my men. But for now, I must sleep. In just 36 hours I would begin my new role as a combat medic. It would be a long time before I would be allowed to sleep again in a cot with a roof over my head and boots on the floor. I am sure I must have wondered as I went to sleep if I would be up to the task, how my men would feel about me, and what I would do the first time we ran into Charlie or the NVA. But those were questions that could only be answered in the future. For now I must sleep.

CHAPTER SIX

NEW GUY

"Two are better than one, because
they have a good return for their work;
If one falls down, his friend can pick him up.
But pity the man who falls and has no one to pick him up."
Ecclesiastes 4:9-10

The next day, Tuesday, January 20th, was spent packing up the aid station and getting ready for the battalion's big move. I was given three days' worth of C-rations and filled my canteens with water. I went to supply to pick up a couple of straps for securing my aid bag and bedroll to my pack. Once fully loaded I was carrying up to 70 pounds, including food, water, all of the medical supplies for the platoon, and personal items. I would soon learn five canteens were inadequate, especially if it was hot and we were doing a lot of humping. A minimum of six and as many as eight canteens were carried by each soldier. In addition to drinking, water was also used for washing and shaving and wasn't always available from other sources. I needed to be ready to go as soon as we made the move to LZ English, where I would catch a supply chopper to the field.

Wednesday morning, January 21st, we were loaded into the back of trucks for the 30-mile move north. The trip took us through a beautiful, lush valley with green rice paddies all around. It was some of the most beautiful country I had ever seen and stood out in contrast to the harsh realities of war, which I was yet to experience.

After pulling into LZ English and unloading from the trucks, one of the first things I noticed was a pungent odor that filled the air, something I hadn't experienced yet in Vietnam. I had no idea what it was. It was a smell I would often experience in varying degrees. At some point, after I was in the field, I got up enough nerve to ask someone what it was. "It's the smell of dead bodies," he said. "We don't bury the enemy. We just leave them to rot."

It was the stench of death that would fill the nostrils of every soldier who dared to walk through the jungles and rice paddies of Vietnam. I would come to experience many smells of war; but this one would be the worst: the stench of war that can never be forgotten. It becomes part of you, staying with you long after you leave the battlefield, never to be washed away.

The medical platoon sergeant walked me to the helo-pad to catch my ride. This was the first of many rides on the infamous Huey slicks, the workhorse of the infantry and Airborne units in Vietnam. As a kid I had been fascinated with helicopters, and now I was finally going to ride in one. It seemed strange that we hadn't gotten any training in helicopters at Basic or A.I.T. Everything there was simulated, including loading and unloading stretchers into and out of vehicles and choppers. I guess they figured we would catch on soon enough once we were in Vietnam.

The roar of the engine and rotors was deafening, and dust kicked up everywhere. In front sat the pilot and commander, and on each side of the aircraft at the back of the doorways sat a machine gunner, his M-60 always ready if needed. The side doors had been removed to make it easy to get in and out of and to quickly load and unload supplies. I stooped, held my helmet on my head and made my way to the door throwing my gear in. Climbing in, I sat on one of the canvas seats in the middle of the chopper and waited. The slick, as we called them, loaded with supplies, slowly lifted off the pad and, with its nose tilted forward and tail in the air, gaining altitude as it went, headed toward the mountain range, which loomed in the distance.

As we passed over the rice paddies, I could see the South China Sea to the east and a village with its grass huts surrounded by now dry and barren rice paddies below. Out in the ocean were navy ships with their big guns ready to give artillery support to our troops if needed. Passing over the village and rice paddies, the chopper came around to the mountains and, after circling, touched down on top of a mountain designated Hill 474 for its altitude. I jumped out and grabbed my pack as others came and started unloading supplies from the chopper.

I was quickly introduced to the platoon leader, whose name was also Mike, and the platoon sergeant, whose name was James. The medic I was replacing threw his things on the chopper and returned to LZ English without so much as a hello or goodbye. That's the way it happened all of the time. Cherries would come in on a resupply chopper and an old timer leaving the field either to go on R&R or home because his tour was up would hop on the same chopper and be gone just like that.

There were two platoons on top of 474 along with the Company Commander, Captain William (Bill) Ohl, his R.T.O. (Radio Telephone Operator), Ronnie Pierce from Oklahoma, and the senior medic, who always traveled with the captain. It was not uncommon for platoons to meet up for re-supply on occasion or to work together on missions, though most of the time we moved in platoon-sized elements.

As I was introduced to some of the men in 1st platoon, it didn't take them long to start looking over my stuff. They knew that as a "cherry" I had no clue what I was doing and wanted to make sure I wasn't humping anything more than I needed to. When you went through supply they threw every piece of standard issue equipment at you and you signed for it not knowing if you really needed it or not. You just assumed they knew what they were doing. But of course, the supply clerks had never humped a day in their life, outside of Basic Training, and were simply following S.O.P.s (Standard Operational Procedures) handed to them by somebody else.

Somebody grabbed the gas mask and the flak jacket and said, "You won't need these. The gooks don't use gas and the flak jacket is too heavy for humping these mountains in the heat and humidity." When the next chopper arrived, they were promptly thrown back on along with some other things to be returned to LZ English. I was a bit shocked equipment I was responsible for was suddenly being taken from me and returned without any way of showing from whom it had come. For all I knew it wound up on the black market rather than back in supply, but then, as the novice I wasn't about to question the judgment of those who had already been living in the field for some time.

When I was introduced to the senior medic, he asked me if I had any questions. I couldn't think of any at the time, so he told me if I ever had any I could call him on the radio for advice. Since the captain liked to rotate among his platoons, there would be times when they would be with us, but most of the time they would be with one of the other two platoons.

The men in my platoon were scattered around the top of the mountain in various places reading the mail they had just received, opening packages, and cooking lunch. There was very little vegetation on top of the mountain to hide in, though there were some boulders and some brush here and there. As I was taken around and introduced, a black soldier by the name of Eugene Wilson was cooking a canned ham with pineapple he had just received from home, and he invited me to share some of it with him. Cooking was done on top of an empty C-ration can with holes punched into it for ventilation. The can was turned upside down, and a heat tab or a small amount of C-4 explosive was placed underneath it and lit. In this case the canned ham was placed on top of his makeshift stove to heat it up.

I soon found out it was common practice to share whatever you had with your fellow soldiers. These were the guys you would depend on for your life, and it only made sense to share your good fortunes as well as the bad.

I noticed some of the guys wearing pieces of green camouflage cloth tied around their necks and asked one of them what the significance of it was. "It's a drive on rag!" he said. "It's from a blanket we took from a dead gook. The idea is to wear it until the day you go back to the real world, for good luck. You know, to keep you drivin' on. Do you want one?" he asked.

"Sure!" I said, wanting to do everything I could to fit in. Taking his off, he tore a strip from the edge of it and handed it to me. I tied it around my neck as a symbol of my newfound acceptance and commitment to the men I had just met, and apart from taking it off to tear in half again to share with someone else, it remained there for the next ten months, until the day I stepped on the freedom bird that brought me home again. I still have it among my memorabilia as a reminder of the closeness we had as a platoon, the common bond that moved us to share anything and everything we had, and to keep driving on for each other.

My reception was probably a bit different from a novice rifleman or "Shake-'n'-Bake" NCO2 who were often looked upon with a degree of suspicion until they had gained the experience they needed to earn the trust of their fellow soldiers. New guys made the kinds of mistakes that often got people killed. Seasoned grunts also tended not to get close to new guys too quickly, because you never knew when they might get blown away and getting close just made it hurt that much more.

As the medic, however, I was there to meet the medical needs of the platoon and not to perform any tactical function. Knowing they needed to be able to count on me to take care of them, perhaps I was received with a greater degree of warmth. Still, I would have to prove myself. Until I experienced combat and demonstrated I could do my job under fire, I was an unknown quantity, an untested grunt, the new guy to be looked on with a degree of suspicion and caution.

I was part of the C.P. (Command Post). That meant I slept in the relative center of the NDP (Night Defensive Position) near the lieutenant, his R.T.O., and the platoon sergeant. This was practiced not just for the safety of the C.P. members but also for tactical purposes. Being in the center of the NDP enabled the Lt. and me, as the medic, to respond to any emergency or attack regardless of where it occurred on the perimeter.

During the day when we were on the move, we traveled single file, spaced apart ten to fifteen feet from each other, and I was about six men back from the point, behind the Lt. and his R.T.O. for protection, yet close enough to the point to get there in a hurry if the point man stepped on a booby trap or walked into an ambush. Platoon leaders had one of the shortest life spans of any soldier in Vietnam; R.T.O.s and medics were not far behind.

As I looked around from our vantage point on top of the mountain, I could see the dry rice paddies down below in front of us with the village a mile or so away and the South China Sea a few miles beyond that. In the other direction were more mountains covered by thick jungle. Known as the Crows Foot Mountains, this area was also referred to as Combat Alley because of the frequent contact with the NVA and VC.

The field units of the 3/506 had moved into this area just a few days before on January 16th, and Company A had already run into the NVA on two different occasions.

On January 18th, their 3rd platoon engaged a small group of NVA near Hill 474, killing one of them who had a diary on him indicating he was from the 7th Battalion of the 22nd NVA Regiment. This was consistent with information gleaned from a North Vietnamese soldier captured in the upper An Loa Valley on January 2nd. He was with the 9th Battalion of the 22nd Regiment, and it was learned his battalion, part of the 3rd NVA Division, had moved into the southern part of Binh Dinh Province. With their 7th Battalion to the north in the vicinity of Hill 474, they hoped to wreak havoc during the coming TET Offensive and disrupt pacification efforts going on in that area.

The very next day, January 19th, the same platoon continued to sweep the area and was ambushed by what was thought to be another squad-sized NVA element, killing their point man, Pfc. Robert Mitcheltree, Jr. of Longview, Texas. A significant firefight ensued, with 3rd Platoon being pinned down. Battalion Commander LTC Joseph N. Jaggers, Jr. brought in elements from Companies B, C, and D to support 3rd Platoon. Eventually the enemy broke off their engagement and disappeared into the rocky crags and well-hidden caves characteristic of this area.

Of course, all of this was information I learned much later, as no mention of it was made to me the day I arrived or in the days that followed. Pee-ons, what we enlisted personnel called ourselves because that is how we felt we were treated, were generally kept in the dark about such things. For now, my job was to get to know my men and be of whatever help I could, including making sure they all took their daily and weekly anti-malaria pills. The daily pills were small white tablets the size of an aspirin, and the weekly pills were much larger orange "horse pills" we called Monday-Mondays in order to remind us to take them on that day. A failure to take these pills almost always resulted in a soldier getting malaria, which could then plague him the rest of his life.

I settled into the C.P. and made myself something to eat from my Cs. As the sun went down and it began to grow dark, I found a level spot to roll out my poncho and liner. Word was we would be moving out in the morning. For now I would try to get some sleep in order to be ready for whatever lay ahead.

CHAPTER SEVEN

CHERRY DAYS

*"Keep me safe, O God,
for in you I take refuge."*

Psalm 16:1

I am sure I must have slept fitfully the first night, wondering if anything might happen. Plus, I had to adjust to sleeping on the ground.

As dawn broke, people started rolling up their bedrolls, washing, shaving, and fixing something to eat. Squad leaders sent people out to retrieve the trip flares and claymore mines set out the night before.

A flare was tied to the base of a bush or small tree and a trip wire was strung from it to another bush or tree to which it would also be attached. Then a rectangular crescent-shaped claymore mine about 6 inches tall and 10 inches wide, filled with ball bearings and C-4 plastic explosive was placed between the trip wire and the perimeter of the NDP facing outward. An electrical wire was attached to the claymore mine and run back to a guard position, a foxhole if we had time to dig one, and attached to a detonator we called a "clicker" because of the sound it made when you hit it. If an enemy soldier tried to sneak up on you, or accidentally walked into your position, he would hopefully trip the wire causing the flare to light up. Whoever was on watch at that position would hit the appropriate clicker to blow the mine and hopefully blow away Charlie along with it. Each squad in a platoon would set three of four of these up, and there were three or four defensive positions on the perimeter of your NDP, depending upon the strength of your platoon, one for each squad. At least two of these positions would have M-60 machine guns in place.

Once the claymores and trip-flares were picked up, it would be safe for guys to make their way out of the perimeter to a semi-private spot for their morning "business," being sure to take their weapon along with them and never going out too far. An entrenching tool (a small collapsible shovel) was also supposed to be taken to dig a cat hole, though this was sometimes ignored. It was important to try and leave as little evidence of your presence behind as possible and also to maintain a sanitary environment in case you used the same NDP over a period of time. Before going out, though, it was also important to notify whoever was on watch so you didn't get shot coming back in.

After eating and cleaning up we packed our gear and got ready to move out. Our platoon was to make its way down the backside of the mountain and work its way through a valley to the rice paddies in front of the mountain where we were to set up ambushes along the trails running from the mountains to the village. Intelligence reports indicated the VC and NVA were going into the village for food at night.

After the Lt. briefed the Platoon Sgt. and squad leaders on the mission, the order was given to saddle up. People began to get their backpacks and web gear (used to attach smoke grenades, hand grenades and other equipment to backpacks) on when all of a sudden a blood curdling scream came from one of the squads: "Medic!"

I grabbed my aid bag and ran in the direction of the screams. There writhing in pain was a black soldier by the name of Bob Asbell, desperately struggling to get his web gear and shirt off. "Scorpion!" someone said. "He's been stung by a scorpion!" Sure enough, when I looked at his back, he had several significant welts. A scorpion had gotten into his web gear and stung him several times in the back when he tried to put the gear on.

I had never imagined my first emergency in the field would be to treat scorpion stings, and I wondered what I should give him. I also had to decide whether this was something that could be treated in the field or if he needed to be evacuated. The other platoon had already pulled out so I told the Lt.'s R.T.O. to get the senior medic on the radio, which he did. He told me to give Asbell six ornade capsules, which were an antihistamine, then call in a medevac and send him in for observation. The antihistamine helped reduce the effects of the poison until he got to the aid station for further treatment. Even if he didn't suffer any long-term effects, he would be in far too much pain for a while to be able to carry his gear, which was essential for a grunt in the field. I filled out a medical tag and attached it to his shirt, which he was able to put back on loosely. When the medevac arrived, he and his equipment were whisked back to LZ English, from which I had just come the day before.

The excitement over, we were once again given the order to get our gear on and get ready to move out. It was another beautiful sunny day, and we had clear visibility as we began to follow a trail along the ridge heading north. The point man had to keep his eye out not only for Charlie but also for booby traps that might be hidden along the way.

One of the guys in the platoon complained he was not feeling well. He had apparently already been treated for malaria once and was running a fever again. Every couple of hours we would stop, and I would take his temperature, give him some aspirin, and try to cool him off with a little water.

After spending all day slowly making our way down the mountain through thick forest and vegetation, stopping only for short rest breaks and lunch, it was decided we had better find a good spot for our NDP. We set up on a small hill overlooking a valley and a stream that ran through the valley and out toward the rice paddies. Squads were sent out, one at a time, to do what we called a clover leaf, to make sure Charlie wasn't lurking nearby. A squad would go out a short distance and circle back covering one-third or one-quarter of our perimeter. Then another squad would do the same thing and so on until the whole perimeter area had been checked. If it was felt the area was clear, trip flares and claymores could be set out for the night.

Because it was a clear moonlit night, visibility was good, and it was quite beautiful and serene. I kept an eye on the soldier with the fever, which had risen through the day, reaching 102.4. We weren't allowed to evacuate a soldier with a fever until it reached 104. At 7 PM it finally broke, and I was able to hit the sack, exhausted from the day's hump.

I am sure I slept better than the night before. As part of the C.P., I also pulled my first two-hour radio watch from 1 AM to 3 PM. Every hour on the half-hour we would call each squad's guard position on the radio for a situation report (SITREP). This helped ensure those on watch at the squad positions were awake and alert. Then every odd hour on the half-hour (e.g., 1:30 AM and 3:30 AM) we would call the Company C.P. and give them a platoon SITREP. They were always brief, only a few words spoken in a whisper to maintain as much silence as possible.

The night was uneventful, though we heard sporadic gunfire in the distance that sounded like M-16s. I wrote home G.I.s were probably just trying to keep Charlie awake, as there was no contact that we knew of.

The next morning, the 23rd, after breakfast, we saddled up and continued our journey toward our objective. We worked our way down the hill and into the valley that ran between the mountains. It would still take us time to work our way through the valley and out to the rice paddies. The valley floor was covered with tall elephant grass, and we knew we would be easy targets for mortar from the mountains if we weren't careful. We made our way carefully to the stream, which we thought would be a good place to rest and refresh ourselves in the heat of the day. The terrain there also provided us with some measure of cover.

Once we reached the stream, we were able to relax. Squads were sent out to cloverleaf our position for any signs of enemy activity. The Lt., his R.T.O., and I always stayed with the rest of the platoon. If a squad on cloverleaf did get hit you didn't want to lose your platoon leaders and medic, and a fire team could always take me to their location if need be.

I took my boots off and soaked my feet in the stream, and so did some of the other guys. The guys talked about how great it was to have such good weather. Prior to this it was extremely rainy, which made things miserable in the field. During monsoon season the grunt is always wet and cold and at risk of developing trench foot and other wet weather maladies. They were glad to be able to get their boots and socks off and air their feet out. I joked with them saying I had brought the sunshine with me.

As I soaked my feet, I took time to write home letting my family know of my arrival in the field and hump down the mountain. As always, I tried to assure them I was okay and felt relatively safe. *"We've got lots of men in this gorge and on these hills,"* I wrote, *"so if Charlie's here, he'll probably either stay hidden or try to leave the area. Nobody here really cares to meet up with him."*

That really did reflect the attitude of most grunts in Vietnam. Even though our mission was to search out and destroy the enemy and his supplies, we often joked our real mission was to "Search and Avoid." Instead of referring to ourselves as the Screaming Eagles, the motto of the 101st Airborne Division, we sometimes called ourselves the

"Squawking Chickens." You had to have a sense of humor about what you were doing there or you would go crazy.

Of course there were all too many in the ranks of leadership, career officers out to earn that next promotion, who were gung-ho about the war and anxious to get a body count. Men like that were dangerous and tended to put their troops at risk in order to achieve their own personal goals. It was these who often found themselves the victims of "fragging," a term made popular in Vietnam, which was the practice of throwing a grenade into a bunker or hootch to kill an officer or other soldier who wasn't liked.

We set up our NDP somewhere near the stream that night. It would be another four days before I wrote home again.

Every third day was re-supply day, when we would get C-rations, water, clean fatigues, munitions, batteries for the PRC25 radios, medical supplies, and, of course, mail, which everyone looked forward to. The list of supplies needed was radioed in the day before.

When the clean clothes came, they were in a pile, all mixed up, and you had to dig through to find a pair of pants and shirt that would fit. I was surprised to find there were no boxer shorts, just fatigues, t-shirts and socks. Because of the humidity most guys felt wearing undershorts contributed to jock itch and so chose to dump them. If you wanted undershorts the only option was to keep what you brought with you to the field and wash them by hand. In all my time in the field I only knew of one guy who did this. His name was Fredricko Gapassin. We called him Ricko. He was from Guam and was meticulous in his hygiene.

After re-supply it was time to continue our mission, so we saddled up and began making our way once again through the valley toward the rice paddies. We humped until we were pretty close to where the valley opened up to the rice paddies and decided to stop there for the night. It was getting late in the day, and we needed time to scout out the trails in front of the mountain and decide where to put our ambushes. We could do that tomorrow.

That evening we set up our NDP in the valley floor in the tall elephant grass to give us some measure of cover. Though there was some risk of being mortared from the nearby hills, the valley floor gave us good visibility of our perimeter, and we felt it would be difficult for the enemy to sneak up on us if he was in the area. Clover leafs were sent out to make sure the surrounding area was clear, and then the trip flares and claymores were put out as it grew dark. Once it was dark there wasn't much to do except hit the sack until it was time for your watch. Maintaining silence at night was essential. The grassy valley floor was much more comfortable to sleep on than the rocky ground on top of Hill 474. I slept until it was time to pull my watch, and then I went back to sleep as all seemed quiet.

CHAPTER EIGHT

CONTACT

"He who dwells in the shelter of the Most High
will rest in the shadow of the Almighty.
I will say of the LORD, 'He is my refuge and my fortress,
My God in whom I trust.'"

Psalm 91:1-2

On Sunday, January 25th, just before dawn, I awoke to the sound of commotion in the camp. The soldier on watch at the position facing Hill 474 thought he heard movement on our perimeter. The VC were known for their ability to crawl up to your perimeter undetected and turn your claymore mine around so when you hit the detonator it would blow on your own position. This made it critical soldiers on watch were alert to any sounds or movement beyond the wires. Every effort was made not to let the enemy get too close, unless of course you were laying a well-concealed ambush and wanted them to walk into the kill zone. The Lt. gave the order to launch a couple of M-79 grenades. After they exploded there was silence. Everyone was alert as we waited to see what would happen. No more movement was detected. As soon as the sun came up and we could see our perimeter was clear, we retrieved the trip flares and claymores and a squad went out to check the area of suspected activity.

A trail was discovered leading up the side of the mountain; tracks indicated it had recently been used. However, there were no blood trails, and we could not be certain there really had been anybody out there that morning. An animal could have made the noise. If Charlie had been there, though, he most likely used that trail coming and going. The decision was made to send a squad to check it out right after breakfast. (In his book *The Protected Will Never Know,* Don Meyer attributes the movement on our perimeter to a lion, something I had never heard until reading his book. Though I believe there were panthers and even tigers in Vietnam, I do not believe lions are indigenous there.)

When the squad returned, they reported they had discovered a small cave among some large boulders on the mountain. At the base of a tree was a stack of firewood, indicating the cave was either in use or had been used recently. But for now the area appeared deserted.

After calling in the report to the company commander, the platoon was ordered to move in and investigate. Making our way up the trail, we moved into the area surrounding the cave. Someone was sent into the cave to investigate. Because the entrance was small, he carried a .45 pistol and a flashlight, as was customary for tunnel rats. When he returned, he reported the cave was empty with the exception of an old NVA backpack and some documents he brought back. When this was radioed in by the Lt., the order was given to set up a defensive perimeter and wait for further instructions. By this time the morning had passed, and it was time for lunch. Since we seemed to have good cover among the massive boulders and there didn't appear to be any activity, we broke out our C-rations.

It was another beautiful day in Vietnam, bright and sunny, but not too hot. The foul weather of the monsoon season had passed, my delay at Camp Campbell having spared me, at least for the time being. It seemed as if God was really watching over me. After all, here I was seven weeks into my tour and other than a false alarm at LZ Uplift and this morning's scare, nothing serious had happened. I was doing okay.

For the most part the C-rations provided a well-balanced and fairly decent variety of meals. Some things almost everybody hated, like the scrambled eggs and the lima beans and ham. On supply days everybody picked through what they wanted, traded what they could, and the cans nobody wanted were punched full of holes and buried in a pit to keep the enemy from using them. A lot of guys carried Worcestershire and hot sauce sent from home to add some spice. Among the favorite foods was the pound cake and canned peaches or fruit cocktail. I especially enjoyed taking the pound cake and mixing it with the peaches for desert, and that's what I decided to do this day. I was getting pretty good by this time at using the little can opener that came with the rations. It was about one in the afternoon, and the warm sun felt good as I sat on a small boulder opening the can of fruit, my mouth watering in anticipation of the sweet taste.

What I didn't know as we ate was someone told the Lt. of fresh signs of gooks in the area in the form of human waste and we should get out of there. But apparently the Lt., a West Point graduate, ignored the warning, and we continued to eat.

Suddenly, all hell broke loose as shots rang out, and our guys opened up against an unseen enemy uphill of us. "Medic!" someone urgently cried from the rocks above me. "Medic!" came the cry again. Dropping my peaches, I grabbed my aid bag and scrambled to my feet. Climbing up over some boulders, I could see a soldier lying on a large flat boulder. His name was Victor San Nicholas, but we called him "Guam" because he was from there.

Tom Landers, nicknamed "Horoscope" because of his interest in such things, had been sitting just to Guam's left. As the Assistant Gunner, he quickly joined one of the machine gunners to help feed the ammo, but the safety on the gun was jammed, as it hadn't been cleaned properly for a while. Tom jumped up and shot off a burst of tracers from his

M-16, then yelled out, "Jean Dixon was right, you mother *expletive*!" referring to some prediction he had heard and believed applied to the situation at hand. He finished his clip of tracers, which overheated his rifle, forcing him to drop it. By this time the machine gunner had gotten the safety released, and together they unleashed a volley of fire up the hill.

Jumping down to Guam, I looked for a wound and saw he was bleeding from the abdomen. Checking his back, I saw a bullet had gone through him exiting near the spine. Fortunately, both wounds were fairly small, and the bleeding was minimal. I used two compresses, tying them around him to secure them over the wounds, and then, with the help of another soldier, picked him up and carried him to a more secure location.

Once I had him in a more secure place, there was little I could do for him other than try to comfort him. "My legs!" he said. "I can't feel my legs!"

"They're okay," I told him as I held him in my lap. "They're right here, and you're going to be okay. We're going to get you out of here." Of course, I knew the bullet might have severed his spine, and I had no idea if he would be fine or not, but as the medic, it was my job to do everything I could to aid and comfort the wounded, saving them if I could. Calming them by telling them they would be okay even if you thought they might not be was important to keeping their spirits up. Hope is always one of the greatest factors in anyone's survival. Leaving him, I made my way a short distance to the lieutenant, who was on the radio calling in air support. "We need to evacuate Guam as soon as we can." I told him. "He's been gut shot and will bleed to death internally if we don't get him out."

Down below us a short distance, maybe 50-75 meters, was a meadow large enough for an LZ. There was also some brush between us and a well-worn trail leading down to the meadow. The Lt. ordered a squad to secure the LZ and requested a dust-off (a medical evacuation helicopter also known as a medevac) from LZ English. While the squad cut its way through the brush with a machete and headed down the trail, I got my poncho liner out and three men to help me carry Guam to the LZ, with one man on each corner. In the meantime, the fighting raged on.

Making our way to the trail, we got on our knees in an effort to stay as low as we could. With two men on the lower end of the blanket and Benjamin Garcia and me at the head of the blanket, we started to inch our way forward, hunching over as we went. Suddenly Benjamin, who was parallel to me on my left, sat straight up with a startled look on his face. Then he released the blanket, slumped to his left, and tumbled down the embankment, disappearing in the tall grassy meadow.

Immediately the other two men and I hit the dirt. At the same time a panicked cry, "Medic! Medic!" came from the foot of the trail where the squad, sent to secure the LZ, had gone. Looking at the other two men I told them to take Guam back up into the rocks where it was more secure. With my aid bag on my back, I low-crawled down the trail as quickly as I could. At the foot of the trail, I found one soldier, Jeff Miller, shot in the head, the bullet having entered just above his right ear. A second soldier, Smitty, was lying on his back on the side of the hill with a bullet wound to his right thigh. A third soldier, Neal Rogers, the R.T.O., lay next to him in a state of shock. The radio on his back had been hit and was disabled, but luckily he was uninjured. The radio, which made him an easy target, had, in this case, saved his life.

Recognizing Jeff was unlikely to survive, I turned to treat Smitty. "No! Miller first!" he insisted. I tried to explain Jeff wouldn't make it, but he insisted again I treat Jeff first. Turning to Jeff, I bandaged his head wound as quickly as I could. He was still alive but unconscious, and his breathing was very shallow and labored. Then I went back to treat the other soldier. The bullet had gone all the way through his thigh and didn't appear to have hit the bone or any arteries, so I was confident he would be okay.

While this was going on, helicopter gunships had arrived and were unleashing a torrent of rockets, cannon, and machine gun fire on the enemy who had us pinned down. The Lt. and platoon sergeant had popped smoke grenades to mark our position for the gun ships, so the medevacs would know where to land. The smoke grenades that had been thrown down into the meadow to mark the LZ caught some of the grass on fire, which created even more smoke.

As soon as I finished bandaging the leg wound, I grabbed my aid bag and crawled off into the meadow to look for Benjamin. Making my way through the tall grass, I found him a short distance away. He wasn't breathing, and there was no pulse. In an effort to revive him, I administered C.P.R., breathing air into his lungs and then compressing his chest in an effort to get his heart going. The burning grass crackled not far away, and the smoke it created probably worked to my advantage, giving me some cover. After several minutes, I checked his pulse again but had no response. Since I couldn't see any blood, I tore his shirt open to see where he had been shot. A bullet had entered his right side just below the armpit ripping into his chest. Undoubtedly, it had pierced his lungs and heart, killing him quickly.

Later, when I had time to think about it, I came to realize the bullet that killed Benjamin must have been meant for me. Benjamin was sitting to my left parallel to me, and the enemy was uphill to my right. His arms would have been forward as were mine, as we held onto the blanket carrying Guam. The bullet had to pass by me first in order to strike him where it did. Clearly, I was the target!

Realizing there was nothing more I could do for Benjamin, I grabbed my aid bag and again crawled back to the foot of the trail. As I did, a dust-off piloted by Warrant Officer (WO) Stephen L. Tomooth from El Monte, California, tried to come into the LZ, not realizing we were in no position to load our wounded. Bullets tore through the chopper, seriously wounding the crew chief and forcing it to turn back. Returning to LZ English, the crew chief was rushed into the aid station for treatment, and the chopper was declared a total loss.

Another medevac commanded by Chief Warrant Officer (CWO) Terry M. Zinger of Grenada Hills, California and piloted by WO Samuel J. Siverd, Meadville, Pennsylvania took off. While the gunships blasted the enemy positions in an effort to give the dust-off the cover it needed, WO Siverd brought the chopper in and hovered over the meadow. As it did, the enemy let loose a heavy volley of small arms fire striking the engine and flight controls. Rocking under the heavy fire, the chopper lifted and turned out over the trees that lined the meadow heading back to LZ English. However, unable to make it, the chopper was forced to land about two miles away near a firebase.

By this time the crew of the first dust-off had secured the use of another chopper and was in the air. As they approached the LZ, the enemy again riddled the chopper with small arms fire. Bullets pierced the windshield spraying the pilot, WO Max Owens of Fort Knox, Kentucky with Plexiglas. As he fell back into his seat, WO Tomooth, the commander, grabbed the controls, preventing it from crashing into the hill, and, turning it away, disappeared over the trees and into the valley below.

Unable to communicate with the rest of the platoon, the other soldiers and I lay at the foot of the trail waiting to see what would happen. We couldn't risk going back up the trail and had no way of letting the Lt. know our condition. Realizing we were without communication, the Lt. ordered his RTO, Ken Wydeven, whom we called "Professor," to bring one of the other radios down to us. As he crawled down to us, however, his radio bumped up against some of the rocks, and when he reached us, it didn't work.

(Ken, a tall lanky fellow from Wisconsin, was a college graduate. He had managed to avoid the draft for four years while he earned his teaching degree, and then, just three days after graduation, he received his draft notice from Uncle Sam. Three months later, he was sent to Vietnam and became the lieutenant's RTO.)

While this was going on, the rest of the platoon was trying to maneuver into better fighting positions. While they did, Sgt. George Spillers was struck by a bullet in the forehead at the bridge of the nose, breaking his black army-issue glasses in half and killing him instantly. Tom Landers and some of the others decided to retreat down the hill twenty-five feet to a safer position, leaving their rucksacks behind. The enemy then moved into their old position and, finding some grenades left with the rucksacks, began tossing them down the hill. Fortunately, the grenades fell down into the crevices of the boulders before exploding. Tom Landers put his hands over his ears and opened his mouth to relieve the pressure from the concussion of the explosions, knowing he was going to get hit by shrapnel. Amazingly, no one was hit.

Realizing they had left the only working radio behind, somebody yelled, "Landers! Go get the radio!"

Tom responded, "Wow, man!" and then asked Jesus to tell him when to go. Yelling, "Cover me!" he began running up the hill from rock to rock until he reached the radio. Grabbing some canteens of water that were also there, he threw them down the hill, and then, with the radio in hand, asked God one more time to show him when to head back down the hill.

Running as quickly as he could, he reached a passageway between the rocks and stopped, but Sgt. Schrang yelled, "Get out of there! That's where everyone is getting shot!"

Of course, it wasn't, but in the fog of battle there is a lot of confusion.

Sgt. Schrang got on the radio and was talking to the battalion commander, who was flying over the battlefield in his OH-6A Cayuse (LOcH) firing M-79 grenades at the enemy and trying to coordinate the battle at the same time. Pulling the handset from his ear, Sgt. Schrang looked at Tom and said, "He wants us to get on line and assault." Of course, this was the standard military maneuver for taking a hill, if you had the men and the firepower to do it. But we were undermanned as a platoon even before the battle began.

Tom, who wasn't about to go back up that hill, pulled the hand set away from Sgt. Schrang and yelled into it, "Look, you *expletive*, you *expletive* come down here and you *expletive* get on line and assault!"

Apparently LTC Jaggers had no idea who said this to him as Tom was never court martialed but was instead awarded the Army Commendation Medal with a "V" Device for valor for retrieving the radio.

The Lt. decided to try and bring Guam down to the LZ again. Guam had told Professor, "I need to get out of here!" and I imagine he was saying that to anyone who would listen. The Lt. grabbed Sgt. Rudy Boykins, a black squad leader from Covington, Tennessee, and with one of them at each end of the blanket headed down the trail on their knees with Guam in tow.

When I looked up and saw them coming down the trail, I yelled, "Get down!" Immediately they hit the dirt, but it was too late. Sgt. Boykins took a bullet through his right elbow, entering from the back and exiting through the inner aspect. The Lt., having escaped injury, crawled the rest of the way down to us. Grabbing my aid bag, I crawled up to Rudy. I looked at his arm and saw he was bleeding profusely. I also looked over at Guam and saw he had been hit by another bullet or two in the side of his face and head, and seemed to be breathing his last, gasping for air.

Looking back at Rudy, I realized I needed to stop his bleeding quickly. It appeared to me the artery in his arm had been severed, and there on the trail I had very little room to maneuver. I had to try to treat him lying down. Ideally, I should have used a compress, or even surgical clamps to stop the bleeding; however, being on the trail with limited mobility and time and still under fire, I felt I had no other option. I asked the guys below me if anyone had anything I could use as a tourniquet and one of them handed me a piece of rubber tubing he carried just for that purpose. Quickly I wrapped it around Rudy's arm just above the elbow, and, using an ink pen, twisted it tight to cut off the circulation. At the same time, I talked to Rudy to try and calm his nerves. I made small talk, asking him if he went to church back home. He said he did, and I told him I did, too. I also told him I thought this would be a good time for us to pray for help, and he agreed. With the bleeding stopped, I grabbed Rudy by the collar of his shirt and pulled him down the trail to where the others were. Guam breathed his last breath and was gone.

It was getting pretty late in the afternoon, and the fighting let up. As dusk was setting in, the decision was made to pull the rest of our men down into the meadow for the night, as it would be too easy for the enemy to sneak up on us in the rocks. One by one, they made their way down the trail. We pulled our dead into one spot on the edge of the meadow and our wounded into the center. One of the men, Mike Wilson, who had been firing one of the machine guns all afternoon and lost his hearing, also stayed with me. The rest of the platoon then spread out in a circle like spokes in a wheel forming a perimeter. They had to pair up and take turns sleeping. Someone gave me the canteen-and-a-half of water retrieved by Horoscope to use for the wounded. Taking my outer shirt off, I used it to cover Rudy, who was cold. During the night, I tried to keep him awake to make sure he didn't go into shock and gave him and Smitty drinks of water to keep them hydrated. As the night wore on, I lay on my stomach on top of my bare arms in an attempt to keep from being eaten alive by the mosquitoes and drifted off to sleep, totally exhausted by the day's events.

CHAPTER NINE

ESCAPE

"Surely he will save you from the fowler's snare
and from the deadly pestilence.
He will cover you with his feathers,
and under his wings you will find refuge.
His faithfulness will be your shield and rampart."
Psalm 91:3-4

When I woke up, it was just starting to get light, and I
could hear the lieutenant and platoon sergeant talking
about what we should do. Obviously, we still needed to
evacuate our wounded, but the meadow had already proven
a death trap, and no helicopter had been able to get in the
day before. There was no reason to believe the enemy wasn't
still holed up in the rocks and caves above us, and during the
night they had most likely moved into our former positions
and taken our supplies, including grenades, trip flares, and
claymore mines. We would later learn that, according to the
gunship pilots the day before, the enemy would just pull into
the caves and rocks for protection, and then come back out
shooting after the gunships made their passes.

As I shook the cobwebs from my mind and tried to clear
the sleep from my eyes, I noticed a sharp smell I did not rec-
ognize and a strange stickiness about my hands. Looking at
them in the early morning light, I realized they were covered
with the dried blood of the dead and wounded from the day
before. I hadn't noticed it the night before, but now that the

blood had dried, it was sticky and pungent. In addition, my efforts to protect my arms by sleeping on them had failed, and they were now covered by hundreds of mosquito bites that began to itch.

As the Lt. and Sgt. Schrang talked, someone thought they could hear the sound of running water nearby. I had used up the canteens of water during the night with the wounded, and they needed more, especially if it was going to be a while before we could evacuate them. Sgt. Schrang said he would take the canteens and see if he could find the stream.

Crawling off through the tall grass, he disappeared. After about fifteen minutes, he returned with full canteens. Sure enough, about fifty meters away was a small stream completely covered with brush. In fact, the brush actually formed a natural tunnel over the stream. "If we could crawl to the stream, we could possibly walk down the mountain without being seen," he said.

It didn't take long for the lieutenant to agree it was worth a try. In fact, it seemed like our only option at this point. The only problem was Rudy would not be able to crawl with his bad arm. Above the tourniquet, his arm was swollen like a balloon, and he was extremely weak. I would have to carry him on my back.

To do this I took a utility belt and worked it under Rudy's body. I then rolled him onto his good side and maneuvered myself next to him on my other side with my back to his. I then had someone hand me the other end of the belt, and, wrapping it around the two of us, I strapped it tight to my chest. Then I carefully rolled onto my stomach, pulling Rudy on top of me. As I began to crawl, Rudy began to have difficulty breathing. "I can't breathe! I can't breathe!" he whispered in a panic. Rolling back over to my right side, I quickly released the belt freeing Rudy. I hadn't considered the fact that Rudy, in his weakened condition, might not be able to handle the constraint of the belt around his chest.

As the medic, it was my responsibility to make the call, and I informed the Lt. that I didn't think Rudy would make it this way.

There weren't many options open to us. We couldn't leave Rudy behind, and it didn't make sense to leave a squad behind while the rest made their escape. What chance would a squad have the platoon did not have? Sgt. Schrang (a gung-ho lifer from a long line of decorated army officers who carried in his backpack an American flag that had flown over the nation's Capitol) volunteered to stay with Rudy and let the rest of us go. As if that would have done a lot of good! The only option that made any sense was to see if we could get another medevac to come out. Maybe we could catch the enemy by surprise and get the wounded loaded and out before the shooting started again.

When the lieutenant called in, one of the pilots from the day before had just come into the radio shack to see if they had heard anything from us. He had been unable to sleep, knowing we still had wounded men out there. When he heard our call, he volunteered to get a crew and another chopper to come out, as he knew exactly where we were. Together with CWO Michael Haeusserman of Beverly Hills, California and medic, Spec. 4 Timothy M. Coogan of Chicago, Illinois, he headed to the tarmac to get their chopper in the air.

While we waited, I wasted no time getting ready. Using my shirt and someone else's and two M-16s from those who had been killed, I made a stretcher for Rudy. Three others would help me load Rudy on as soon as the dust-off touched down, and Wilson, the soldier who had lost his hearing, would help Smitty get on.

The pilot flew his helicopter through the morning mist close to the valley floor just above the rice paddies so the sound of the rotors would not be heard by the enemy on the mountain. As he approached the mountain, he tried to stay as low as possible, sweeping up the side of the mountain until he suddenly popped up over the tops of the trees, turned and, cutting his engine, settled into the meadow. Jumping up as quickly as we could, we rushed to the chopper staying low and loaded Rudy and the others. Immediately we hit the dirt as the chopper lifted up, turned back toward the valley, and, tilting its nose forward, vanished back down the side of the mountain almost as suddenly as it had appeared.

Our plan had worked. We had indeed caught the enemy off guard. When the chopper got back Spec. 4 Coogan reported, "For some reason the NVA didn't fire at us for several seconds. We were pulling the second and last man through the door when the ship started taking fire." Because of the roar of the chopper's engines and rotors, we were unaware we were being shot at. However, when the dust-off got back to LZ English, like the three choppers the day before, it was declared un-flyable because of the amount of damage it had sustained.

With the wounded safely evacuated, we were now able to execute our original plan. We would have to leave our dead behind to be retrieved as soon as the area was secure. Because we still had two extra rifles, I offered to carry one of them down the mountain so someone else wouldn't have to carry two. One by one we crawled to the stream on our bellies and into the brush that covered it. When I got there and stood up in the stream, I was so happy I felt like shouting out for joy, but I knew we had to maintain absolute silence. Instead, I dipped my hands and arms into the cool fresh water washing away the blood of the dead and wounded. Then I lifted my cupped hands to my lips to quench my thirst and wash away the dust from the trail of death. "Keep moving, Doc!" Sgt. Schrang gestured. There were more guys behind me, and I was holding things up.

We slowly made our way down the stream, the running water covering the sound of our steps. After moving what we thought was a safe distance, we got out of the stream and continued to slowly make our way down the mountain toward the rice paddies, taking advantage of what cover we could as we went.

The day before, our guys had almost run out of ammunition, and because we had lost everything in our packs, we were in desperate need of supplies. Helicopters came out and without landing threw off boxes of C-rations, ammunition, canteens of water, and additional medical supplies. They just threw a bunch of stuff together and brought it knowing we had lost everything.

In the meantime, the battalion commander had moved the rest of the battalion into position to surround the mountain and prevent the enemy from escaping if possible. Jets were called in to bomb the side of the hill throughout the day. Huge spotlights were set up below to scan the mountain at night in search of enemy movement.

It took us two days to make it down the mountain, as we moved carefully in an effort to avoid the enemy. On the second day we set up another makeshift NDP in a field of elephant grass to wait out the night. In the morning, we reached the units set up in the valley floor.

(In a letter dated January 30th to Barbara, I wrote, *"We spent three days maneuvering away and also getting resupplied as we were cut off from all of our equipment and the N.V.A. got it."* However, I also wrote another letter to my mother on the 27th indicating we had received a one-day resupply after moving down the stream and that on the morning of the 27th we had *"moved further down the hill so that now we're at the very foot next to the rice paddies and flat lands." I'm not sure why there is a discrepancy in time between the two letters, but it may be we didn't link up to the rest of the battalion until the 28th.)*

Early that next morning, one of our soldiers thought he heard movement on our perimeter. The lieutenant gave the order to toss a couple of hand grenades. As stupid as it sounds, and it was, out of curiosity I propped myself up just slightly in the hope of seeing the explosion. I should have known better. Though we hadn't had weapons training in Basic, we had been through live fire exercises, and I knew we were supposed to keep our heads down. As the first grenade went off, I felt this tremendous jolt and sharp pain in my left shoulder, by the collarbone. Lifting my t-shirt at the neckline I could see a small entry wound where I had been hit by a piece of shrapnel. Embarrassed by my foolishness, I said nothing to anyone but instead took a Band-Aid from my aid bag and covered it up. For a few days, it was quite sore, but otherwise I experienced no other ill effects, and it healed fine. The shrapnel had come within just a couple of inches of my jugular vein. Even though it was very small, if it had hit me in the neck, it could have killed me. If it had hit me in the eye, I could have lost the sight in that eye. Once again, I was thankful God was watching over me, even in my foolish moments.

A couple of years later, when I needed a chest x-ray as part of a physical exam, the technician asked me if I had ever been shot. At first I was a bit puzzled by the question, and then I remembered the shrapnel and told him about it. It is still there today, a little souvenir of the foolishness of an unlikely warrior. I am just glad to be able to laugh about it. I suppose I could have written myself up for a Purple Heart, but the thought never entered my mind. A few months later I had a guy get a piece of shrapnel in his finger in a firefight, and I treated it with a Band-Aid. The lieutenant made me write him up for a Purple Heart even though I didn't think he deserved it. Technically, he qualified, but what was an injured finger to what a lot of others experienced? I had gotten what I deserved and could laugh about it, but there were many others whose wounds were no laughing matter: men like Rudy Boykins and Smitty. Those were the guys who deserved Purple Hearts, not guys with slivers of shrapnel that could be treated with Band-Aids.

An inspection of the area didn't turn up any evidence of enemy activity. Perhaps we were jittery from the action we had just experienced, but it was better to be safe than sorry.

We moved the rest of the way down to where the blocking force had been set up. I am sure as we came in we had the "thousand-mile stare" I would later see in the eyes of others who had been through tough battles. We had been beaten badly and suffered terrible loss. I hadn't time to really get to know the men who had been killed and wounded, but others had gotten to know them, had depended on them in the field of battle, shared packages from home with them, and talked with them about their hopes and dreams. Until now we had been running on adrenaline, just trying to survive. But now that we were safe, the magnitude of what we had been through began to hit us and we had to deal with the feelings of anger and resentment that always follow such loss. Some tried to deny it, stuffing it deep down inside. Others, like Sgt. Schrang, wanted revenge and hoped he could somehow get his American flag back. Each of us dealt with it in our own way.

This is the way war is, and the way it has always been. We were no longer boys playing in the woods pretending to be brave. We were men with real guns fighting a real war, where real people get hurt and die. War really is hell, as we all instinctively know, but I understood it now for the first time, not just from an intellectual perspective but experientially. I had seen, heard, and tasted it in more ways than one. I had experienced the smells and sounds of war, not just read about it or seen it in the movies. I had the blood of the wounded and dying on my hands. I was no longer the new guy, the unknown quantity. I was a grunt, a soldier, and a combat medic.

That morning after we reached the blocking force in the rice paddies, we received some more supplies before the bombing runs started. The lieutenant asked me if I wanted to turn the rifle in or keep it. "I think I'll keep it." I said. If I ever ran into a similar situation, I knew I had to be prepared to defend myself and the wounded. He also told me he was putting me in for the Silver Star, the third-highest medal for heroism, which surprised me. No one thinks of getting medals when he is in combat. His mind is on doing his job and surviving. No one fights for the medals, but I was flattered by the thought, anyway.

When the award finally came down several months later, it had been reduced to a Bronze Star with a "V" Device for Valor. When I eventually read the commendation, which was based on what was written by the Lt., I understood why. Only I knew what I had really done as the rest in the platoon were busy fighting their own battle. The Lt. couldn't know what I had done to reach those who were wounded and killed. He wasn't with me as I crawled up and down the trail and into the smoke-filled meadow to find Benjamin, and, of course, the wounded had been evacuated, and the dead could not talk.

I never saw my medal or received any formal presentation of it until the day I left Vietnam, when it was handed to me along with an Army Commendation Medal and my paperwork as I processed out. I was going through a processing line and some clerk looked at my papers, pulled them from a glass cabinet like you would candy in a theater, and handed them to me as if they were just part of the process, another item to check off of the list. I have often thought it was no wonder so many G.I.s felt unappreciated and used, even dirty when they came back from Vietnam. Not only did the public ridicule them, but in many cases the very institution they had served failed to properly honor what they had done.

Oh, some medals were presented on occasion. I remember when Captain Ohl presented Army Commendation Medals to three of the guys in my platoon, including Horoscope, and I thought it was pretty cool at the time. I even took pictures. But later, I came to see the inconsistency and the hypocrisy that was often involved with some officers being awarded medals they didn't really deserve. I am sure some did, but many didn't, and that is one thing that has made some Vietnam veterans bitter.

It took over forty years for me to receive one of my medals, which had somehow fallen through the cracks. It was mailed to me along with the written commendation and a corrected DD-214, but it is not the same as being recognized by those you served with and under, even though we didn't do it for the medals. I am thankful my old captain went to bat for me and some others when it was finally learned the medics had been overlooked. But that's not why we did what we did in battle. We didn't do it for the medals. We did it for each other.

I grabbed some paper and a pen that was part of our re-supply and, as the jets dropped their bombs and napalm on the hill, I wrote home. *"Dear Family,"* I began, *"Just a few lines to let you know that I'm fine and to give you the latest. Now, I don't want you to get worried about what I tell you, because for the most part the worst is all over. God has been and is with me, I know. He had to be to allow me to still be here."* I then explained much of what had happened, ending the letter with these words:

> *Right now it's 11:00 AM and we'll be getting another re-supply after the jets are finished. Then we'll go by chopper back to the top of the hill to link with another Platoon, pick up the bodies and comb the area salvaging what we can. I'm carrying an M-16 now and plenty of ammo. I hope I never have to use it, but if put in the position I will. Four dead men in my lap, their heads torn open by bullets, a man who'll lose*

his arm and two others wounded is enough for me. I'm not killing people; I'm only killing death, trying to keep my men and myself alive. God forgive me if I do wrong and help me to do what is right. Your loving son and brother, Mike.

Many have said it before, and it is true: in Vietnam we fought not so much for patriotism or to be heroes but to stay alive and keep our buddies alive. Ask any soldier who has been to war and he or she will tell you the same. It was true then, and it is still true today. Such is the bond of warriors, even an unlikely warrior like me.

That afternoon, after the jets finished making their bombing runs, choppers brought us the rest of our supplies, new backpacks, canteens, and everything else we needed. We also received some new recruits, and some of our troops who had been in the rear for various reasons returned, beefing up our severely-depleted numbers. I can only imagine what the new guys must have thought coming out to this platoon that had just had its ass severely kicked and knowing the battle to take Hill 474 had just begun. The battalion chaplain, Chaplain Bass, came out to conduct a memorial service with our platoon for those who had been lost. Then slicks picked us up and carried us back to the top of the hill, where our mission had begun just six days earlier. Here we would act as a blocking force while the jets continued to do their job for the next five days. It was good to be linked with another platoon for security, and to know that for now we had the high ground. In the days to follow there would be more work to do. The hardened NVA holed up in their caves would not easily let go, and more lives would be lost on Hill 474.

Victor San Nicholas, also known as Guam, killed Jan. 25th, 1970 on Hill 474.
Photo courtesy of Tom Landers.

George Spillers, killed Jan. 25th, 1970 on Hill 474.
Photo courtesy of Tom Landers.

Rudy Boykins in the foreground with Victor San Nicholas behind him.

Army Commendation Medals for Valor during the battle on Hill 474, June 25th, being presented by Company Commander Capt. William Ohl assisted by Platoon Leader Lt. Richard Greig to (from left to right) Tom Landers, Neil Rogers, and Don Meyer.

Chapter Ten

Taking the Hill

"Find rest, O my soul, in God alone;
my hope comes from him.
He alone is my rock and my salvation;
he is my fortress, I will not be shaken."

Psalm 62:5-6

On January 28th, after two days of bombing, B Company's 3rd Platoon attempted to recover the bodies of our fallen brothers. The battalion commander must have thought the enemy had been sufficiently softened up, but he was terribly mistaken. It cost 3rd Platoon dearly. Their platoon leader, Lt. Alan Paul Johnson, 23, from Medford, Massachussetts, Sgt. Steven Orland Dile, 21, of Chambersburg, Pennsylvania, Sp4 Peter D. Guzman, 20, Los Angeles, California, and SP4 Frank Dodge Madrid, 25, Puerto De Luna, New Mexico, were killed.

The death of these additional soldiers proved our platoon's decision to escape, even though we had to leave our dead behind, was a wise one. If we had stayed, we would have surely experienced many more casualties and still would have been forced to retreat. Worse yet, if our platoon had been able to get on line and assault, as the battalion commander had wanted us to, we would have very likely been wiped out. Though the Army and Marine Corps had a long-standing tradition of leaving no man behind, sometimes it was impossible not to do otherwise, at least in the short term.

In time our fallen comrades were recovered and returned home, but not before several more days of intense bombing.

On the 28th, a cold front moved in, bringing with it strong chilly winds and some rain. But by the 30th, the clouds began to break, revealing the sun once again, and I could hear a song bird singing in the distance, a small joy in a time of deep sorrow.

For the next five days, after breakfast, we moved about a click (1,000 meters) down the back side of the mountain, set up a Daytime Defensive Position (DDP) and waited while jets continued to drop their heavy ordnance and artillery units pounded the mountain with their big guns. Even at that distance we could hear the shrapnel flying overhead, sometimes coming dangerously close. I remember a few occasions when large pieces went flying overhead, emitting a low whining *whoo, whoo, whoo* sound as they flew through the air. Late each afternoon after the bombing ended, we returned to our NDP to continue acting as a blocking force.

On one of these nights the Lt., who was making rounds to check the guard positions after dark, fell into a foxhole and broke some bones in his right hand requiring he be evacuated. I later heard he had lost it mentally, really lost it, but one hears a lot of rumors in the field. I really don't know what happened to him. I also heard he received a Silver Star for his part in the action on January 25th. I don't know if anyone thought he really deserved it, anyone who was actually there on the ground that is. In fact, I have talked to some who said he lost it on the hill, was in tears and unable to give direction in the battle. This was at least part of the reason Horoscope, after returning to the States, used his Army Commendation Medal to wipe out a barracks drinking fountain and left it tacked to a bulletin board. For him the hypocrisy of the situation was too much to bear. But again, I cannot say for sure what is true regarding the Lt., since I had my own job to perform and didn't see everything that went on up in the rocks that day.

The good thing about that lieutenant's departure was we got a new lieutenant I came to greatly respect. His name was Richard Greig. He wore thick rimmed glasses and smoked a pipe. Before going to Officer Candidate School, he was an enlisted man, a medic in fact. He was assigned to a hospital in the States and often tended to soldiers who had been wounded in Vietnam. He would ask them what had happened to them, and they invariably told him their platoon leader had gotten them into a bad situation resulting in them getting hurt. He told me he decided to become an officer because he thought he could do more as a platoon leader to take care of a group of men than he could as a medic.

He was right. A good officer could do much more to ensure the safety of his men through good leadership than a medic who could only try to keep his men well or treat them after they had already been hurt. I never got the impression Lt. Greig was there to make a name for himself, to earn another promotion, or to get a body count. I truly sensed his first priority was to take care of his platoon and get them home alive, if at all possible, while also performing his duties.

In the mornings before pulling off the backside of the mountain, we sent out patrols to check for evidence of enemy activity, and there was plenty of it. We found warm coals from cooking fires, and one morning we found a trail marker at the intersection of two trails. The marker consisted of six sticks tied together in the middle in a cross pattern with four sticks pointing down one trail and two pointing down the other trail.

Lt. Greig asked our Kit Carson Scout, Lee Van Tho, if he knew what it meant. Lee was a former Viet Cong who had been captured by 1st Platoon. When a VC or NVA soldier surrendered, if he was cooperative, he was given the option of going to a POW camp or working with the American forces as a scout after going through "Kit Carson School."

The term came from the period in American history when Native Americans worked for the Cavalry as scouts. Though not an Indian, Kit Carson was a beaver trapper who served as a scout for American explorer John Charles Fremont from 1842 to 1846. He also served as a U.S. Scout in the Mexican War and fought for the Union in the Southwest during the Civil War rising to the rank of Brigadier General.

When Lee was given the option to become a scout, he said he would only do so if he could work with the platoon responsible for his capture. He figured any Americans skilled enough to capture him would be a good group to work with, providing him with a greater measure of safety, since as a scout he would also become a prize target for the Viet Cong and NVA.

The VC punished his family, holding his young son's hands over a fire, burning them severely. American doctors were able to repair much of the damage through surgery, giving him the use of his hands again, and rather than dissuading Lee from working with us, the cruelty of the VC made him even more committed. He became one of the best scouts to serve the 3/506, and we came to trust him implicitly.

From time to time we would get other scouts for training, but none proved to be as trustworthy or to have the skills Lee exhibited. One scout we had for a short time, whose name was Troung, was a 16 year-old former VC, and though he was an enjoyable young man, he was too immature to engender the trust of the platoon. Another, Nguyen Van Hung, who was former NVA, proved unreliable. When he was walking point one day, he came upon a VC in the bush, and rather than fire on the VC he simply jumped out of the way, exposing the men behind him. The guys behind him fired on the VC, who got away, but needless to say, we sent Hung packing back to the rear real fast after that.

Lee thought the trail marker might be a sign to other NVA one trail was booby-trapped and the other had an ambush set up on it. We could not know for sure and chose not to find out. Instead we radioed in our findings. For now our job was to guard the top of the hill until the jets and artillery were done with their jobs. Only then would we begin the job of routing out the enemy from his hiding places, but this time it would be on our terms and not his.

As our forces continued to saturate the hill with bombardment, the VC and NVA were at work trying to retaliate where they could, as there were a couple of mortar attacks on nearby bases in the valley resulting in American casualties. However, eight NVA had surrendered and provided valuable information used to further direct our bombing and artillery attacks.

February 2nd was re-supply day, and I received my first letters since arriving in Vietnam almost two months earlier. The letters were from Ralph Morris, an elder and youth group leader from my church, and Mrs. Tragis, a Sunday school teacher from my younger days. Mail from home was the grunt's one connection to the real world and highly valued. No matter how difficult the circumstances, a letter from home could lift his spirits, and there were times when a lack of mail could break his spirits.

On February 3rd I wrote home to let my family know I was safe. I'm sure my previous letter must have caused significant concern. I wrote I was fine and the bombardment was supposed to end that morning, after which we were supposed to begin our sweep down the mountain.

That afternoon we did just that. As a company-sized element we spread out in a long line along the ridge and began to make our way slowly down the mountain. LOcH helicopters flew just overhead to our front "walking our point." In the rear seat on each side of the LOcH sat a soldier with a sub-machine gun. Their purpose was to draw the fire of any dicks left on the hill, before they could hit us.

The bombardment had done tremendous damage, and though we heard an occasional crack of gunfire, we did not encounter any of the enemy that first day. We did however find abandoned caves. On the afternoon of the fourth, I continued the letter I had started the day before:

> *Well, here we are on the side of the mountain where the VC and/or NVA once were. The jets really did do a job on this place, and it's pretty well burned and blown up. But because there are big rock-formations there are still a lot of tunnels intact. But the Dicks are gone. This morning we've hauled out everything from uniforms, rice, canteens, entrenching tools, and Ho-Chi-Minh sandals to rockets, Chikom grenades, dynamite, detonators, AK-47 rifle ammo, and even some medical supplies. Apparently the Dicks were up here when they hit us about 100 to 200 meters below here. We'll probably start down further and into that area tomorrow. There are lots more tunnels and probably lots more enemy supplies. Undoubtedly we've hurt their plans for TET. Hopefully we'll find the stuff that they took away from us. Some of the guys had stuff they want back.*

It became very clear why our platoon had come under such fierce attack. We had walked into the 8th Battalion headquarters of the 22nd NVA Regiment, interrupting their plans for a TET offensive. These natural caves were so deep and complex they even included underground streams. They had a hospital unit and all of the supplies they would need to inflict significant damage on our forces. So entrenched was the enemy that, even after seven days of heavy bombardment, it would still take us several weeks to finish driving them from their stronghold.

Battalion Chaplain Bass and me on top of Hill 474.

A view of Hill 474 from the base of the mountain. After having been heavily bombed, the large boulders where the many caves were previously concealed by trees and other heavy vegetation were now clearly visible. From a distance the mountain looks fairly tame, but up close the massive boulders and cave complexes were quite ominous.

Chapter Eleven

The Ledge

"The angel of the LORD encamps
around those who fear him,
and he delivers them."

Psalm 34:7

Those first couple of days exploring the caves we moved back up the mountain each night to set up a secure NDP. February 5th was a re-supply day in which I received the first mail from my family, four letters and a package of cookies I shared with my platoon. Later that day I wrote to my grandparents in Colorado,

> *Intelligence tells us that the "dicks" who took to hiding in the villages, were supposed to come back to the caves last night. As we all move up the hill away from the caves for the night, they could have very well done that. Also, they are supposed to be trying to get reinforcements from another N.V.A. regiment. Anyway, pretty quick we're supposed to start moving down to the area again. We only hope that either the "Dicks" are gone or in a bad position.*

As we made our way down the mountain it became difficult to find a place to set up for the night because of the steep terrain and large craters left by the bombs and artillery. Late that afternoon as we were setting up, one of the guys started digging in a bomb crater to make a level place to sleep when he uncovered a hand. The NVA and VC were always

107

very good about dragging away and burying their dead, so we could not get a good body count. A lot of body counts reported in Vietnam by U.S. forces were estimates, often inflated to give the appearance of success. If they killed one of ours surely we must have killed ten of theirs. In this case, the NVA had buried one of their own in a hurry, probably at night under the cover of darkness, before fleeing the area. The order was given to dig the body up to see if there were any papers that might provide helpful intelligence. After searching the body, of course, they had to bury it again.

During a break that afternoon, I was reading the small Bible I carried and Lt. Greig asked me what I was reading. When I told him it was a Bible, he asked if I was a Christian, and I told him I was. He said he was a Christian, too. As a result we began to spend some time in prayer together each morning and evening, and he said he'd like us to do some Bible study together, too. Like me, Lt. Greig had a sincere desire to see the men in the platoon come to experience the same kind of faith in Christ we had.

Though I was beginning to have some good conversations with others in the platoon about my faith, to my knowledge none of the others had what I would call a personal relationship with Jesus Christ. Some had been raised in religious homes and had either rejected their parents' religion or were nominal in their faith at best. And then there were those like Horoscope, who were into just about everything with Jesus being part of the mix along with Jean Dixon, astrology, and whatever else might have been popular at the time.

The place we had chosen to set up our NDP that day was at the base of a steep cliff. The lieutenant came to me and said, "Doc, if we get hit tonight, it's going to be from that ledge, so I have to put a squad up there to guard it, and I need you to go with them." Of course, he was right. If the squad was attacked in the middle of the night, there was no way I could get up there after the fact. I would need to be there with them. So, I got my stuff together and joined the lucky squad to make our way up the hill.

Once at the top of the ledge, the squad found a place just a little further up a trail with some large boulders which provided perfect cover for our guard position. They set up the M-60 machine gun and put their trip flares and claymore mines out in front of that. In the meantime, I found a flat spot down the hill near the ledge to lay out my bedroll. It was right on a well-traveled trail, the only spot really level enough to sleep. There was also some cover in the form of brush and trees around it that was important, since much of the cover on the mountain had been decimated by the previous days of bombing.

I could not help but wonder how many NVA soldiers had walked this very trail in the weeks and months before this. We knew they were still around. On February 7th I wrote to Barbara, *"Yesterday morning a young enemy soldier tried coming up the mountain and was spotted. We've got troops all over this hill. He should have known better. Anyway, they had to wound him to catch him and he died on the way to the hospital. He looked about sixteen years old according to those who saw him."*

We worked out a rotation for guard duty, and it would be my turn at 2 AM. The rest of the squad hung out at the guard position, while I prepared to get some sleep. The last thing in the world I wanted to do was to fall asleep on guard duty. As part of the CP I normally pulled a two-hour radio watch, but now, with just a few men in the squad, I needed to do my part on the line.

As I lay down with my M-16 beside me and pulled my poncho liner over me, a frightening thought occurred to me. The squad did not have enough trip flares and claymore mines to cover our flanks. They were able to cover the guard position pretty well, but out to the flanks from where I was there was nothing to keep an enemy soldier from sneaking in and cutting my throat while I slept. We thought we were pretty safe as there was no cover and a lot of loose rock in both of those directions. In addition, we had not run into the enemy since starting down the mountain. But we also knew he was still there hiding in some of the caves, and the potential for one of them sneaking in under the cover of darkness was very real.

As these thoughts played through my mind, I began to pray silently, "Lord, how in the world am I supposed to go to sleep knowing that an NVA could cut my throat in the middle of the night if he wanted to? You know I've got to get some sleep, but if I go to sleep I could wind up dead." Then a scripture came to my mind: "If you make the Most High your dwelling, even the Lord, who is my refuge, then no harm will befall you, no disaster will come near your tent. For he will command his angels concerning you to guard you in all your ways, they will lift you up in their hands so that you will not strike your foot against a stone" (Psalm 91: 9-12, NIV).

I knew the Lord had been watching over me all of this time. He had protected me in the heat of battle before, and He could protect me now. So I said, "Lord, your word says that you give your angels charge over us if we trust in you. So, I am going to believe that there is an angel standing right here at my feet to keep watch over me, and I am going to roll over and go to sleep. Thank you, Lord!" And I did just that. Picturing in my mind's eye a very large angel standing over me dressed for battle with his sword drawn, ready to act in my defense, I closed my eyes and went to sleep.

Early the next morning, as it began to get light, I woke up. Wiping the sleep from my eyes, I wondered what was going on. No one woke me for my watch, and there was no evidence any of the guys had come down to sleep. I was alone in the silence of dawn and wondered if something had happened to them.

I grabbed my M-16, got up, and slowly began to make my way up the trail almost afraid of what I might find. As I approached the guard position, I began to hear the low whisper of voices. It was the other members of the squad talking to each other. Relieved, I continued on up to them. Somewhat confused and even a little peeved at this point, I asked them, "Why in the world didn't somebody wake me up for my watch?" One of them answered, "Well, Doc, you were sleeping so soundly we just didn't have the heart to wake you!"

You can be sure this was the only time something like this ever happened to me. I had to laugh at myself for worrying about God's ability to protect me. Here I was trying to share with others in my platoon the importance of putting their faith in Christ, and yet I had struggled to trust Him myself. Once I settled the issue, though, not only was I able to sleep, but He let me sleep the whole night through.

King David, in the Old Testament, had a similar experience. Driven from his throne by his son Absalom, he had to flee Jerusalem for his life. During this time he recorded his own prayer: "Oh Lord, how many are my foes! How many rise up against me! Many are saying of me, God will not deliver him. Selah! But you are a shield around me, Oh Lord; you bestow glory on me and lift up my head. To the Lord I cry aloud, and he answers me from His holy hill. I lie down and sleep; I wake again, because the Lord sustains me" (Psalm 3:15, NIV). He too knew what it was to be afraid of his enemies in the dead of night, but when he cried out to the Lord, he was able to lie down, go to sleep and rise again, because the Lord protected him.

I have often told people if it were not for my faith in God, I don't think I could have made it through my year in Vietnam. They say there are no atheists in foxholes, and I think that is true, but I am glad I had a living faith before I ever needed a foxhole. It didn't mean I wasn't afraid, but rather I knew where to turn when I was. Later when I went out with squads on overnight ambushes, I set my guard duty to coincide with Lieutenant Greig's radio watch, and we would encourage each other. It was very brief. I would give my situation report in the customary whisper and then would add something like, "The Lord is with you" or "God's angels are watching over us." It was just a simple way to remind ourselves our trust was not in our weapons or military strategy alone. We had someone far greater to trust in, someone who could keep us safe in the most difficult of circumstances. I also have to wonder what Charlie must have thought if perchance he was listening in on our transmissions, as he was known at times to do.

My sneaking suspicion is the members of the squad were too afraid to go to sleep that night. Everyone was afraid, and the person who says he wasn't is either a liar or a fool. But everyone dealt with fear in his own way. Some gave in to it and were driven to do anything they could to get out of the field, feigning sickness or even madness. Some inflicted injuries upon themselves. But most pushed through it, did what they had to do to get the job done and come home alive. Most stayed and fought for their brothers in arms.

I remember one time when a soldier by the name of Steve Kempster from Los Angeles picked up a smoke grenade after it had been popped and had finished spewing its smoke. I guess he didn't stop to think where there is smoke there is fire, or perhaps he thought once it had quit smoking it would also be cool. (It was the same kind of dumb mistake I had made trying to watch a grenade explode.) It was still hot and severely burned the palm of his hand, which turned into one huge blister. I said to him, "You know, I should send you in to the aid station to have this taken care of," but Steve begged me not to send him to the rear. I am sure he felt foolish at having picked it up, and the last thing he wanted was anyone thinking he was trying to get out of the field. He was a true grunt who didn't want to let his fellow soldiers down, and if there was any way I could take care of his hand in the field, that was what he wanted.

Even though I had my doubts, I agreed to try. The blister had to be broken, the dead skin cut away, and the wound cleaned. I bandaged it with gauze and antibiotic cream to try and keep it from becoming infected. After a few days of changing bandages and cleaning the wound, I decided it was too risky because there was just no way to really keep it clean in the jungle. We would go weeks at a time without a bath or shower, and even though we got clean clothes every three days, we were still a filthy sight to see. If I sent him to the rear for a few days, he could shower and keep it clean every day, and it would heal much quicker without the same risk of infection. Against his wishes, I ordered him to take the next chopper in and to have it taken care of at the aid station.

Guys like Steve Kempster made me proud to be part of a platoon of men committed to each other. The bonds forged as we faced the daily battle of trying to survive in the jungles and rice paddies of Vietnam were unlike any other I had ever experienced. I used to introduce myself to the cherries by saying, "Hi there. I'm Doc Dingman, your medic. You take care of me, and I'll take care of you," and I meant it. I was the only medic they had, and I needed them to watch my back, just as they needed me to take care of them, not only in the heat of battle, but also every day as I watched out for their health.

On February 10th, the senior medic came to me and told me we had an influx of new medics at the time, and if I wanted to go to the rear to work in the aid station I could. That was rare, because a medic's rotation was supposed to be six months, and I had only been in the field for two weeks. "No thanks." I said. "I think I'll stay right where I am."

When Sergeant Schrang heard what I had done, he said it was a good thing. I guess he thought I was doing a good job. It was nice to feel appreciated, to be wanted, to know I was meeting a need.

I look back sometimes and think I must have been crazy to say that, but I wasn't. On February 13th I wrote to Barbara and told her what I had done. *"Jesus is really here with me and there are times when I can feel the very presence of His power protecting me. I can sleep on an open enemy trail and know that an angel of God is right here with me standing between any danger and myself, keeping me safe."* It was true, and that's how I could stay where I was. God had taken care of me in the heat of battle, and on the ledge, and I could trust Him to continue to take care of me wherever we went no matter what we faced.

After receiving a camera in the mail from home, I had one of the guys take this picture of me so the family could see what I was carrying up and down these hills. On top of my backpack is my aid bag, and in my left hand is an ammo can used to store medications of all kinds. As the medic, it was my job to diagnose and treat as much as I could in the field before sending someone to the rear for treatment.

CHAPTER TWELVE

DRIVING OUT THE ENEMY

"God is our refuge and strength,
an ever-present help in trouble.
Therefore, we will not fear,
though the earth give way and
the mountains fall into the heart of the sea,
though its waters roar and foam
and the mountains quake with their surging."
Psalm 46:1-3

The rest of the month of February and into March were spent continuing to clean out the caves, running patrols, and setting up ambushes at night. We were trying to catch the enemy coming out of the hills to get to the village for supplies or simply to escape. Because we had troops all over the mountain, it was impossible for the enemy to move in any kind of force, so they tended to move in groups of two or three. One of the spotlights, which had originally been down on the valley floor to scan the mountain at night, was moved up onto a crest on the hill. On Feb. 12th I wrote home,

I'm on a crest now (and last night) with about fourteen men
put here to defend a spotlight (and jeep) that we use at night
to scan the areas where we have troops. The rest of my pla-
toon is just a short hike up on the top of the hill right next to
us. Though I am with the minority of my men, still it's not too
bad as the Lt. went through medic training before deciding to
become an officer. If anything happened up there he should

*know what to do until I could get up there. Also, we figure
that it's usually the smaller element that's most likely to take
casualties anyway, so it's nice to have the medic on hand.
But to add to all of that reasoning, once again, we've got
"buku" (lots of) troops all over this area so it's pretty secure.
The "Dicks" seem to be moving in twos and threes and are
losing at it. Just about half an hour ago B company, over
the hill, spotted three and got one for sure and possibly the
other two. We're setting up security and a possible ambush in
case they try to "didy mao" (leave the area) past us. To put
it simply, "We've got our stuff together, we're up tight!" So,
don't worry; I don't and I'm the one who's out here.*

The morale of the platoon by this time was much
improved from the first few days after our big battle, as we
had received a number of replacements and were now "fat"
with thirty guys. With the number of troops on the hill and
the fact it had been so decimated by the bombing and artillery, we felt we had the upper hand. I was also getting mail
on a regular basis now and received a package with dried
fruit, which I shared with the rest of the platoon.

The NVA, however, were tenacious and would not be
easily driven from their strongholds. As caves were discovered, they had to be searched, which meant a volunteer had
to crawl into the tunnel with a pistol confronting any enemy
that might still be inside. These volunteers were called
"Tunnel Rats," and the job was one of the most dangerous
anyone could perform. At one point, a tunnel rat from one
of the other companies was killed and had to be pulled
out. This caused a great deal of fear among those in Delta
Company, who were going into the tunnels, so our Company
Commander, Captain Ohl, decided to set an example by
requiring the officers of Delta Co. go into the tunnels for a
while. Lt. Greig shared this memory with me:

I don't know how many tunnels the other platoon leaders
went into, but I recall one quite vividly. I didn't take a flashlight with me so I was crawling in the dark, listening every

couple of minutes for sounds of any noise at all. Lumpy had told me to keep my mouth wide open in the event that I had to fire the .45 while in the cave; this would apparently keep my eardrums from being severely damaged. I was more scared during that time in the cave than at any other moment in my life, even during some of our worst firefights. The only "real" flashback I ever had was as a result of that experience and happened more than twenty years afterward while I was in a totally dark and enclosed space during a fire emergency training exercise. I was quite literally back in that cave during the exercise. The decision for the officers to be tunnel rats was a great decision as it allowed us to show leadership and set the example for our men.

When it became too dangerous for the "tunnel rats" and the enemy was unwilling to come out of the caves, a Chinook helicopter was brought in with a bucket or barrels of "foogasse" dangling beneath it to be dumped on the cave entrance and ignited by a flare in an attempt to burn the enemy out.

After the caves were cleaned out, engineers came out and blasted them with C.S. gas, a form of tear gas that stuck to the walls of the caves, making them unusable for at least six months or more. On Feb. 11th, the wind changed directions and blew some of the C.S gas back our way, causing us to have a nice little cry and reminding us of our basic training days when we had to go through the tear gas chamber.

As our battalion continued to put pressure on the NVA still heavily entrenched in the multitude of caves scattered throughout this massive mountain, the decision was made to place two small six-man Tiger Teams from our platoon down at the base of the mountain to catch the enemy who were trying to escape into the valley in small groups. Because the Tiger Teams' survival depended upon having maximum firepower, there was no room on the teams for a medic, so I remained with the rest of the platoon up on the mountain. Squad Leaders Sgt. John Nauman, whom we called "Rags," and Sgt. Porfirio Hernandez were chosen by Lt. Greig to lead these teams.

According to John Nauman, as the orders were being given, two helicopters were already on their way, giving Hernandez and him only a matter of minutes to select and ready their teams for deployment on what would be the most dangerous mission he had ever been assigned. Because they were operating in such small teams, the risk was enormous. If they were to come under attack at night, they would largely be on their own with the exception of artillery and gunship support. If attacked by a sizable NVA force, they might not even have time to call in the support they needed before they were all killed. Therefore, the greatest skills of stealth and combat effectiveness were required.

For five successive nights, the Tiger Teams engaged the enemy thwarting numerous attempts to penetrate their ambush sights. During the day they ran recon patrols and selected new ambush sites for each night. Numerous NVA were killed without a single casualty to the Tiger Teams. They were so effective that on the sixth day, Feb. 21st, a third Tiger Team was added, led by Sgt. Alan "Lumpy" Hunter. On that night Rags's team once again came under attack. I can recall watching from high above on a ridge as tracer rounds poured from their M-60 machine gun and as claymores were blown and grenades tossed in the valley below. This time Rags's Team was not so lucky. Rags was wounded by two pieces of shrapnel from an enemy grenade, one hitting him in the right hand taking off part of a finger and the other in the chest. Undaunted by his wounds, Rags continued to lead his team in defending their position. Once the fighting let up, Rags called Lumpy for help, asking him to come and take over his Tiger Team. Lumpy and one of his men, Ken "Professor" Wydeven, quickly made their way in the dark from their ambush site to Rags's location, and a medevac was called in to make a night-time extraction.

Rags, a consummate warrior and leader, had his ticket home and lived to tell his story to his children and grandchildren. The next day two dead NVA officers were found outside their perimeter, one of whom was very tall for a Vietnamese (at least six feet), leading to speculation these might have been Chinese military advisors.

Other units were not as fortunate. On February 17th, Company B's 2nd platoon went out on a patrol in light battle gear leaving their packs behind. When they returned, they found three NVA soldiers rummaging through their packs and a firefight ensued, resulting in the death of their medic, PFC Joseph Paul Honan, 20, of Scranton, Pennsylvania. Two others were wounded. The very next day the 2nd platoon of Delta Company also found themselves engaged in a firefight with an element of unknown size, resulting in the deaths of two more Americans, Pfc. Daniel Eugene Blevins, 20, of Tram, Kentucky and Sp. 4 Richard Albert Burgess, 19, from Towers, Minnesota.

After the caves were cleared and gassed, our platoon moved to the foot of the mountain to continue ambushes and patrols for the next several weeks. A flat square field surrounded by hedges became our main base of operation during the day with our squads moving out at night for ambush operations and NDPs in other spots. This field had been used in the same way by the Tiger Teams earlier and was dubbed the "Football Field."

For the most part, our days were uneventful. However, on one occasion Lt. Greig went out with a couple of squads on a patrol and encountered what appeared to be a young VC on the trail. The VC ran and was seen jumping into a spider hole to hide. Lee, our Kit Carson Scout, shouted out orders for the VC to come out and *chu hoi,* but he refused. He would pop up and shout something in Vietnamese and then go back into the spider hole. Lumpy volunteered to crawl up to the spider hole and take the VC out with a pistol, which he did, emptying the revolver into the hole and killing him. When they pulled his body out, he appeared to be a teenager, maybe 15 or 16 years old. When the squad returned and I heard what had happened, I was deeply saddened by the event and struggled for a while with negative feelings toward Lumpy. I had to wonder if it was really necessary to kill the young kid. I realize today Lumpy was just doing what he had to do. There was no telling whether the kid had a grenade or weapon in that hole he might use. He had been given the chance to surrender and refused.

There were also lighter, albeit somewhat strange moments. One day Lumpy decided to test our new lieutenant's fortitude as the Lt. had been to Ranger School, and being a Ranger was considered a big deal. In an ambush a few days before, an NVA soldier was killed by a claymore blast and his mangled body lay decaying in a stream not too far away. Lumpy challenged the Lt. to accompany him to the stream and join him in eating a can of beans while standing over the decaying body. The Lt., not wanting to appear weak, accepted the challenge, so off they went with a squad of men for security. Neither backed down and the feat was accomplished while others stood watch. The Lt.'s reputation was secure.

The presence of streams on the mountain turned out to be a real blessing beyond the fact one had provided our way of escape on January 26th. On February 22nd, I wrote home, *"The other day we got to take baths in a stream and that was really great, especially in this hot weather. It had been over a month since I bathed."* Later that same night at 10:25 PM I added to the letter by moonlight, *"Today I got another bath in the same place, as we haven't moved. WOW! But tomorrow we're supposed to get on down the hill, so that may be it again for a while."* One of the things I didn't mention was during that time one of the guys had spotted an ear floating down that same stream, apparently from the body of a rotting enemy soldier somewhere up the hill. I was sure glad I learned about it after taking a bath and not before.

In spite of the passage of time and the devastation we wreaked on the enemy, there was still some bitterness in my spirit about the men we had lost on Jan. 25th, bitterness I was probably not even aware of until one day when we were on patrol on the side of the mountain. We spotted a group of Vietnamese in their "black pajamas" and their pointed sampan hats at the base of the mountain going through one of our dump sites. After resupply, we always did our best to render excess C-rations useless by opening the cans and burning and burying them in a pit. The enemy was known to raid these garbage pits, looking for materials they could use in a myriad of creative ways, including booby traps. In this particular case, the Vietnamese were probably farmers from the nearby village who worked the rice paddies. However, the area they were in at the base of the mountain was a "free fire" or "Red" Zone where we had the liberty to shoot first and ask questions later. As we watched them, I suddenly felt agitated as the rage hidden in my heart came to the surface, and I said something to the effect we should fire them up and get our revenge. After all, we knew the NVA had been using this village to get supplies, and these could be VC with weapons hidden under their clothing. They were in an open area, and it would have been like shooting ducks in a pond. I recall the Lt. looking at me in surprise and saying something to calm me down. He radioed in a report about the activity and was told to leave them alone, which we did. Afterward I had time to reflect on what had happened and was thankful for a cool and calm leader who knew how to gently handle someone like me.

In another incident on Hill 474, I came very close to being seriously wounded or killed. It was another situation in which the bulk of the platoon remained at the DDP while the platoon sergeant led the rest of us out on a short patrol. We were working our way down the hill on a narrow trail, and the man right behind me suddenly stumbled over a rock. As he stumbled, his weapon fired. Whenever we went on patrol, we did so with our weapons locked and loaded, a round in the chamber and our fingers on the trigger ready to fire but with the safety on. In the event a situation required it, one could easily flip the safety with his thumb and quickly fire at his target. However, in this case the safety on this man's weapon had somehow become disengaged, so when he stumbled, his finger pulled the trigger, discharging it. Of course, we all reacted instinctively by ducking and then realized what had happened. Sgt. Shrang was furious and immediately began to dress the soldier down with a verbal lashing. "You could have killed Doc!" he said. He then ordered the soldier to get back up the hill with the rest of the platoon, and he would deal with him later. Thankfully, the rest of the patrol went off without incident, and I have no recollection of any further action being taken, though he could have been hit with an Article 15, resulting in a loss of rank and pay.

Because we had lots of slack time during the day, I wrote home profusely, including letters to Barb, even though I had yet to hear anything from her. In a letter dated February 23rd, I told her about one of the other platoons losing one of their men, though I did not describe, nor do I recall, what the circumstance was. I went on to explain,

> *This week our company has killed about ten enemies and captured about four. This too is a sad thing and yet because you realize that even though these people have gone through some horrible things, still, for your buddies, it's them or us. And because war is a hard thing to understand about the only choice left is to accept it and do your best to stay alive, judging no man. What a day it will be when Jesus returns and wars will be no more! Then the wiping away of tears will come and blessings will be in store. ... It's tiring to even talk about Vietnam; just to think about it gives one a headache. And yet, when I see the Lord working here in the hearts and*

minds of individuals who are sincerely searching for Him,
then I praise God and am brought to rejoicing. Serving Him
is such a joy even here because one rejoices to see others
come to love Him and grow in Him.

Apparently I was having some significant conversations
with some of the men about spiritual things and was encouraged by their response. The Lt. even suggested I might
consider holding services on Sunday mornings because we
rarely ever saw a chaplain out in the field.

Because I hadn't heard from her, even though I had been
writing since getting to Vietnam, I encouraged Barb to write
back, even if it was just to tell me I should stop writing:
"...[E]ven though it has been over a year now since we
broke things off, still I have faith that the Lord has a time
for us, and I am praying it will be after Vietnam, after the
Army. Maybe for you that's too long. Maybe you don't feel
the same way or want to even take the chance of it's [sic]
not working out again. But at least drop a note to say one
way or the other."

As the medic it was my job was to take care of everyone
in the platoon, and sometimes that meant being the bad
guy. As the days turned into weeks and contact with the
enemy became rare, our guys became careless in their
sanitation practices. Every soldier was supposed to carry
an entrenching tool for digging fox holes and taking care
of his morning "business" by digging a "cat hole," which
was essential for good sanitation and for minimizing our
footprint. However, as we began to use the same DDPs and
NDPs, some of the guys became lazy and stopped digging
holes. I told the squad leaders this was becoming a problem
and if they didn't start practicing better sanitation, I would
have to take further action. Whether it was my laid-back,
mild-mannered personality that failed to impress them or
simply stubbornness on their part, nothing changed. So, one
day when we moved to a new night defensive position, I

told the Lt. the men had still not been properly burying their "business," and so I wanted each squad to dig a slit trench just outside the perimeter for that purpose. Needless to say, the men were not happy about having to do extra work, but the exercise solved the problem, and I never had to talk to the men again about it. From then on, whenever a man went out for his morning constitution, he took an entrenching tool with him and dug a proper hole.

In a letter home dated February 25th, I thanked my mom for a letter she had sent that took ten days to get to me. I also mentioned I was anxiously waiting for a package that included some kind of powdered drink mix to add to my water, like Start or Kool-Aid, some canned fruit, and an Instamatic Camera and film so I could take pictures for them showing what it was like to be a boonie rat. I also wrote, *"Tomorrow we get to go to the beach for two days."* And, *"I may get another bath this afternoon if they don't bring in an air strike. Otherwise we'll have to move out of range."*

The two days at the beach were a welcome break, after having spent over four weeks out in the field in the grueling heat, climbing up and down Hill 474, cleaning out caves, and pulling ambushes. (I no longer remember how we got there, but since there weren't any roads nearby we were probably picked up by chopper and taken to a base, from where we were transported by truck.) We had tents and cots to sleep in, cold beer and sodas to drink, and hot meals to eat. They brought in a portable MARS Station so we could call home. The MARS Station was a radio truck that made contact with a shortwave radio operator in the States, who would in turn make the call to your home and patch you through. It meant using radio protocol, and we were only allowed a couple of minutes each to talk, so everyone would get a chance to call. It was about 1:00 AM in the morning when I got to make my call, making it around 8 or 9 AM at home, I figured. We were instructed NOT to mention where we were, as our calls might be intercepted by the enemy, but once I was connected I was so excited I forgot and mentioned we were at the beach, resulting in an immediate frown from the radio operators.

Back at Hill 474, I wrote home on March 1st saying how good it was to talk to them. *"We had a really good time at the beach, sunburn and all. The only things they didn't have enough of were sodas and time; but can't have everything."* I went on to explain,

> *We aren't doing too much during the days, but setting ambushes at night. The object of an ambush supposedly is to offensively catch the enemy by surprise while they are moving from one local to another. But so far I've found no one who really wants to run into the enemy at all, offensively or not. So, believe me, we're not hardened veterans out here driving on to destroy the enemy and win the war! We're just a bunch of men bound together doing what we're told to, at the same time, as the men might put it, "trying to keep our (expletive) together."*

On March 6th, I wrote a short note to Barb. A letter I had sent to her had an inadequate address and had been returned, so I was resending it to her, having finally received my address book from home. In the note I mentioned one of the newer soldiers in my platoon, Crilly, for whom I had asked prayer, had *"realized his condition before God and told the Lord about it. I really believe he is being, or was, born again, so keep on praying."* I also told her about a new Kit Carson Scout, Troung, just 16 years old, who had been VC but surrendered when his group walked into an ambush and his buddies were killed. *"The VC then killed his father and five year old sister. So, now Troung is fighting for SVN and for his G.I friends. He's a good kid."*

In the "Football Field," from left to right, Kit Carson Scouts Troung and Lee Van Tho and me, enjoying a meal together prepared by the Scouts. Behind us is Platoon Sgt. Calvin Clemons, an old-timer who had served in the Korean War. After getting into some trouble, he had been busted in rank and sent back to the field as a Platoon Sgt. replacing Sgt. Schrang.

My first haircut in the field, given by Scout Lee Van Tho.

CHAPTER THIRTEEN

HOT LZ

*"Suddenly, in an instant, the LORD Almighty will come
with thunder and earthquake and great noise,
with windstorm and tempest and flames of devouring fire."*
Isaiah 29:3b-6

As a special task force detached from the 101st and on loan to other divisions in II Corps that needed extra help, one of the jobs of the 3/506 was to have units available as a fast reactionary force prepared to be moved within forty-five minutes of being called. That meant being able to quickly load up and get to a Pick-Up Zone for a Combat Assault (CA) to a new LZ. Since the activity on Hill 474 had become quiet and our days were rather easy, they brought in choppers one day so our platoon could practice rapidly loading and unloading as we would do if called upon to make such an assault.

It wasn't long before the call came. A Long Range Recon Patrol (LRRP Team) somewhere in Combat Alley was in trouble and needed us to come help them out. It was late in the afternoon and wouldn't be too many hours before it would be dark. The Huey slicks came, picked us up, and we were on our way, adrenalin flowing. As the medic, I loaded onto the second chopper. The Lt. and his radioman were on the first chopper so he could assess the situation and direct the others as they came in. It took five or six choppers to move an average platoon, with each chopper carrying five or six guys. Two guys would sit in each doorway on either side of the slick with their legs hanging out, ready to disembark quickly, with two more sitting on the floor in the center of the chopper. On this occasion I chose to load into the center and let others take the doorways.

This was my first actual combat assault, so I had no idea what to expect. Would we come into a hot LZ with guns blazing, or would it be quiet and easy?

As we made our way out of the valley and into the mountains, we were escorted by gunships. (Primarily two types of helicopter gunships were used in VN: Cobras and Hoggs, which were Hueys outfitted with rocket launchers on each side and M-50 machine guns. The slicks we were riding in had M-60 machine guns in each doorway, with a door gunner sitting behind them.) As we made our way toward the LZ, the gunships made runs ahead of us, peppering the area around the LZ with rocket and machine gun fire. The door gunners in the slicks also opened up as we approached the LZ, a grassy meadow in a slightly elevated area above a stream which ran about a hundred meters to the left of where we were coming in. As my chopper came in, we quickly off-loaded and spread out in a circle, falling into a prone position with rifles pointed outward to secure the LZ as we were trained to do. The meadow was smoky as the dry grass on the edge of the field had caught fire from the rocket blasts. It didn't take long for us to realize something was not right. We were the only ones on the LZ. The Lt. and first squad, which were on the first chopper, were nowhere to be found. To this day I do not know how it happened: the pilot of the first chopper went to the wrong LZ. I am sure the Lt. was equally confused when none of the other choppers were behind, and he found himself and the first squad all alone. We quickly established communication, and the first chopper went back to pick up the Lt. and his squad and brought them to our location.

Once we were all together, an assessment was made. There was no enemy fire, so technically it was not a "hot LZ," as they were called when you came in under enemy fire, but the grass fire ignited by the rockets was growing, and we needed to get away from it. It would also be dark soon, and we needed to find a good position to set up our NDP. Across the stream was a hill that would give us good elevation (you always wanted to have the high ground, if possible), so the decision was made to make our way to the stream, cross it, and climb the hill. The stream would act as a barrier between us and the fire.

By the time we made it across the stream and to the top of the hill, it was getting dark, so our squad leaders went to work setting up a perimeter by setting out the claymore mines and trip flares. Two of the squads had M-60 machine guns at their guard positions and the other two squads were defended by rifle and M-79 grenade launchers.

The rest of the night was quiet. Looking across the stream the next morning we could see the burned out field that had continued to smolder throughout the night. I don't remember what happened to the LRRP Team, but apparently their situation resolved itself. Either the enemy broke off and skedaddled, which was a common hit and run tactic, or the LRRP Team was able to extricate themselves, because we never did have to go in and get them. We spent the next day relaxing on the hill watching jets make bombing runs in the distance and writing letters home. Eventually the choppers came back and returned us to the Hill to continue our patrols and ambush operations. I was thankful even though the fire at the LZ had given us a bit of a scare, it was a far better situation to deal with than an actual hot LZ. I was also very happy we did not have to go in to rescue the LRRP team.

"Tiny," so called because of his stature, reading a newspaper on the hill overlooking the burned-out Landing Zone we had been choppered into the evening before. Tiny later left the platoon to go work with the LRRP Teams.

Chapter Fourteen

Wrapping Up

"I exalt you, O LORD, for you lifted me
out of the depths and did not let my
enemies gloat over me."

Psalm 30:1

On March 11th I wrote another long letter home thanking my family for another package and talking about how glad I was to have the camera and film they sent. I also talked about how I was 10 days away from completing two months in the field, which would leave me four to go. I then explained what we were doing at this point.

> *Yesterday morning we were CAed to the top of Hill 474 again, LBE (Light Battle Equipment) and swept down the rocks again to check the CS gas in the caves. This time there were just 30 men from our platoon instead of the whole company and I was really afraid that the VC may have come back to the area. But we were able to make it all the way back to the foot of the hill, where we've been the last couple of weeks, without any trouble at all.*

> *Then, today (this morning) we (one squad) had to hump back up the hill to this last area of caves we checked. Again, we went LBE but it was still quite a hump, even without packs. Our head scout found fairly fresh tracks, but again we didn't find the Dicks that made them, and thank goodness.*

The CS was still real good in all of the tunnels except for one section in these last ones. The explosives didn't work in those and we didn't have the stuff to set them off. So, tomorrow some more men will have to hump back up and set them off and plant some booby traps. As I'm the medic and we only have one of me (unfortunately), I'll probably have to go back up with them. What a bear! But that's life I guess, the price for being a medic (or Quack as my men tease me with).

We finished the task of setting off the explosives in the remaining section of the cave and spent the next few days doing what we had done the last couple of weeks, setting up ambushes and NDPs without any significant results. Things at Hill 474 were quiet; our mission of driving the NVA from their stronghold and rendering it uninhabitable for at least a few months was accomplished.

In the March 30th edition of *The Screaming Eagle*, the 101st's newspaper, the following article appeared:

3/506 Inf. Routs NVA Battalion

LZ North English – In a hard hitting series of clashes the 8th Bn., 22nd NVA Regiment has been routed by the Screaming Eagles of the 3rd Bn. (Ambl.), 506th Inf., northwest of Bong Son, Binh Dihn Province in northern II Corps.

The deeply entrenched NVA Battalion concealed in the caves and crevices of Hill 474, initiated a series of fire fights with heavy AK-47, B-40 rocket, RPG, and RPD light machinegun fire against the Currahees.

As the conflict progressed sorties of F4 Fighter-Bombers were brought to bear on the enemy positions. In coordinated airmobile assaults, Lt. Col. Joseph N. Jaggers Jr., battalion commander began an encirclement of the NVA. Further air strikes and artillery bombardment prevented the NVA battalion from fleeing their camp.

With the NVA surrounded, the air and artillery bombardment was intensified with the Currahees directing this massed firepower on observable targets. Further combat assaults were made by the airmobile troopers, placing them in command of the enemy routes of escape.

The NVA, under the continuous punishment of small arms, air and artillery fire, attempted to exfiltrate hill 474. Despite the enemy's advantage of terrain, Lt. Col. Jaggers continually shifted his forces by helicopter, caught the NVA battalion and systematically destroyed the enemy force.

In the clashes that followed, the hardened veterans of the 506th never lost the initiative and drove against the NVA breaking them into smaller and smaller elements.

The NVA lost 90 dead as a result of the engagements. Twenty AK-47 assault rifles, 5,000 rounds of small arms ammunition, three RPD machine guns, four RPG rocket launchers, 25 B-40 rockets, twenty-five Chicom grenades, 3000 pounds of rice, a typewriter and substantial quantities of medical supplies, entrenching tools and clothing (were captured).

In spite of the enemy supplies we captured, the personal items and equipment we lost on January 25th were never recovered. My assumption is whatever munitions were not used against us in the battle and skirmishes that followed and all of our personal items were taken out of the area by the enemy as they escaped in the early days of the bombardment. The C-Rations would have likely been consumed by the dicks hiding in the caves, and all of my medications, which were in an ammo can and not in my aid bag, would have been quite valuable to them.

Like many military reports, though perhaps technically correct, the article failed to tell the real story of the battle for Hill 474: the blood, sweat, and tears of those who fought on the ground; the missteps that resulted in the loss of American lives; the bravery of the medevac pilots who, against incredible odds, flew in to try and save the wounded and dying; the narrow escape of a battle ravaged platoon in the shelter of a brush-covered stream; the decision to leave the dead behind and more lives lost trying to recover them; the myriad of ambushes pulled night after night by everyday grunts like me; and the personal stories of pain and loss. Fortunately, other articles in other papers told the story from the vantage points of the soldiers and pilots who fought the battles, articles in *The Currahee* (the battalion paper), *Firebase 173* (the paper for the 173rd Airborne Division), and *The Overseas Weekly – Pacific Edition*, copies of which I sent home for safe keeping and still have. But the deeper stories, the personal stories of those who were there, are left to be told by the survivors, those who experienced the battles, handed down by oral tradition, or in books just like this one, written by unlikely warriors like me who can never forget war is not glorious but ugly and painful, even when necessary. The battle for Hill 474 was finished, but my year in Vietnam had only just begun.

CHAPTER FIFTEEN

THE TIGER MOUNTAINS

"I love you, O LORD, my strength.
The LORD is my rock, my fortress and my deliverer;
my God is my rock in whom I take refuge."
Psalm 18:10-12

On March 16th our battalion was combat assaulted into an area known as the Tiger Mountains, several miles southeast of Hill 474 and Combat Alley, for a mission that lasted 11 days. *The Stand Alone Battalion, A Pictorial Chronology of the 3-506 Vietnam Odyssey (1967-1971)*, written by Jerry Berry and John R. Alexander, describes this area as a "rugged insect-infested mountainous AO, located immediately south of the Song Lai Giang River and between Hiway [*sic*] QL-1 to the West and the South of China Sea (which) proved to be more inhospitable than the elusive enemy." Fortunately for my platoon, we were placed in the lowlands to act as a blocking force and to pull ambushes while our other two platoons were CAed into the mountains to cut LZs and work their way down to our location. Other companies and LRRP teams were inserted in other areas to search for the elusive enemy. It had been some time since any GIs had been in this area, so I suppose the mission was to check to see if the enemy had returned and to interdict them if we found them. On March 17th I wrote home, *"Our job is to make it unhealthy for the Viet Cong and easily accessible for our friendly forces."* I went on to write, *"The weather has been real warm, but as we're not humping around it's not too bad. But I wonder how long it will last. So far it's lasted quite awhile [sic].*" I went on to say tomorrow would be resupply day, which meant we would get some sodas. We paid $5.00 a month to get three sodas each resupply day and enough ice for each person to have maybe one cold soda. I continued, *"One doesn't realize how much of a luxury ice is until he has to go without. Too bad, it won't stay frozen in a package. When I think of home I think of a tall glass of coke full of ice!"* That was really true. Sometimes I'd think about how wonderful it would be just to have a glass full of ice to enjoy.

The next day, March 18th, I got a letter from home and started writing another one to which I added over the next three days. I had been writing to my mom about the possibility of her and my step-dad joining me in Hawaii for seven days. I had requested a seven-day leave from my medical platoon Sgt., and he had assured me I could get one as long as it was in May, since we had a lot of medics going home in June, and I would be needed then. Initially, my mom was favorable to the idea, but as time went on, it became clear she didn't think they could go. It was probably more of a pipe dream for me than anything else, but it gave me something to look forward to. I would still get my one week R&R after six months in the field and planned to go to Japan to visit a church friend working with a short term missionary team at the Osaka World's Fair. I also went on to explain things were fine. *"The most excitement I've had lately medically is one snake bite patient (not serious), a tooth ache case, and urine tests to be sent to the rear. Sounds like an easy job, doesn't it? Well, it is. I just hope it stays that way."*

The snakebite incident was not really a snakebite at all, I later concluded. We had come to a stream on the 19th and chose to rest there a while, giving the men a chance to take off their boots, soak their feet, and rest in the shade. Suddenly came the cry "Medic!" down by the stream. I grabbed my aid bag and ran down to where the call came from only to find a man holding his foot. On his ankle were what appeared to be fang marks. "A snake! I was bitten by a snake!" he said. I asked him what it looked like, and he said it was a small green snake swimming in the water. There were certainly poisonous snakes in Vietnam, including one called the "two step" because of its deadliness. Supposedly if you were bitten by one, you would be dead before you could take two steps.

I had not seen any snakes yet in Vietnam, so I was a little suspicious. It was also not uncommon for men to use whatever means possible to get out of the field. Guys would even put bars of soap under their arms in an attempt to clog their pores, in the hope it would raise their body temperature imitating a fever. That's one reason we weren't allowed to evacuate anyone until they had a temp. of 104 degrees, impossible to achieve with soap under your arms. "Did anyone else see the snake?" I asked the other men who were nearby, and all they did was shrug their shoulders saying they hadn't seen anything. The soldier continued to insist he had been bitten by a snake. Not wanting to call him a liar, and with no one willing to stand up and say he had faked the bite, I felt I had no choice but to evacuate him for observation in the rear. Better to be safe than sorry on my part. To my knowledge he never returned to the field, which was maybe just as well. Years later this soldier's squad leader told me how angry he was at him for using such a ruse to get out of the field.

During this mission we came across another stream and beautiful pool of water with about a five-foot waterfall flowing into it. Because we had not encountered any dicks yet, we felt secure enough to take some time out for a swim, setting up guard positions on both sides of the pool for security. Once again, moments like these were especially cherished after living in the jungle or mountains for weeks at a time without a bath. At one point we decided to see if there were any fish in the pool, so we cleared the area, and someone dropped a concussion grenade or two into the pond. Unfortunately no fish floated to the surface, so C-rations would have to be it for dinner that evening. We returned to this spot one or two more times for another leisurely swim before leaving the area.

Though things were quiet for Delta Company, some of the companies and recon teams were making enemy contact in their areas of operation (AOs). Battalion Operational Reports indicate the following:

On March 16th 2nd Platoon, Alpha Co. engaged three NVA, killing one and capturing an AK-47 with ammo, some miscellaneous equipment, a rice bag, and materials including a picture indicating the KIA was an NVA officer. Gun ships were brought in to support the contact and later another partially buried NVA KIA was found.

On March 19th 1st and 2nd platoons of Bravo Co. engaged and killed one NVA in a cave. Some miscellaneous equipment including 82mm mortar rounds were found in the cave.

On March 20th Bravo Company's 1st platoon found some miscellaneous items in another cave, and Bravo Company used CS gas, as had been done on Hill 474, to render them inhospitable for enemy use. Charlie Company's 1st platoon had three WIAs from an unknown type of booby trap requiring evacuation.

On March 21st Recon Team 2 killed one VC/NVA capturing an M-26 grenade, writing paper, and 1.5 pounds of documents, which contained a count of VC, ARVNs, and a list and count of personnel at Lo Dieu OP. Diaries, personal letters, and propaganda materials were also found.

In the meantime, Recon Team 1 engaged six VC/NVA, who returned small arms AK-47 fire. Two gunships were brought online, resulting in one VC/NVA killed inside a hootch 6'x15'x18' and one secondary explosion. Another 6'x6'x6' hootch was also spotted in the area.

One thing that amazes me is what each soldier remembers from his time in Vietnam and what they have, for whatever reason, completely forgotten. For example, I have absolutely no recollection of the following, but it is both documented by the Operations Reports and has been repeated to me by Lt. Greig and others from the platoon. On March 22nd our platoon swept through the Recon Team 1 contact area from the day before and found one female VC KIA wearing black pajamas. She had an ID card and papers. She was in the larger hootch and appeared to be a VC doctor, as there were also medical supplies, canned food, tobacco, shaving cream, a hammock, poncho, sewing kit, mosquito net with blood stains, and some marijuana there. It was estimated the hootch may have been occupied by as many as seven people. After checking out the area, our platoon set the hootches on fire so they could not be used again by the enemy.

How I could not remember this event I will never know, but again it is a testament to the fact every man's memory of what he experienced in Vietnam is at best imperfect and differences in firsthand accounts of the same events are sometimes a reflection of those imperfect memories.

I write all of that to show that even though our platoon had it relatively easy during this particular mission, it didn't mean that other units were not engaged in contact during that same period or that there weren't any casualties. The reality was that no matter where we operated as a battalion, some platoons might see relatively little activity while others would see more. For myself, I am thankful that the Tiger Mountains proved to be uneventful for 1st Platoon, Delta Co.

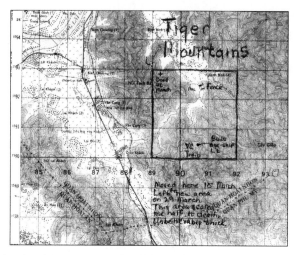

A map showing the area we were operating in with notations made by Lt. Greig indicating where the dead VC woman was found, the pool where we went swimming and where we built an LZ so U.S. troops would have better access to the area in the future. Map courtesy of Richard Greig, Cpt. U.S. Army, ret.

Enemy hootches being burned. If you look closely you can see the feet and dark figure of the VC Doctor lying on the ground in the middle of the hootch. Photo courtesy of Richard Greig.

CHAPTER SIXTEEN

THE CROWS FOOT MOUNTAINS PT. 1

"In the presence of God and of Christ Jesus,
who will judge the living and the dead,
and in view of his appearing and his kingdom,
I give you this charge: Preach the word;
be prepared in season and out of season,
correct, rebuke and encourage –
with great patience and careful instruction."

2 Timothy 4:1-2

Having completed our mission in the Tiger Mountains with little enemy contact, Task force 3/506 was C.A.ed by chopper to the Crows Foot Mountains on March 27th. (The Crows Foot Mountains was the range of mountains where Hill 474 was.) Still riding on the second chopper, I was now sitting in the doorway with my legs dangling out, my back-pack being the only thing holding me in. I had decided that I wanted and needed to be able to get out quickly, especially if the LZ was hot and there were casualties from the first lift. The mountainous terrain below was beautiful. I pulled out my Instamatic camera to take a picture and the door gunner sitting next to me signaled for me to give him the camera. Taking it he leaned out of the helicopter, holding onto a pole that was between us, and looking back took a picture of me holding my fingers in a "V" pattern for "Victory."

There was no resistance at the LZ making the assault uneventful. The weather and terrain were similar to what we experienced in the Tiger Mountains; it was hot and relatively rugged with plenty of thick overgrowth. On March 31ˢᵗ I wrote home: *"things here are fine as I am sure you have already gathered from the preceding few words. We finished cutting the LZs in the tiger mountains and, believe it or not, we have been moved to another hill with the same number as the one before, hill 474. but it is hardly like the last one in its features and hopefully not in its deadliness. So far, in checking it out, it seems pretty safe. I think things should be alright."*

(Hills were identified by their elevation, so this hill was also 474 meters above sea level as was the previous mountain on which we had engaged the NVA.)

I also included a letter I had received from Rudy Boykins, the soldier on whose arm I had to use a tourniquet back on the first Hill 474, who lost his arm as a result of our inability to evacuate him until the next morning. I had sent a letter to him, and he wrote a touching letter back to me:

Dear Doc:

I got your letter the other day. I was glad to hear from you and the rest of the guys. I'm sure things have cooled off some by now.

I also got letters from a lot of the other guys, but I haven't had time to answer them yet. I'm home with my wife, and boy, am I having a ball! She's writing this letter for me now. I could have written it, but she wouldn't let me.

I want to thank you for doing everything you did while I was wounded because without your help and God's I probably wouldn't be here, especially keeping me awake all night (smile). I haven't seen Smitty since I left Japan. Tell the rest of

the guys I will be answering their letters soon. It was indeed
nice knowing guys like you.

A Friend,
Rudy & wife

It was a great comfort to receive this letter, as I often wondered if I could have stopped the bleeding without using a tourniquet. Many years later I reconnected with Rudy and found out he and his wife were doing well, and he had no bitterness about what had happened. He was grateful to be alive and praised God for His goodness over the years.

Contrary to what I wrote home to my family about what I was experiencing at this time, the Crow's Foot Mountains were a hotbed of enemy activity by both VC and NVA forces, as indicated by the situation reports for that period. The area was filled with enemy bunkers, caves, and well-used trails. Various platoons encountered small groups of the enemy or found enemy supplies on almost a daily basis. For example, on March 30th 2nd Platoon of Alpha Co. found eight NVA KIA, though the Operational Reports do not describe how they were killed. Weapons, ammo, and other miscellaneous items were also found. On the same day 1st Platoon, Alpha Co. also found a host of enemy equipment, including eight NVA rucksacks, various munitions, documents, clothing items, medical supplies, cooking utensils, and even a bicycle. 1st Platoon, Bravo Co. engaged an unknown size enemy force near a stream using grenades but with negative results. Continuing their sweep, they engaged another lone NVA with small arms fire but again with negative results. On March 31st a natural cave complex was found and searched. On April 2nd 3rd Platoon, Alpha Co. engaged 3 VC/NVA killing one; 1st Platoon, Bravo Co. also engaged two enemy soldiers with negative results and various small items were found, including medical and payroll records, personal letters, notes, and numerous notebooks. During this time some units and fire bases were hit with mortar rounds at night, though no one was injured.

The Operational Report lists activity for every day of the mission except April 5th and 6th. April 4th was a particularly busy day for our 2nd Platoon, Delta Co. finding a bunker with one NVA KIA in a shallow grave. He had apparently been dead for about a month and a half, killed by a gunshot wound to the head. 3rd Platoon, Alpha Co. found eight spider holes along with a number of miscellaneous personal items. They also engaged and killed one lone NVA and captured more miscellaneous items. 1st Platoon, Bravo Co. found a very old trail and tripped a booby trap that killed one of their soldiers and injured two others.

I could go on, but really that is not the purpose of this book. It is not meant as a chronology of our battalion's activities but of my own personal experiences.

The reality is when we were out in the field, we didn't really hear or know much about what was happening with the other platoons and companies unless, of course, it affected us in some way. At least I didn't. I can only assume the same was true for the other men in my platoon as well. I suppose it is possible the Lt. knew some of what was happening with the rest of our company and battalion and would have known what our mission as a platoon was in relationship to them. But for the most part, as I understood the way things worked, each company had an Area of Operation to search and that AO was divided among the platoons, with each platoon working its own area. Sometimes all three platoons in a company would meet up at the same LZ for resupply, but not always.

As a platoon, our focus was on doing our job and staying alive. Generally speaking, it consisted of covering ground, humping each day from one objective to another in search of the enemy, and setting up ambushes when and where appropriate. Some days were exhausting if we had a lot of ground to cover and the terrain was rugged, especially on the first day after resupply when our rucksacks were full. If it was hot, we sweated like pigs, and our pores became clogged on our shoulders and backs where the rucksack straps and packs pressed themselves against our flesh, resulting in prickly heat.

As platoons we had enough to worry about without also worrying about what was happening with other platoons and companies. Not knowing kept us from getting discouraged or overly fearful.

On April 5th I wrote a letter to Barb in response to a card she sent me. This was the first communication I received from her in the four months I had been in Vietnam. She had indicated in her card she was going through some struggles, so I tried to encourage her with some words about God using trials to refine our faith, pointing to Job from the Old Testament as an example. I then continued,

> *The sky has been dropping rain all day today, and I'm writing this letter during a lull in the hopes that I can get it finished before it starts again. It's around 2:30 pm now and not much is happening. Last night, however, another soul was cast into eternity ... He was most likely an NVA soldier and he walked into one of our ambushes last night at midnight. He tripped a trip flare and was surely killed almost instantly by the blast of the claymore mine detonated by one of our men at the guard position. His body was so mangled by the explosion that even to describe it on paper would be most gruesome.*

Just as I no longer have any memory of the VC Doctor we found dead in the Tiger Mountains, I have no recollection of this particular incident, though again I have no doubt it happened. I may not have been with that particular ambush but obviously had seen the body of the dead NVA the next day.

I do remember another incident, however, that I recounted in the same letter. Easter Sunday, March 29th, Lt. Greig asked me if I would conduct services for the platoon. Because we were in the jungle on Search and Destroy, we would need to do it squad by squad, which meant doing it three or four times. In any event, the mini-sermons were well received even though at one point the Lt. had to come and remind me to keep my voice down. That was quite a challenge for me, since I competed in high school as an orator and my sermons at home were always quite high energy. In fact, some years later I was told by one of the men from my church it was not uncommon for them to turn the microphone down or off when I preached because it was not needed, since I had a voice that carried quite well.

I continued to write, *"It's not uncommon to have a man tell me he's learned more from my ministry than at any time under the ministry of a church at home. How wonderfully the Lord can work here! How thankful I am for the prayers of others and the power of our Lord Jesus. I can truly sing, 'How great Thou art!'"*

In the same letter I went on to tell Barb about an effort by one of our chaplains to reach the VC and NVA for Christ by giving Bibles and Christian literature to Christians in the platoons to be left in strategic places.

> *We are even trying something new with the backing of our battalion Chaplain now. He's provided us with some Vietnamese Bibles (New Testaments) and Gospels of John, along with some tracts and we will leave them in likely places to be found by the NVA. Hopefully they will take them and out of curiosity read them. Perhaps some will even make their way back to North Vietnam itself. We are backing the project with much prayer and know that we will probably have to wait until eternity itself to know the results. But if only one of the 300 pieces of literature should be found and one soul saved as a result, then it will be worth it and far more. God's grace will have been made known to one more and Christ glorified.*

As I recall, the Bibles had a nice red cover and were packed into zip lock plastic bags with little packets to absorb humidity. I remember the day when the chaplain, a young fellow, came out to the field and asked me if I would be willing to carry a few in my pack and leave them along the way. Of course, I did not want to say no to the chaplain, even though none of us really wanted to carry any more weight in our backpacks than we had to. The reason we were called "grunts" was because of the noise we would make whenever we got up with our packs on. It was not easy and was accomplished by sitting down, slipping the straps over our shoulders with a towel wrapped around our necks and across our shoulders for padding. We would then lean forward, roll over onto our knees, and stand up with a grunt, adjusting the 60- to 80-pound ruck to fit as comfortable as possible. In any event, I took several of the packets in deference to the chaplain. I seem to remember the Bibles and literature were provided to the chaplain by his church back in the States. Sometime later someone sent me a small article that had appeared in my hometown newspaper, the *Gresham Outlook*, and explained we were trying to "spread Christianity" by dropping Bibles. I don't recall who sent it to the paper and was quite surprised to receive it.

I do not remember much of what happened the next few days. Surely they were spent humping the hills, setting up more ambushes, perhaps finding and destroying a few abandoned bunkers, and maybe cutting an LZ or two, but nothing major for us in the way of enemy contact. I would not write home again until April 13th.

I do remember our cutting some LZs either here or in the Tiger Mountains. Lt. Greig's map of the Tiger Mountains Operation shows we did cut one LZ there. We were provided with chain saws, but, of course, that also meant having gasoline and dealing with breakdowns. We also used C-4 plastic explosives that were attached to a tree trunk and then blown from a distance, knocking down the tree. Our guys actually enjoyed blowing LZs, since we didn't often get to work with C-4.

Soldier drops Bibles on tour

PFC Clarence M. Dingman, 20, son of Mrs. Robert J. Morsman, 235 NE 19th, Gresham, is spreading Christianity while serving in Vietnam.

He is a medic and on his tours drops Bibles that will be picked up by the Viet Cong. They are wrapped in water proof material because of the damp climate.

It is one way some of the soldiers in Vietnam are trying to teach Christianity to the enemy.

This article appeared in my hometown newspaper, *The Gresham Outlook*.

A picture of me on a Combat Assault, taken by the helicopter door gunner while he leaned out of the chopper hanging on to a support pole at a high altitude.

CHAPTER SEVENTEEN

THE CROW'S FOOT MOUNTAINS PT. 2

"I trust in the LORD.
I will be glad and rejoice in your love,
for you saw my affliction
and knew the anguish of my soul."

Psalm 32:6b-7

T he next letter I wrote home was not a pleasant one. In just a few days I had gone from praising God for all the good things that were happening to a point of discouragement and despair. The events of the previous few days had weighed heavily on me, and the final straw was when I didn't receive any mail on the next resupply. Mail for the grunt in Vietnam was his only connection to the real world back home. Letters and packages from home lifted one's spirits and gave encouragement, unless, of course, the letters brought bad news. Letters and care packages were the two things that told us people back home still cared about us and about what we were going through. When things were not going well and we were tired of living in the jungle for weeks on end, facing the prospect of death on a daily basis, and then you didn't receive any mail, it was especially disheartening. So, before the next resupply I sat down to write another letter.

As already mentioned, I had been writing to my mom and step-dad about meeting me for a week in Hawaii. By this time it was clear they were not going to be able to come, and so it was on this topic I began to write.

Dear Mom, Bob and Family:

Just a few lines to let you know that I am ok and am thinking of you often. I'm hoping to hear from you soon again about Hawaii. If your second answer is still that you don't think you should go I've decided to take the 7 day leave anyway. I may go to the Philippines and visit Uncle Roy if he's still there. If not there, then I don't know where. But I'll go someplace as I need the break. Maybe I'll get a letter from you tomorrow.

Day before yesterday was the first resupply since I've started getting mail that I didn't hear from a single person, family or friends. I had noticed a little slackness in the mail but didn't think it would come to a total halt. It's a real shame when a G.I. is sent to a place where he didn't ask to go, has to do a job he didn't ask to do and live a life he shouldn't have to live, not knowing whether he or his buddies will get hurt or killed next and then he doesn't even get mail from home. But I've seen a lot of G.I.'s go without more than once and I imagine I'll see it happen a lot more yet.

The last few days have been kind of rough on my nerves. I guess that's why I'm being so frank. I really don't mean to sound angry or anything because I'm not. I know you all really do worry about me over here and I wished you didn't have to. I know you love and miss me and rest assured I love and miss you a lot too. Most of the guys manage to write home without telling their families about what's really happening, but I can't do that. I really feel that God wants us to be honest with each other, sharing our problems and encouraging each other. Else how can we know how to pray for each other and with what urgency or how to help each other in what manner of service? But God wants us to have faith in Him too, believing that He sees and understands our problems and that He will provide. If we can share our burdens honestly, pray for and encourage each other, and trust, really trust that God is with us, then our sorrows are turned to rejoicing and our burdens are made light. Knowing that one is in God's hands through Jesus Christ makes all the difference in the world.

The 9th, one of my men walked into a booby trap and had his right leg nearly blown completely off just eight inches below the knee. I was just a few men behind him in the file, so I was able to reach him fairly quickly and apply a tourniquet and give morphine.

I can't imagine how that must have struck my mother to go from reading in one paragraph about my not getting mail to reading in the next one of my men had been seriously injured by a booby trap just a short distance in front of me. But as I had already explained, I thought it was important to tell them exactly what was going on. In reality, looking back, I realize now it was my way of dealing with it, of getting it out rather than keeping it in. I needed to vent, and that wasn't something we could do in the field. We had to keep it together and focus on our job.

I remember the incident well and can still picture the scene in my mind. The NDP where we had set up was in an open grassy area just big enough for our platoon, surrounded by jungle and uneven terrain. The weather was warm, and everything seemed to be going well. We had not had any serious incidents or injuries since the battle on Hill 474.

That morning after breakfast and cleaning up, the Lt. decided to take a two-squad patrol out, leaving the rest of the platoon at the NDP with our gear. I don't remember how far we got outside of the perimeter, but it couldn't have been too far when suddenly there was a huge explosion to the front of us: "KABOOM!" The earth shook beneath our feet, and, with a great billow of smoke, dust and debris flew everywhere, accompanied by screams of horror. Immediately we hit the dirt, and then instinctively I began to make my way forward. At the same time the squad leader, Bob Asbell, who was second in the profile, made his way back to me. As I looked at him to see if he was injured he said, "Don't worry about me! My point man! My point man!" Almost immediately the point man, Mike Kosky from Arizona, called out, "No sweat! No sweat!"

In my letter I wrote to my mother,

> *That was odd but a great relief as I hadn't expected to even find him alive, let alone conscious and calm. I came back with, "Mike, are you alright?" and then he gave me another turn-around; He came back with a very straight and emphatic, "No! I'm (expletive) up!" Though it seems funny now, it wasn't at the time. The screams of horror and pain that had just followed the explosion and preceded the conversation wouldn't let it be. The torn flesh and pool of blood prevented it. The thought of someone dying or just being seriously hurt, the visions of your buddies injured or killed put you in anything but a funny mood. It puts a pit in your stomach, a throb in your head, and fear in your mind, but you drive on hoping to save your buddy and maybe yourself. War really is hell!*

When I reached Mike, he was still conscious but obviously in bad shape. I could see the lower part of his left leg was nearly severed. He was bleeding profusely as the sheer impact of the blast had not only nearly severed the lower part of his leg and foot but had also split the insides of both of his legs. I knew I had to act quickly to save his life, so I grabbed two tourniquets from my aid bag and applied one to each leg just below the groin area to stop the bleeding. When the Lt. made his way to my side, he made some comment about how quickly I had put the tourniquets on, as if to question my judgment. Having been trained as a medic prior to becoming an infantry officer, he knew tourniquets were to be used only as a last resort. However, as the medic it was my job to make that decision, and I felt in this case it was necessary to save

Mike's life. I also gave Mike a shot of morphine to help with the pain and pinned the empty morphine ampoule to his shirt collar, so the dust-off medics and hospital personnel would know he had received it and how much.

While I continued to give aid to Mike, a call was made on the radio for a dust off. However, we would first need to get Mike to an LZ, and to do that safely we needed a stretcher. It wasn't long before a chopper made it to our location and dropped a stretcher down to us. The chopper was on its way to another emergency and indicated it would be back as soon possible. This gave us time to get Mike to the LZ. I told a couple of the other guys who were there to give me a hand lifting Mike to the stretcher. Immediately I could see no one was anxious to deal with his nearly amputated leg, so I told the other two to get their arms under his shoulders and torso, and I would take his legs. As gently as we could, we lifted him to the stretcher, and then we made our way to the LZ. Bob Asbell, who had been right behind Mike, had only suffered minor lacerations but needed to be evacuated with Mike. A third man had completely lost his hearing due to the blast and also needed to be evacuated.

At the LZ, the rest of the men secured the perimeter, and we waited for the return of the medevac. For me it seemed like an eternity. I couldn't believe how long it was taking. Mike remained conscious, and a couple of his buddies along with the Lt. stayed by his side. I made my way around to the other men to make sure they were all doing okay, as there was not anything more I could do for Mike except wait. I really began to fear he would die before the chopper returned. Finally the medevac came back and whisked Mike, Bob, and the other soldier off to the aid station where Mike was stabilized before being evacuated to a hospital.

In my letter home I continued, *"They're all ok, but the one man did lose his leg. Thank the good Lord it was below the knee as this will allow him to walk without a limp and*

*live an almost normal life, limiting his activity only slightly.
That is, after he learns to use his new leg."*

I went on to explain the real shame was the booby trap
was one of our own. Our platoon sergeant, Calvin Clemons,
an older veteran who had served in Korea, had shown us
how to set up claymore mines using a trip wire across a trail.
Sgt. Clemons, part Inuit Eskimo from Alaska, had replaced
Sgt. Schrang who had been court martialed for threatening
to kill our Lt. The mine was attached to a flashlight battery,
so when the wire was tripped the mine automatically deto-
nated, killing whoever tripped it. We called them "automatic
claymores." Each morning the squad leaders were supposed
to see they were picked up, along with the regular trip flares
and claymores protecting our perimeter, but in this case one
of them had forgotten his. Fortunately for Mike, the claymore had been poorly positioned, or he would have been
killed instantly.

On April 11th, two days after the above incident, our
platoon was CAed to a new location a few miles west, where
we were supposed to go up against the 3rd NVA Division. We
were to relieve an ARVN unit that had already been working
the area. I remember our coming into a small clearing on
top of a hill, and as we got off the choppers the awaiting
ARVNs got on and were lifted out. In the three months I had
been in the field, I had yet to see any ARVNs, so this was my
first glimpse of an ARVN unit, and I wasn't impressed. They
looked pretty ragged and were not nearly as well equipped as
we were. But since they had already been working this area,
I figured it couldn't be too bad, at least not right there.

Once we got organized, our platoon began to make its
way off the hill top down a steep trail through the jungle.
Suddenly shots rang out, and we hit the dirt almost in shock.
We hadn't gotten more than 50 or 75 meters down the hill,
and we were already under attack! The point man, Jim, was
hit by the burst of fire and cried, "Medic!" Slipping my

backpack off, I proceeded to un-strap my aid bag. We didn't have quick release straps back then, and for some reason my bag was strapped on especially tight. I was having difficulty getting them loose. The Lt. looked at me and said, "Hurry up, Doc!"

Getting it off, I prepared to head down the steep trail to Jim when I noticed he was trying to make his way back up to me. This gave me great relief, as I figured if he could move like that he must not be too seriously injured. "Keep down, Jim!" I hollered

He came back with, "But I've got to get to you, Doc! I'm hit bad!" I could see he was hit in the left arm in the bicep as his arm dangled limply and was covered with blood. I slipped down the trail meeting him half way, examined the wound, and applied a compress to his arm to stop the bleeding. I also gave him a shot of morphine for the pain and used a pistol belt as a sling to immobilize his arm.

In my letter home I explained, *"Though the wound wasn't too serious and should heal with proper treatment, still it was very painful as the bone was surely broken and the exit hole extremely large having a lot of flesh and muscle torn away. As I tried to calm him telling him that he would be alright, he cried, 'I know, but it's the pain!' and he began to recite a Catholic prayer he had probably learned as a child."*

Jim was able to walk with the help of a fire team back up to the LZ, where he was evacuated for treatment. In the meantime, a squad was sent out to circle around and find the culprit that had opened fire on us. The rest of us lay still, waiting. After about 45 minutes shots rang out again, and the squad reported they had gotten him.

In my letter I continued to write,

While these things are happening, it's pretty scary. But after it's all over and I think back, sometimes I laugh. For example, Jim's comment, "I've got to get to you, Doc!" is funny the way it came out, because usually I go to them. Just before

that the Lt. had hollered, "Are you alright, Jim?" and he answered with a strained, but very emphatic, "No, Sir!" I thought it funny that he'd answer in that manner. I'd of expected something more like, "Hell no! I'm hit!" instead of the respectful, "No, Sir!

My frustration with the whole situation came out further in the following complaint.

One thing that makes a G.I. mad is when those working in the rear go around telling all sorts of war stories and complaining about how bad it is over here. They've done nothing but sit behind their typewriters, or drive their jeeps and maybe had to sweat a couple of mortar attacks while the boony-rat is the one who is doing all the fighting and sweating it all the time. They sit in the rear drinking all of the cold sodas they can get, watching all the movies and USO shows, and eating three hot meals a day while the boony-rat may have one hot meal every three days flown out to them by chopper, and are lucky if they even get in to see a movie or USO show. When he does get in he's usually put on K.P or guard duty while there until he's sent back to the field. Don't get me wrong! . . . Any boony-rat who could work in the rear would. I myself, being a medic, will get to do a few months in the rear too. I only wished that they'd realize how good they've really got it and tell it like it really is.

In a few days, 15 or so, we may get to go to the beach for three days again. That'll really be nice. A break from the constant sound of jets bombing, dropping napalm, and shooting their cannons; gunships and Cobras firing their rockets, automatic 79ers and machine and mini-guns; artillery shells whistling over head [sic], exploding shortly after in the distance, and sometimes not so far in the distance. It'll be a nice break! Maybe I can call you from a mars station again.

Clearly I was using this opportunity to vent my frustrations, and in so doing was being a bit melodramatic. But I was tired, weary of war after seeing a couple of my guys seriously wounded, frustrated by the senselessness of it all, especially Mike being injured by one of our own mines, and disappointed at having not received any mail. So, in that respect the thoughts expressed exactly what I was feeling at the time.

I also wrote a letter shortly after this to Jim, who had been shot in the arm, and received the following back from him written on May 4th.

Doc,

I was sure glad to hear from you. You're the only person who took enough time out to write me, and I want to thank you very much for the letter.

You are so right about me sleeping like a baby between clean sheets and eating good solid meals. And I am going back to the world, with my left arm still on my body.

I hear tell, from the 101st liaison officer, that you people are pretty sure you got the dick that shot me. I really do hope so. Tell me, Doc, was I hit with an AK or an M-16? All I heard was a loud pop, like a fire cracker. You must of [sic] heard the shots, so would you please write back and let me know just what I got hit with? And also, I don't know if you noticed or even saw that I was shot twice in my left arm. I never felt the second round, just the first. The second one was a clean straight through wound and was in between my elbow and wrist, on the bottom side of my arm which has already completely healed up. But the top wound is still in the healing stage.

Here's what all is wrong with my arm. I no longer have a left upper arm muscle, it was blown away, plus I have nerve damage pretty bad. I have feeling in just two fingers, my little finger and the one next to it. All the rest have no feeling and I am unable to move them. I'm going to have to see a nerve specialist back in the World so that I can use my hand and fingers again.

That (expletive) Dick did a job on me, and what's even worse, I never saw him or got a chance to fire him back. But I shouldn't complain at all, because if he had been a better shot, I wouldn't even be writing you this letter, right? So, I can see that someone up there was watching over me.

He went on to explain he was in a hospital in Japan and would be leaving to "the world" that week, so to hold up on writing to him again until he could write me from there and give me his new address. He ended the letter, *"Give my best to everyone and be cool and keep your head and ass down low to the ground. I'd hate to see any more people get fired up like me. From a Boonie-rat going HOME, Jim."*

The truth is I did not see the wound in his lower left arm because it was a clean through and through shot and apparently did little damage. Because the damage to his upper arm muscle was so massive, I was focused on treating that and the pain. If I saw blood on his lower arm, I probably thought it was from the upper arm injury. He didn't mention whether the medevac medics or the doctors at the hospital he was evacuated to caught it.

I also remember there being some question as to whether the enemy soldier we killed was the actual shooter, due to some confusion about whether Jim had been hit by an M-16 or an AK-47. The dick killed was carrying the later, but some thought the shots fired sounded like they had come from an M-16 instead.

We continued to operate for several more days in the vicinity where we had killed the lone shooter and would often walk past his body as we moved along the trail. I don't recall any further significant contact, but I do recall watching the wretched process of decay and the maggots that filled his mouth, eyes, and nose by about day four. The loathsome smell of death I had noticed when I first arrived in the field was present once again after having been free from it during our time in the Tiger Mountains. It may have also been in this AO that the smell of a decaying body became so overpowering that after a couple of days the Lt. ordered a squad to go out and find the body and bury it. The sights, sounds, and smells of war were not over for me. I had been in the field for just under three months now and had at least three more to go with no idea of what lay ahead.

I finished my letter home with the following: *"Well, in the meantime, take care and write when you can. One of my buddies says for me to tell you we miss all of you back there, and we do. But remember, I'm ok. After all, I've got God on my side and with a partner like Him how can I lose. Love always, Mike."*

Chapter Eighteen
Consequences of War

"As a father has compassion on his children,
so the Lord has compassion on those who fear him,
for he knows how we are formed,
he remembers that we are dust."

Psalm103:13-14

After the incident in which Mike Kosky lost a leg walking into one of our own automatic claymores, Jack (not his real name) who had forgotten to pick it up that morning was pretty much ostracized by the rest of the platoon. If there was one thing we needed on the battlefield, it was the ability to count on each other. My men needed to know they could count on me to be there for them, and I needed to know they were watching out for me. If I were killed or wounded, I would not be able to give them the life-saving aid they might need. So, when Mike was nearly killed, it was only natural for the rest of the platoon to distance themselves from Jack, to treat him like an outsider. As the medic, and having reached out to him spiritually in the past, I did my best to encourage him and assure him of God's love. But it was clear he was depressed, and I was concerned about his well-being.

At some point over the next eight days, we set up camp on top of a hill where we remained for the next two or three days. On one side of the hill a steep slope swept down about two hundred meters to a grassy meadow where yet another platoon set up their camp. This is the only time I can remember having two platoons set up so close to each other. Here Jack came to me one day complaining he had fallen out of his hammock (I do not recall ever seeing anyone use a hammock in the field, but this may be yet another memory that has slipped my mind) and landed on his back on a rock. I issued him a muscle relaxant to see if that would help, but a day or two later he was still complaining of significant back pain. Seeing this as an opportunity to get him out of the field for his own protection as well as for the morale of the platoon, I decided to have him evacuated to the rear, where his back pain could be more effectively treated.

Two significant events took place at this location. One was a couple of soldiers from the other platoon made their way up the hill toward our location. I do not remember why they were coming up to our position, but no one had radioed us they were coming, and when the soldier at that guard position saw movement on the perimeter, he opened fire before he could identify the target. This was common practice, because whenever we were out in the jungle we were operating in what was considered enemy territory, a "free fire zone," which meant our men were instructed to shoot first and ask questions later. One of the two soldiers was shot in the thigh. Though not life-threatening, the injury necessitated he be medevaced to a hospital for treatment.

The second incident happened in the middle of the night. A burst of M-16 fire rang out from the meadow below, waking us instantly from our slumber. There were sounds of panic and commotion, with people yelling and screaming, and then radio traffic as a medevac was called in to make a nighttime extraction. The next day we learned one of the other platoon's soldiers had a nightmare, and in a disoriented panic bolted to his feet, rifle in hand, and started shooting, spraying the area with bullets. I do not remember how many of his comrades were wounded or if any were killed before he was tackled by one of his fellow soldiers, but the damage was already done.

The incident was a significant reminder of the effects war has on many soldiers. Tragedies such as the one that struck our platoon had devastating consequences not only for Mike, who lost a leg, but also for Jack. The soldier that wound up injuring or killing some of his own men because of a nightmare had to live with the memories of that event the rest of his life, and those wounded with the after-effects of their injuries. The scars of war are not always visible, and it is easy to see why many find talking about their experiences almost impossible. Who can understand how a simple slip of the mind or a horrible dream could have such tragic consequences? The wounds of each are real, visible and invisible, and the consequences of war horrible.

Needless to say, I was deeply saddened by these incidents but also very thankful God was watching over me, keeping me safe.

On April 21st Task Force 3/506 was pulled out of the Crow's Foot Mountains and flown from LZ English to Camp Radcliff near An Khe, home of the 4th Infantry Division, which was preparing to launch a new offensive called "Operation Wayne Wind." In preparing for this operation, the 1st Brigade Commander of the 4th Infantry Division, Colonel Harold Yow, specifically requested the 3/506 be transferred from the 173rd Airborne Brigade's control (OPCON). We became OPCON to the 4th Infantry Division on April 20th and were released from OPCON to the 173rd Airborne Brigade on April 22nd with Operation Wayne Wind beginning on April 25th. We were now part of a new task force called Task Force PURSUIT. The operation would take place in the Doc Payou Valley area known as "VC Valley," where it was believed the 3rd NVA Division was operating.

Loading up for the short trip from LZ English to An Khe.
Photo courtesy of Tom Landers.

CHAPTER NINETEEN

BOOTS AND MORTARS

"The LORD delights in the way of the man
whose steps he has made firm;
though he stumble, he will not fall,
for the LORD upholds him with his hand."

Psalm 37:23-24

On April 23rd I wrote another letter home: *"This week we left the 173rd Airborne Div. (we were helping them in Bong Son) and now we're with the 4th Infantry Division near An Khe. Things are sure a lot nicer here. They pulled us from the field Tuesday and we've been partying since. Saturday we're to go back to the field. But our company may wind up on a firebase building bunkers for a while."*

I went on to explain I had not slept on a bed since January 18th and was thankful finally to have a roof over my head. It had been over three months of living in the jungles, mountains, and rice paddies of Vietnam with only one two-day break at the beach. What was especially exciting was with the facilities here to house us, they would be able to pull us out of the field every so often for breaks and entertainment. In fact, that afternoon we were going to *"get to see a USO show with back to the world type girls and everything."* I went on to talk about how I had less than three months to spend in the field, and I could even get pulled out earlier if they got enough new medics to replace those in the field sooner. The one thing that wasn't going to happen was getting the seven-day leave I had requested. As I had already explained, we were going to be short medics in June so it would have to happen before then, and here it was near the end of April, and it didn't look like it was going to be possible.

One of the only recollections I have of those few days at Camp Radcliff was the adjustment I went through. Sleeping in a barracks in what was supposed to be a relatively safe area after three months in the field seemed strange. I don't believe we had cots the first couple of days, so we slept on the floor. I wondered whether the base might get mortared at night or whether sappers might try to break through the wire. Because I was so used to being on alert at all times, I didn't feel comfortable taking my boots off at night. We slept with them on in the field, and for at least two or three nights I slept with them on at Camp Radcliff. I remember thinking to myself, "I wonder if it is safe to sleep with my boots off?" After thinking about it for a while, I decided it was. So I did.

On Sunday, April 26th or Monday the 27th Delta Co. was lifted from Camp Radcliff and CAed to Firebase Mattie in support of other companies out in the field. A firebase is an artillery base with cannon and mortar for fire power and, in this case, even a couple of Hueys for air support. Our first responsibility was to build bunkers and establish a secure perimeter with concertina wire. On May 2nd I wrote a letter home telling them where we were and adding we had been there for a week. *"I'm glad we're here on a firebase and hope we stay for awhile. But it's got its bad points as well as good. We have to be ready for mortar attacks at night and also on guard for sappers trying to sneak through our wire with high explosives. We've had a couple of mortar attacks but we're pretty uptight to keep sappers out. Our bunkers protect us from the mortars and our guards, wire, mines, and trip-flares from sappers."*

The reality was the mortar attacks were terrifying. Though brief, usually taking place at dusk and consisting of only three or four mortars each attack, there was little we could do but hunker down in our bunkers and hope we didn't take a direct hit. The reason for only launching three or four mortars each night was likely so we would not be able to pinpoint their exact location and respond with return fire. I am not sure when they first began, but it had to be just a day or two after we arrived.

There wasn't much to do other than to make sure my guys took their Monday Mondays and daily malaria pills. I don't remember any particular medical issues during that time, and the weather was relatively nice, other than a heavy rain shower some afternoons. I remember during one downpour one of the engineers or artillerymen took a shower on top of his bunker, bar of soap and all.

The first or second night we were hit by mortars we all dove into our bunkers for safety. "Incoming!" someone yelled as the whine of the first mortar roared overhead, landing with a loud "BOOM!" The ground shook, and dust fell from the rafters of the bunkers when the first mortar struck. Then it happened, the panicked cry of a soldier from a nearby bunker: "Medic! Medic!" Immediately I began feeling around in the dark for my aid bag but to no avail. The reality was I couldn't remember where I had set it. Again, those terrifying words rang out between mortar explosions, "Medic! Medic!" I was struck with both panic and a sick feeling deep in my stomach as I thought of this soldier in need and my inability to find my aid bag. It was probably only a minute or so before the mortars stopped, and so did the cries of the nearby soldier. Shortly afterward I learned another medic had made it to the bunker and found a soldier, probably one of the artillerymen, who had gotten some dust in his eyes as he dove into his bunker. Using some water, the medic was able to rinse them out, and he was fine. I was greatly relieved the soldier was okay but also terribly ashamed I had allowed myself to become so relaxed I didn't even know where my aid bag was. "What if that had been one of my guys, and what if he had been seriously wounded?" I thought to myself. I vowed I would never let anything like that happen again.

A day or two after that an order came down the next time we were hit by mortars we were all to empty one clip of M-16 rounds into the tree line around the perimeter before heading to our bunkers. It was thought the enemy might have a forward observer (F.O.) hiding in the trees giving direction to the mortar team firing at us. The next time we got mortared, I was outside the bunker when the first round came in. Quickly I leveled my M-16 to the tree line. A clip only held about 18 rounds (they would hold a few more but tended to jam if we filled them full), so it didn't take long to empty on automatic. However, as I fired I could hear Lt. Greig in the bunker frantically saying, "Where's Doc? Where's Doc?"

My clip empty, I quickly made my way into the bunker. "Here I am! I was following orders emptying a clip into the tree line!" I don't think he was very happy with me, and I don't remember what he said to me after that, but it was probably something about not waiting to get into the bunker. Maybe he thought I should be exempt from the order as the medic, since there was only one of me, and I would be needed if someone was hurt. But I felt I had done my job, and if there was an F.O. in the tree line, it would take all the firepower we had to either scare him or knock him out of the tree.

It may have been that night one of the artillerymen on the other side of the firebase was killed when his sleeping position took a direct hit. There was nothing anyone could do as the artilleryman was literally blown to pieces.

The Battalion Commander, LTC Jaggers, was getting tired of the enemy's ability to lob mortars at us so easily, so the next night we got mortared the order came down for first platoon to go out and find the dicks responsible and silence them. Because the mortars always came in at dusk, it was already getting dark, but the choppers came in and picked us up anyway. Lt. Greig was not about to risk his platoon hunting the mortar team in the dark. When we landed in the jungle in the vicinity they thought the mortars were coming from, we quickly found a good spot for an NDP and set up for the night. The next day our platoon searched the area but found nothing. After that the mortar fire seemed to stop.

I closed my letter of May 2nd with these words: *"Well, that's about it. It's rained the last three days around 4:30 PM and it's about that time. The clouds are right on-time, so I'd best close. Write when you can. Love Always, Mike."*

My wish we could stay on the firebase for a while in spite of the mortars, like so many other desires, was not to be. On the very next day we received orders to quickly tear down the firebase, and we were lifted back to An Khe in preparation for the biggest and potentially most dangerous mission we would ever face.

The Platoon Command Post Bunker on Firebase Mattie under construction. Lee Van Tho in the doorway and me lying on the sandbags. Photo courtesy of Richard Greig.

Lt. Richard Greig taking a much-deserved break.

A Flying Crane either picking up or delivering supplies to a firebase.

Chapter Twenty

Out of the Frying Pan, Into the Fire

*"Have not I commanded you? Be strong and courageous.
Do not be terrified; do not be discouraged,
for the LORD your God will be with you wherever you go."*
Joshua 1:9

On May 3rd Firebase Mattie was quickly disassembled and bunkers destroyed to the best of our ability. Materials that weren't needed were burned to avoid use by the enemy. Huge Flying Cranes swept in to lift out the remaining supplies and equipment in huge cargo nets, their massive rotors churning up dirt, rocks, and whatever else might be picked up by the gusts of wind they created. A bandolier of M-16 ammo left too close to one of the burning fires had to be pulled out before it started cooking off. Chinooks hauled away artillery pieces, and, last of all, the grunts on the ground were picked up by slicks and whisked away, back to Camp Radcliff, near An Khe for a mission we knew nothing about.

Back at Camp Radcliff, the entire battalion was put on a 24-hour stand-down, during which time we took hot showers and enjoyed the amenities of the rear, all the time wondering what lay ahead. Why, after just a week in the field on Operation Wayne Wind, was the battalion so hastily removed? We were used to being moved from one AO to another, a platoon or company at a time, but never had the whole battalion been so hastily removed without any indication of what lay ahead. While at Camp Radcliff, troopers were issued new ammunition, which seemed unusual, especially for my platoon, because so much of our ammo had already been replaced after losing most of our supplies and equipment on Hill 474. Nevertheless, it was clear the higher-ups thought we needed fresh ammo for the new mission we were about to embark on.

It was great having a barracks to sleep in again, but that too would be short lived. I am sure most of us slept somewhat fitfully that night, not knowing what the next day would bring. Still, even one night in the rear was a welcome break from sleeping on the hard ground, in a dark bunker, or in the pitch black darkness of triple canopy jungle.

The next morning we were loaded onto deuce and a half trucks to be convoyed (motor marched) to Camp Holloway, Pleiku, just thirty miles from the Cambodia border. As the massive convoy snaked its way east via highway QL 19 through the Man Yang pass, Cobra gunships and Huey Hoggs flew up and down the highway providing security. Additional security was provided by mechanized units.

When we arrived at our destination, we were housed in tents. That afternoon we saw wave after wave of slicks coming in and parking along the edges of the airstrip. I remember walking over to the airstrip and being overwhelmed by the sheer number of choppers assembling there. Clearly something very big was about to happen.

Later that day we were briefed about our new mission. We were told we would be going into Cambodia to seek and destroy enemy supplies and installations in what was known as Base Camp 702. Primarily ARVN, along with some US troops, had already invaded Cambodia to the south, down by Saigon, beginning on April 29th, and President Nixon decided to launch another offensive from the northern part of South Vietnam. The assignment was given to the 1st Brigade of the Fourth Infantry Division, and by a quirk of fate the 3/506 would now be part of that invasion. Several key members of the leadership, including the battalion commander of 1st Brigade's 3rd Battalion of the 12th Infantry Regiment, had been killed in a chopper crash on April 27th, downed by enemy fire. The 1st Brigade commander decided the 3/506 would take their place. In fact, according to Major John Gibbs, Battalion S-3 Officer, when Colonel Yow looked at his battalions he decided the 3/506 had more experience fighting the NVA, due to our recent engagement on Hill 474, and were better prepared than his own for the fight. Therefore, the Currahees were not only selected to replace the 3rd of the 12th, but we would also spearhead the invasion, meaning we would be the first to hit the ground.

Unlike the invasion in the south, which was primarily a mechanized ground invasion involving tanks and APCs, this would be entirely an air assault with two brigades from the 4th Infantry Division, consisting of six infantry battalions, artillery units, engineers, and the 40th ARVN Regiment inserted in a single day: a miniature, albeit not insignificant, D-Day invasion. As Jerry Berry writes in *Twelve Days in May,* "Never before in the Vietnam conflict had so many aircraft amassed for a single purpose; this was history in the making. Operation Binh Tay 1 (Tame the West), the northern thrust by South Vietnamese and U.S. Forces into Cambodia, was about to commence. The Cambodian campaign would be the last unrestrained offensive use of U.S. ground forces in the Vietnam War" (86).

The 4th Infantry Division commanders had only been given two days to assemble their forces for the invasion, receiving warning orders sometime in the afternoon of May 2nd and brigade commanders receiving their warning orders that night at 2000 hours (8:00 PM). This meant all of their forces had to be pulled out of the field, given a 24-hour stand-down, and be resupplied with new ammo and additional weapons.

Then they needed to be transported to the departure points in Pleiku, and all the aircraft, fuel, munitions, rations, other supplies, and additional personnel needed to support such a mission assembled ready to go for the May 5th invasion: a logistical nightmare! This explained the urgent tearing down of our firebase and the rapid movement of our battalion along with 1st Brigade of the 4th Infantry Division to Camp Holloway and other nearby bases after such short notice.

That night was undoubtedly a restive night for all of the troops going into Cambodia the next day. Rumors floated around the 3/506 the Kit Carson scouts were refusing to go into Cambodia with us. While we slept, or tried to sleep, B-52s dropped their heavy loads of bombs on the areas where we were expected to land the next day. Though I have no recollection of it, Lt. Greig remembers feeling the tremors of the bombs as they tore through the Cambodian countryside. This is something I would later experience and clearly remember as I lay silently on the jungle floor inside Cambodia the following week. The dull rumbling of loud explosions in the distance like slow rolling thunder shook the ground beneath, sending shock waves in rapid succession for miles through the earth's crust, waking me from my slumber.

On the morning of Tuesday, May 5th, we, along with the rest of the 3/506, moved to the airfield to board the choppers for the approximately 60-mile, 30-minute ride out of the frying pan and into the fire. Despite what the other scouts may or may not have done, our highly respected scout, Lee Van Tho, was still with us. Sixty slicks, half of the 120 choppers which included Chinooks, Flying Cranes, dustoffs, and gunships committed to this operation from all over II Corps, lined up on both sides of the runway, their fuel tanks full and their rotors beating the already hot humid air, awaiting their precious cargo of human flesh weighed down by heavy backpacks and all the armament we could carry.

Lt. Greig, his RTO Don Meyers, and four other grunts lumbered into the first chopper. Along with five others, I loaded into the second, followed by the rest of our platoon, company, and battalion on down the line until all 300-350 men were loaded into the 60 slicks. One by one the choppers lifted from the ground, tilting forward with their tails in the air, rising into the sky with their heavy loads, a sea of fire-breathing dragons making their way to the NVA strongholds across the border. Helicopter gunships, Cobras and Hoggs, led the way and prepped the LZ for the insertion of our troops. Adrenalin rushed through our veins as we watched the countryside pass below and anticipated what lay ahead. If we landed in the order we took off, my chopper would be second on the ground, and I would be one of the first twelve men to hit Cambodian soil in the northern invasion.

As the gunships made their first run into the LZ, they drew heavy small arms and .52 caliber machinegun fire from well-concealed enemy positions and bunkers in the wood line. The slicks began their descent toward the LZ, as the gunships raked the area with their fiery rockets and deadly machine-guns. Attempts to silence the enemy were met with such fierce resistance the decision was made to turn back the troop carriers and move on to an alternate LZ. As the gunships zeroed in on the second site for insertion, they were once again met with lethal resistance while the troop carriers held in a circling pattern waiting for clearance to make their approach. This site too was deemed to be too hot to insert our troops. Battalion Commander LTC Jaggers made several attempts to land his CC Chopper at several other sites in an effort to find one safe enough, only to be met by significant hostile fire at each of the other locations. By this time, the choppers were beginning to get low on fuel and the gunships on ammo. The choppers had to break off their assault and return to base for refueling.

After refueling, LTC Jaggers took to the air again, this time with Alpha Company in the lead and the necessary gunships in another attempt to find a suitable LZ for the insertion of his troops. The choppers carrying the rest of the battalion followed shortly behind. More than four hours had passed since the first choppers had lifted into the sky that morning, and LTC Jaggers was determined to get his battalion on the ground before the day was out.

On the first two attempts of the afternoon, LTC Jaggers's CC Chopper and the accompanying gunships were once again met with heavy enemy fire. At the third site, however, after the gunships made their runs on the potential LZ with rockets and machineguns blazing, the decision was made to go ahead with the landing. Alpha Company was quickly inserted and secured the LZ with only light resistance. Soon after the first artillery unit was brought in, and the "go ahead" was given for the remaining infantry companies to be inserted in their successive order: Bravo, Charlie, and Delta Companies, followed by the remaining artillery units. By 1430 hours (2:30 PM) the Stand Alone Battalion was on the ground and ready to begin its mission with Alpha Company securing the firebase and Bravo, Charlie, and Delta Companies moving out in different directions to search for the enemy, his base camps, and supplies.

Because it was already mid-afternoon, there was not much time to engage the enemy. Finding suitable NDPs for each company was a high priority. However, as they moved out, Bravo Company's 2nd Platoon encountered two NVA on bicycles riding down a well-worn trail. 2nd Platoon engaged the enemy, killing one and wounding the other, who escaped. About thirty minutes later, while following the blood trail left by the wounded NVA, 2nd Platoon came under fire from an unknown-size enemy force. Because it was already getting late and darkness was closing in, the decision was made to withdraw and join the rest of the company at their NDP for the night.

After the insertion of the 3/506, attempts were made to insert the next battalion, the 1st of the 14th Infantry, only to be repelled in LZ after LZ. Finally the decision was made to return again for refueling and then to wait until the next morning to continue the invasion. On the first day of the invasion, the 3/506 of the 101st Airborne Division was the only unit to make it into Cambodia. The Stand Alone Battalion would be on its own for the first night and into the second day.

Much of this information I learned many years later by reading Jerry Berry's excellent book *Twelve Days in May*. Much if not most of that first day's events has long been washed from my memory by the sands of time. Without the assistance of others who were there, especially Lt. Greig, I could only give a bare sketch of what Delta Company and my platoon experienced.

Berry summarizes the day's events well:

> By the end of D-Day, May 5 only one battalion with its supporting elements was operational in Cambodia– the 3-506th, ironically nicknamed "The Stand Alone Battalion." The media ... did not mention the fact that the 3-506th was the only 101st Airborne Division unit to participate in the Cambodian Incursion... Nor did the media or Vietnam historians afterward give credit to the 3-506th for spearheading the 4th Infantry Division Cambodian Operations as well as the fact that it was the only American infantry unit to successfully land its forces on Cambodian soil in the initial assault. Despite the intense enemy small arms and anti-aircraft fire that forced the other 4th Infantry Division forces to abort their assaults on D-Day, the tenacity and combat spirit of the 3-506th prevailed once again, living up to their motto of "stand alone" (99).

Chapter Twenty-One

On the Hunt

"Be self-controlled and alert.
Your enemy the devil prowls around
like a roaring lion looking for someone to devour."
1 Peter 5:8

That first night in the jungles of Cambodia was filled with a great deal of apprehension. With the initial assaults met with such fierce resistance before finding a suitable LZ, we had no idea how many of the enemy might be out there or how soon we would encounter them in any sizable force. The experience of Bravo's 2nd Platoon earlier that day was proof enough they were here. This was their backyard, and we were the intruders. Our maps were from 1965, and our officers weren't sure how accurate they would be, an important factor to give proper coordinates to artillery units for fire support in the event of an attack. Our greatest security would have to be in our size as company elements, the defenses we set up for our NDPs, and the alertness of the individual infantryman on watch.

Don Meyers, Lt. Greig's RTO, recalls shortly after we had set up our NDP, one of the perimeter flares was tripped. Immediately the soldier at that guard position hit the clickers on his claymores, and their thunderous results simultaneously shook the earth beneath us. Immediately afterward were screams of pain and a rustling about as if someone was running, followed by a dull thud as if someone had run into a tree. After that was silence. Everyone was on full alert, but the rest of the night was uneventful.

The next morning, May 6th, when a recon of the area was done, what looked like spokes from a bicycle were found along with a blood trail. Apparently a lone NVA soldier riding along the trail had tripped the flare and been injured in the blast, but not enough to keep him from getting away along with his bike.

After eating breakfast and cleaning up, Delta Company headed out in search of the enemy. It wasn't long before we came upon some abandoned hootches and bunkers. The bunkers were more like bomb shelters than fighting positions. There were no enemy supplies, so we simply set about destroying the structures as best we could.

That evening we set up our NDP in the same general area as the hootch and bunker complex. Capt. Ohl ordered ambushes set out in the hopes of catching some hapless NVA moving down one of the trails. One of those ambushes consisting of troopers from 3rd Platoon had just such an encounter around midnight, when several NVA singing and talking loudly walked right into their ambush site. Spec. Four Ronnie Leonard blew his claymore and opened fire, after which everything became silent. The rest of the night was uneventful, and we slept as best we could, knowing tomorrow could be a different story.

The morning of May 7th the ambush team found blood trails but again no bodies. After performing our usual morning rituals, we set out in platoon-sized elements to see what we could find. If any one of our platoons got into trouble, the others could easily come to reinforce them. The area we were operating in was relatively easy to move through. It was basically level with some rolling hills. The trees were smaller and more spread out and the undergrowth more sparse than the Tiger and Crow's Foot Mountains where we had previously been. In fact, it had more of a state park feel to it rather than the rugged jungles and mountains in which we were used to operating. It was easy to see why the NVA had chosen this route for their supply lines along the border of South Vietnam, where they would not face interdiction from the US and ARVN troops until now.

A LOcH flying reconnaissance with a Cobra (a Pink Team also known as a Killer Team) had spotted a hamlet nearby, and we were to check it out. Late that morning our platoon found a complex of hootches and bunkers, including one structure containing an estimated 3 tons of rice. This complex was abandoned like the complex we had found the day before, so we burned the rice hootch and destroyed the other structures with grenades so they couldn't be used by the enemy.

In the meantime, that same morning, about 0730 hours, 3rd Platoon discovered a network of trails and began to follow them. Before long they spotted a bamboo bridge in the distance and another hootch complex. As a point squad cautiously approached the base camp, they observed four NVA soldiers near the first hootch going about their various chores. At about the same time, the rest of the platoon that had stayed a short distance behind heard voices, and eight NVA soldiers were observed coming down the trail towards them from the other direction. The two squads engaged the enemy immediately, killing two of them. The other remaining five NVA returned fire initially but then fled back up the trail from which they had come. Hearing the firefight going on behind them, the point squad, which had approached the base camp, opened up a barrage of fire on the complex with their M-60 machinegun, M-76 grenade launcher, and M-16s. With cover from his platoon, Lt. Hall moved forward toward a bunker from which they were taking fire and lobbed in a grenade, killing several more NVA. During these firefights, three of 3rd Platoon's soldiers were wounded. With the enemy fire silenced, 3rd Platoon moved in to search the bunker and hootch complex and found one lone surviving NVA, whom they took prisoner.

A medevac was called in to evacuate the wounded from a nearby LZ, during which time the dustoff and an accompanying Cobra came under fire from two NVA soldiers hidden in the wood line. 3rd Platoon was able to successfully evacuate their wounded in spite of the enemy fire and went to work silencing the attackers. Later that day and throughout the evening artillery was called in to pound suspected enemy positions.

In *Twelve Days in May*, the above action is described as two events, one involving 1st Platoon on May 7th and the other involving 3rd Platoon on May 10th. However, after a careful reading of the two events, including an article from *The Ivy Leaf*, 4th Infantry Division's newspaper, also included in Berry's book, extensive conversations with Lt. Greig, examining the unit history along with a map from Lt. Greig of our Cambodia operations with notations of daily activity, and rereading some of the letters I wrote home, I have come to the conclusion these were one-and-the-same event involving 3rd Platoon. Neither Lt. Greig nor I remember the action attributed to it or to him on May 7th. Nor do we recall having three WIAs from our platoon that day, something I am quite certain I as the medic and Lt. Greig as the platoon leader would remember. The *Ivy Leaf* article states 3rd Platoon had three wounded in action, confirming for me this was indeed what happened. A reference on Lt. Greig's map stating thirteen rucksacks and one NVA soldier were captured and seven NVA KIAs, together with the unit history, which also mentions the seven NVA KIAs on May 7th, further confirms it. The last piece of evidence came in a letter I wrote home on June 2nd, in which I wrote the following:

> *I don't know if I mentioned we had News people [sic] with us in Cambodia, but we did for one day, and they did have a motion picture camera with them. They were even mad at*

themselves because they hadn't brought their tape recorder with them and it was the day our 3rd Platoon made contact killing 6 NVA, capturing one POW and thirteen rucks. They had to get out that evening so they could get their film to Saigon for developing and use. So, I guess it's possible it was us, but unless Ron knows more about what was going on in the film I couldn't say.

Apparently, someone back home thought maybe they had seen our unit in a news report. I believe what happened was 1st Platoon picked up the news crew from an LZ and then linked up with 2nd and 3rd Platoon to search the base camp and help destroy it. Lt. Greig remembers an NVA prisoner who was at first very fearful after his capture, who then became very friendly once he realized we weren't going to kill him. Neither he nor I remember the bamboo bridge, though the sands of time may have something to do with that. I believe I have heard others from our platoon talk about it, though, at some of our reunions.

None of this is meant in any way to disparage Jerry Berry's excellent work in trying to produce an accurate account of the northern thrust into Cambodia, which was an enormous undertaking. In fact, I have depended on it heavily for much of the information you have read here. However, it is only reasonable to expect in the process of compiling such an extensive work there might also be some inaccuracies.

Needless to say, May 7th was a busy day for Delta Company. May 7th would have also been a resupply day. My assumption is it must have happened later in the day after the above described activity, which began early in the morning. There was no mail from home, likely because it had not caught up with us yet after the rapid move from VC Valley. But I do have a recollection of Lt. Greig giving Lee Van Tho, our scout, a pass to go home and see his family. None of the other scouts had come in with us, and Lt. Greig apparently thought Lee deserved a reward for his faithfulness. In talking with Lt. Greig these many years later, he has no recollection of Lee having gone into Cambodia with us or of this event. However, it so impressed me I never forgot about it and have recounted the story on numerous occasions. I was not only impressed by Lee's commitment to our platoon but also by Lt. Greig's concern for Lee and his desire to reward him.

That night there was no contact with the enemy, and we were all able to get some welcome sleep.

Lee Van Tho, Photo by Tom Landers

Kit Carson Scout, Lee Van Tho.
Photo courtesy of Tom Landers.

CHAPTER TWENTY-TWO

THE BIBLE

"Blessed is the man who finds wisdom,
the man who gains understanding,
for she is more profitable than silver,
and yields better returns than gold."
Proverbs 3:13-14

The next day, May 8th, was also uneventful. There were no major finds by Delta Company, though Jerry Berry mentions a half-ton of rice was found, which, of course, would have been destroyed like the rest.

It may have been on this day an incident happened that would later give support to the premise the term "Military Intelligence" is indeed an oxymoron.

I was still carrying the packets of Bibles given to me by the chaplain back in the Tiger Mountains in March. I had yet to leave a single Bible on any trail. To be honest, I felt a little awkward about leaving a Bible on a trail for the enemy to find. As an infantry platoon, we were there to kill the enemy and destroy his supplies, not to convert him. Secondly, leaving a Bible on the trail would give away the fact we had been there. Nonetheless, I was feeling a little guilty about having not dropped any of them during the last six or seven weeks. I was also getting tired of packing them around in my rucksack.

It was on one of these uneventful days I was out with my platoon, walking one of the well-worn trails, when we came to a "Y" in the path. One trail went off to the left up an incline along an embankment, while the other trail continued on to the right on level ground. At the "Y" where the two trails came together was a very large tree stump. I do not recall seeing a fallen tree there, so it was as if someone had cut the tree down for firewood or to use in the construction of their hootches.

We stopped to take a break so the leaders could talk about whether or not this would be a good place to set up an ambush. Obviously these were well-used trails, and this junction point would be an excellent place to catch the enemy coming from any one of three directions.

As the leaders looked at their maps and talked, I couldn't help but think what a perfect place this would be to leave a Bible, right there on the tree stump where it could clearly be seen by anyone coming down the trails. In spite of the conflict I felt, I decided I was going to finally do it. I slipped a Bible packet out of my backpack, and, when the order was given to saddle up and continue on the patrol, I walked over and as discretely as possible set the packet on the stump, hoping no one had seen me do it. I then took my place with the rest of the platoon on the trail, and we continued on our way.

It must have been at least two or three weeks later, after we had left Cambodia and were on yet another mission, that someone handed me a copy of one of the Army newspapers we occasionally got out in the field. I do not remember if it was a battalion or division publication, but it had an article in it about an important piece of intelligence found in Cambodia. Apparently another platoon had been on patrol on the same trail we had been on just a day or two later. As they approached the "Y," they observed three NVA soldiers in their khaki uniforms and pith helmets standing at the "Y" by the tree stump. One of them, who looked like an officer, had a red book in his hand and was looking at it. All three seemed to be talking about the book. Of course, the platoon didn't watch long before firing up the enemy. When they did, the enemy dropped the book and made off as quickly as they could, apparently uninjured. The platoon reconnoitered the area. Picking up the book, they were unable to decipher what it was. After all, it was in Vietnamese. However, since it was in the possession of three NVA soldiers, at least one of whom looked like an officer, they figured it must be important. So, it was sent back to Battalion Intelligence.

At Battalion Intelligence, it did not take long to figure out this was a Bible. With a little research they also learned a battalion chaplain had given them out to soldiers to be left on trails back in the Bong Son region of South Vietnam. Therefore, since the Bible was found in the hands of the NVA in Cambodia, it must be important evidence of the movement of NVA troops from Bong Son to Cambodia and vice versa.

Needless to say, I was somewhat stunned by what I was reading. I was also a bit embarrassed I would be the cause of such a blunder in intelligence. Nevertheless, I was not about to tell anyone I had left the Bible there and that the important find was *not* evidence of enemy troop movement at all but rather of US troop movement. If Army Intelligence was not smart enough to figure that out, I certainly was not going to rain on their parade or burst their bubble. There really is some truth to the saying "Military Intelligence is an oxymoron."

May 9th proved to be a fruitful day. In the morning our company found another hootch and bunker complex. There were about 30 pigs and 50 chickens running loose. We also found about four tons of rice, some miscellaneous clothing, and four SKS rifles. The pigs and chickens were disposed of as best we could, and the rice and complex destroyed before moving on.

Not far from the first complex, we came across two more large hootches, with one containing an estimated 520 tons of rice, which turned out to be the biggest cache of rice found throughout the Northern Cambodian operation. This amount of rice would have fed a very large number of NVA for several months had we not found and destroyed it. Also found were four more SKS rifles and a Chicom radio. According to Lt. Greig's map notation for this day, we also captured one more NVA soldier. According to a letter I wrote home on the 11th and 12th, he was just a teenager. How he was captured I do not remember.

That night again passed without incident.

Based on the intelligence reports and minimal contact, it appeared the majority of NVA in the area, estimated to be about 1500, had chosen to evacuate just before and after our initial assault, taking whatever supplies they could with them, leaving behind small elements to slow our progress. Needless to say, we were not unhappy about the limited resistance we were running into. By this time our company had traveled about 10,000 meters from our original insertion point, Firebase Currahee. The days ahead would prove to be a different story.

Chapter Twenty-Three

The Rescue

"The LORD is my shepherd, I shall lack nothing.
He makes me lie down in green pastures,
he leads me beside quiet waters, he restores my soul.
He guides me in the paths of righteousness for his name's sake.
Even though I walk through the valley of the shadow of death,
I will fear no evil, for you are with me
your rod and your staff, they comfort me."

Psalm 23:1-4

May 10th was resupply day. This time our mail finally caught up with us, and I received two letters from home and a card from Barb. I also received three packages, two from my sister, Cheryl, and one from friends in L.A., mostly cookies I shared with the platoon and a few canned goods that went into my backpack.

Though the day was uneventful for Delta Company, we were undoubtedly busy going out on platoon-sized searches for the enemy, as I did not begin to write my own letters home until the next day.

While Delta Company was experiencing a respite from contact and any significant finds, Bravo Company on the other hand found themselves in a fight for their lives.

From the time they first landed at LZ Currahee, Bravo Company had been in contact with the enemy every day with the exception of May 9th. They had one trooper wounded in contact on May 6th and another on May 7th. They killed several

NVA in these skirmishes, found and destroyed a couple of small hootch complexes, and captured several weapons.

On the evening of May 9th, as Bravo Company was setting up their NDP within the wood line on the north side of a large cultivated clearing, they spotted the grass rooftop of a hootch in the wood line on the southeast side of the clearing. Captain Waynbright reported the finding to Operations (S-3), figuring it was likely part of a larger hootch complex, and requested a resupply of ammo, water, and C-rations. Because it was already late in the day, a full resupply wouldn't be possible until the next day, but an emergency supply, called a "kick out," could be made. As the chopper and an accompanying Cobra came into the clearing to drop its load, it came under fire from NVA in the wood line on the other side of the clearing. However, the crew was able to kick out the supplies successfully and continue on their way, despite the enemy fire.

Bravo Company was ordered to stay put, and artillery was called in to pound the suspected enemy locations, after which a large group of people and barking dogs could be heard moving through the jungle to the southeast. In the early hours of May 10th, movement was detected on their perimeter. Claymores were set off and a barrage of fire was focused on the area, after which it was quiet. The next morning, blood trails were found in the area where movement had been suspected, but no bodies were found.

Shortly thereafter elements of Bravo Company moved into the now-deserted complex of nearly 40 hootches, determined to be a hospital complex, and went about destroying it. Finished by around 1100 hours, they were instructed by LTC Jaggers to investigate another hamlet nearby, which he had spotted from his command and control chopper. As they moved toward the complex, they came under heavy attack, and a battle developed that raged on throughout the day and into the evening. *Twelve Days in May* describes this battle in great detail. Bravo Company pinned down by the enemy in a deadly ambush suffered eight killed and thirty-five wounded, and there were fears at the brigade level the company might be completely lost.

Delta Company was far enough away from the action that we were unaware a battle for survival by Bravo Co. was even under way, with the exception of Capt. Ohl and the platoon leaders who may have been briefed about the situation sometime that afternoon. Early that evening, as we were setting up our NDP for the night, Cpt. Ohl received orders to break camp and move to reinforce Bravo Company.

Moving through the jungles of Cambodia during the day was certainly dangerous enough, but moving through the jungle in the pitch black of night had to be one of the most harrowing and dangerous experiences anyone could ever have. I can remember clearly the sense of fear and trepidation that hung over us as our squads retrieved their mines and trip flares, and we prepared to move out. Cpt. Ohl had tried to persuade Command it would be better if we could wait until morning, but his appeal fell on deaf ears. Bravo Company was in desperate straits, and we were the closest unit to them. How our Command expected our leaders to follow a trail or read their compasses to get a proper bearing in the dead of night, I will never know, not to mention the difficulty a point man would have seeing booby traps or detecting an ambush on the trail.

Slowly, we moved out, a full-size company, about ninety men, trying to move as quickly and quietly as possible in the dead of night. Because of the difficulty seeing, we could not spread out as much as we normally would have during the day, a dangerous situation in itself. If we were to come under attack or the point man was to hit a booby trap, we would be bunched together, resulting in even more casualties. Because of the snail's pace at which we had to move, it would also take us several hours to get to Bravo's location. After about forty-five minutes and very little progress, the decision was made to stop and set up a makeshift perimeter as best we could on the trail. We would wait out the night and move out again at first light. There was little we could to do to evacuate their dead and wounded until first light anyway.

The next morning at daybreak, we moved out as quickly as possible. There was no time for breakfast or the other usual morning rituals. Our first and only priority was to reach Bravo Company and aid in their extraction.

In those early morning hours, Bravo Co. continued to receive incoming fire from small arms and RPGs. However, as Delta Company drew near, the enemy broke off and faded into the jungle.

I don't remember how long it took us to reach them, but when we did somberness penetrated the air like a thick fog. Delta Company encircled Bravo to provide security, and I made my way into Bravo's perimeter to see how I could help. There was little conversation and what little there was, was in whispers. As I looked into the faces of the men who had struggled for their lives the day before and through the night, there was the deep empty stare of men who were totally exhausted, not only physically but also emotionally. There were also in some respect feelings of great relief upon seeing us, much like the joy I felt when I stepped into the cool, wet stream that had become our salvation on Hill 474. That relief however was greatly subdued by the tremendous sense of loss they were feeling.

I found one of the medics and asked if there was anything I could do, but there wasn't. All that could be done for the wounded and dying had been done. What Bravo Company needed now was simply to know we would take care of them while they carried their dead and wounded to the PZ for evacuation. For some reason Battalion was unwilling to let the choppers land in the clearing where Bravo Co. was ambushed, so the dead and wounded had to be carried about

500 yards to another clearing. Because the clearing could only accommodate one helicopter at a time, it took quite a while for the extraction to be completed.

Once Bravo Company was extracted, members of Delta Co. made a sweep of the area. The enemy who continued to harass Bravo Company in the early morning hours apparently pulled out when they realized reinforcements were closing in. Though reports were as many as 47 NVA were killed, neither Lt. Greig nor I have any recollection of seeing a single body. The NVA, like the Viet Cong, were very good about taking their dead with them so we could not get a body count. With the amount of munitions expended against them that day there is little doubt they must have suffered significant casualties, but there was no way of proving it based on bodies found.

Delta Company also had the responsibility of policing Bravo Company's rucksacks and securing them until they could be picked up and returned to them the next day.

After Bravo Company was safely evacuated to the firebase, Alpha Company, which had been securing the firebase up until now, was CAed into the same clearing Bravo had just been picked up from. (Bravo's rucksacks were possibly loaded onto the choppers Alpha Company used, as I don't remember that happening the next day.) DDelta and Alpha Companies were to work in tandem, moving through the jungle on parallel lines in an effort to find the NVA who had hit Bravo Co. After Alpha Company arrived and got organized, Delta and Alpha moved out in different directions from the LZ to set up their NDPs.

Sometime that day I began a letter home to my mother. The first two thirds of the letter mentioned the mail I had received, including some pictures I had taken and sent in for development my mother sent to me. Apparently I was interrupted, since I did not finish the letter until the next day.

The night passed quietly, though I am sure all of us were extremely on edge.

CHAPTER TWENTY-FOUR

THE CONFUSION OF WAR

"Unless the LORD had given me help,
I would soon have dwelt in the silence of death.
When I said, 'My foot is slipping,'
your love, O LORD, supported me,
your consolation brought joy to my soul."

Psalm 94:17-19

On the morning of May 12th after eating breakfast and cleaning up, Delta Company moved out in search of the enemy. After a couple of hours of uneventful humping through the jungle, we stopped to take a break. The company spread out in a circle, with each platoon taking one third of the perimeter, just as we did at our NDPs. The area was relatively flat ground with small trees and marginal undergrowth. A dry stream bed was just outside our perimeter on one side.

It wasn't long before Alpha Company contacted us on the radio and said they were approaching our position and would be passing through, so not to fire them up. A few minutes later they entered one side of our perimeter and exited the other.

I don't remember why we broke as long as we did, but after humping for a couple of hours with 60 to 80 pounds of weight on your back, a break is always welcome. It was a chance to break out a snack, eat lunch, or maybe even jot out a few lines in a letter home.

It may be at this point that I finished my letter home and told them where I was.

> *I suppose I shouldn't mention this to you until it's over with, but it's best you hear it from me than someone else, as I have mentioned it to others. It's really not anything serious, but I know you'd worry anyway. We are on a fourteen day mission out of Pleiku in Cambodia. We came in May 5th, so it's already half over with. We travel as a Company instead of platoons here, to insure [sic] plenty of security. So far things have gone well for my Company. We've destroyed over 520 tons of rice caches and about five hutch and bunker complexes. Our Company has killed six NVA and captured two, along with fourteen rucksacks and about 12 weapons. Three men in 3rd Platoon were wounded but are ok. My platoon's been pretty much out of the action, thank goodness. Soon, this operation will be over with though, and we will maybe get a couple of more days in the rear. That'll be nice. We're all waiting for it.*

After a couple of more paragraphs about things at home I finished by saying I needed to quit and write to my sister and some others. *"Thanks for writing as often as you can. Love to hear from you. Love, your Son, Michael."*

At some point I left the CP area to check on my guys to see how they were doing. As I moved to the edge of the perimeter on one side and talked with some of my men, shots suddenly rang out. M-16 and M-60 machine guns opened up in a torrential rain of fire, and immediately I hit the ground, hugging it as closely as I could, the adrenaline rushing through my veins. There was a rucksack on the ground near me, so I reached out and grabbed it, raising it on its side in front of my head, as if somehow that would protect me. I could literally hear bullets whizzing by me, passing within inches, or so it seemed.

The shooting probably lasted less than a minute, but it doesn't take long for a few guys with automatic M-16s and M-60 machineguns to lay out a significant volume of fire. Moments like that were called "Mad Minutes," in which everyone let out a volume of fire to confront a threat. "Cease fire! Cease fire!" came the cry. At the same time, the cry every medic dreads came from multiple directions, "Medic!" "Medic!"

As I looked to my right, back in the direction I had come from just a few minutes before, I could see Don Meyer, the Platoon RTO, writhing in pain and holding his foot. I quickly made my way to him and grabbed my aid bag. A bullet had passed right through his boot and the ankle area, in one side and out the other. He was in excruciating pain, but I had to get his boot off so I could treat his wound. I gave him a shot of morphine to help with the pain. The wound was serious enough to be his ticket home. While I was tending to him, another one of my guys on the perimeter was being tended to by others. He had a shrapnel wound from a grenade to the thigh. Two additional men from my platoon also received wounds, though they were not serious.

It did not take long for us to realize the firefight was not with the enemy but with Alpha Co., who had come back around from their patrol unaware they were approaching our DDP. Jerry Berry writes in *Twelve Days in May*,

> Somehow, Alpha Company had mistakenly wandered into Delta Company's area of operation; and upon seeing 'soldiers' on their flank, promptly opened fire – sadly, on Delta Company. The case of mistaken identity had inflicted senseless casualties, as well as the death of a squad leader in 1st Platoon, Alpha Company – Sgt. James Vincent Ballay. Their greatest fear concerning inaccurate maps had come to fruition, causing the unnecessary death of a young Currahee who had less than a month left in his Vietnam tour of duty (221-220).

In addition to the death of Sgt. Ballay, one other soldier was wounded in Alpha Company. It was difficult enough when you had guys wounded or killed in a fight with the enemy, but when it was the result of friendly fire, it was especially disheartening.

As soon as the wounded were tended to, they and the KIA were moved to a nearby PZ and evacuated. Alpha Co. then moved on to another location, and Delta Co. settled down to digest what had just happened. I took time to write a letter home to Barb. The card I had received from her mentioned she was having a hard time and was kind of "down in the dumps," so I decided to try to encourage her.

May 12, 1970
Dear Barb,

I received your card and am sure sorry that you're down in the dumps. But perhaps I can cheer you up. Think about this:

Less than 30 minutes ago bullets were flying within six inches to a foot of my head. Four of my men were wounded; one fairly seriously. One man in another (Alpha) company was killed and one wounded.

Yesterday morning our Bravo Company had six killed and over 20 to 25 wounded and our company had to go in and get them out; we had tried to reach them the night before in the dark, but couldn't.

Today, and since May 5ʰ, I'm sitting in the jungles of Cambodia some 50 miles West of Pleiku, S. Vietnam, on a search and destroy mission. I've seen four NVA killed and two captured, one just a kid. We've burned their hutches and destroyed their rice. We've killed and been killed. Daily we live in a type of hell but look for deliverance. Daily we suffer loss.

"Now, listen to this! Christ Jesus is the one who died, rather who was raised to life and is at the right side of God. He pleads with God for us! Who can separate us from the love of Christ? Can trouble do it, or hardship, or persecution, or

hunger, or poverty, or danger, or death? As the Scripture says, for your sake we are in danger of death the whole day long, we are treated like sheep that are going to be slaughtered. No, in all these things we have complete victory through him who loved us! For I am certain that nothing can separate us from his love; neither death or life, neither angels nor other heavenly rulers or powers; neither the present nor the future; neither the world above nor the world below – there is nothing in all creation that will ever be able to separate us from the love of God which is ours through Christ Jesus our Lord" (Romans 8:34-39).

And, "This one thing I do, forgetting those things which are behind, and reaching forth unto those things which are before, I press toward the mark for the prize of the high calling of God in Christ Jesus. ... For I can do all things through Christ who strengtheneth me" (Philippians 3:13-14; 4:13 KJV).

And there are many others, Phil. 3:8, Hebrews 12:1-4, 1 Cor. 2:9, and Romans 8:28 just for example. Then let us, for the moment, stop and rejoice, not that we loved Him, but that He first loved us and gave Himself for us while we were yet sinners. Let us be still and <u>know</u> that He is God; <u>know</u> that He knows our problems and hears our prayers; <u>know</u> that everything is for the <u>best</u>!

Well, Barbara, I think I had best stop as I'm very tired and have others to write. Just remember that somebody up there cares–and so do I.

Yours in Him,
Michael.

Romans 8:34-39 as written above must have been my own paraphrase, as I can find no translation that uses the exact same verbiage, though the language is similar and the meaning is the same. In the next-to-last paragraph of the letter I also quote and even mix other verses together without citing their references as I knew Barb would be familiar with them. It must be kept in mind I was writing this in the jungle just shortly after having gone through a traumatic experience. Barb and I had both read through the entire Bible and committed many passages to memory at bible school where we met.

The rest of the day and evening passed without incident. May 11th and May 12th had been difficult days. May 13th would be a new day, and soon we would be leaving Cambodia to return to South Vietnam.

CHAPTER TWENTY-FIVE
WHEN FEAR STRIKES

"Sing joyfully to the LORD, you righteous;
it is fitting for the upright to praise him.
. . . We wait in hope for the LORD;
he is our help and our shield."

Psalm 33:1, 20

The morning of the 13th, Capt. Ohl called the platoon
leaders together for a morning briefing. 1st Platoon was
assigned responsibility for conducting the morning patrol.
2nd and 3rd Platoons remained at the DDP in reserve in case
we ran into any trouble. We left our rucksacks at the DDP
and went in light battle equipment (LBE). With my aid bag
on my back and my web-belt on, from which hung a couple
of canteens and my ammo bag, I picked up my M-16 and
assumed my position six men back from the point man, with
the Lt. and his RTO in front of me.

The terrain in Cambodia was beautiful in many ways, a
lush green forest with rolling hills and no rugged mountains.
The undergrowth was moderate, and the jungle floor was
covered with a web of well-worn trails, leading to the hootch
and bunker complexes we had been finding. Known as the
infamous Ho Chi Minh trail, the NVA moved their troops and
supplies from North Vietnam down along the border through
Cambodia and Laos entering SVN at strategic points along the
way. Units like the one we encountered on Hill 474 undoubtedly came in along the border where we were now seeking

199

to interdict the enemy and his supplies. We had already done significant damage to his food supply and destroyed many facilities, but we knew there were more to find.

It was another beautiful day in Cambodia, hot and humid like it had been pretty much the whole time we had been there. The shade of the double canopy jungle helped to temper the heat as we moved out and walked along the trail.

Once again it had the feel of walking through a state park back home. The tree trunks were relatively small compared to the great Douglas Firs of the Northwest where I had grown up, and they were spread out giving us good visibility. Suddenly a thought struck me as we made our way through what would otherwise have been a serene scene were it not for the fact we were in the middle of a war: if our visibility was so good because of the sparse undergrowth, then so was the enemy's. Since this was his territory and not ours, the odds were he would see us long before we ever saw him. Of course, this was also true back in Vietnam. The enemy was always much more likely to see us long before we ever saw him. But for some reason the thought gripped me at this moment as it never had before. My heart began to race as the fear we might get ambushed filled my thoughts, and then I experienced something that had never happened to me before. Suddenly, and without warning, my knee caps began to dance up and down.

I had heard of people being so afraid their knees shook or they lost control of their bladder or bowels, thus the saying, "You scared the crap out of me!" I have read of soldiers to whom this happened, but I had never experienced anything like it myself. Up to this point when something happened I was too focused on doing my job to think much about my own life being at risk. Not that I wasn't afraid, because everyone was to one degree or another. I had just never been this afraid before.

As my knee caps did their ditty I thought to myself, "Oh, Lord! How am I going to keep putting one foot in front of the other?" I was literally on the verge of having a panic attack! I knew I had to do something to get control, so I began to sing to myself every song I could think of from Sunday school.

I couldn't sing them out loud, so I sang them silently to myself. I don't recall exactly which songs they were, but words like "Jesus loves me, this I know," and "every day with Jesus is sweeter than the day before" filled my mind and spirit as I worshiped in my inner man. As I sang to myself and to the Lord, my heart rate began to decline, my breathing slowed down, my knees stopped dancing, and I was once again able to focus on doing my job. Singing helped remind me God was watching over me and I did not have to fear whatever lay ahead. As I had told a soldier back in SEARTS training, "my trust is in the Lord and I know that he has my life in his hands."

As we continued along the jungle floor, the point man suddenly stopped, took a knee, and raised a closed fist, indicating we should stop, take a knee, and be silent. Lt. Greig made his way to the point to see what was happening. Up ahead in the was a hootch complex, thatched roofs clearly visible in the distance.

After evaluating the situation, Lt. Greig decided to divide the platoon in two, with half the platoon moving on line (as opposed to in line) toward the hootch complex from the left flank and the other half moving on the right flank. As part of the CP I remained with the Lt. and his RTO in the right flank element. Platoon Sgt. Clemons took the other half of the platoon and flanked left.

As both flanks moved forward toward the hootches, shots suddenly rang out, the sharp crack of an AK-47 opening up on the left flank. Immediately we hit the dirt. I threw myself into the prone position between two other soldiers, pointing my weapon in the direction of the hootches. Adrenalin flowing, my mind focused like a laser, looking for any potential target, wondering where the shots had come from. My mind was so focused on being prepared to defend our platoon I was only slightly aware of the commotion going on over the radio between Lt. Greig and Sgt. Clemons. One of the squad leaders, Jeff Haggedorn, had been hit. No one was crying "medic" though, so it appeared it wasn't too serious.

In fact, when Jeff hit the ground in the prone position, a bullet from an AK-47 hit the ground in front of him and ricocheted up, striking him in the left cheek bone an inch or so below his left eye and to the left of his nose. Initially it knocked him unconscious, stunned by the force of the blow. In fact, some thought in going down he had hit his head on a rock and been knocked unconscious. Shortly, however, he regained consciousness and, other than being in significant pain, he seemed to be okay. There was minimal bleeding, and it appeared the bullet, having lost much of its force after hitting the ground, had lodged somewhere in Jeff's nasal cavity. His vision seemed to be okay, and he didn't seem to have any other side effects.

Forty-three years after the fact the details of what happened next are a bit murky. At what point I got to Jeff to tend to his wound I do not remember. I do know we still had to deal with the fact there was at least one enemy soldier in the hootch complex, and who knew how many more. Before we could do much of anything else, we had to deal with the threat, and since Jeff seemed to be okay, we resumed our movement toward the hootches.

The brief burst of AK-47 fire from the hootch area had ceased almost as fast as it had begun, and, without a target to shoot at, we did not return fire. We cautiously moved close to the hootch complex, which appeared to be abandoned other than a few pigs and chickens running around. There were three, maybe four large hootches. A search of the hootches revealed nothing significant. Apparently the lone gunman who had fired at us escaped, disappearing into the jungle behind the complex. Perhaps his shots were meant only to slow us down or as cover for others who may have been with him but were making their escape. We would never know.

Rather than kill the animals and give away our position with a lot of noise, the Lt. decided to let them go. My assumption is we set fire to the hootches, though neither Lt. Greig nor I recall what we did to the complex at this point.

After finishing our work at the complex, we headed for a nearby clearing for the purpose of evacuating Jeff. I am not sure exactly how it developed, but somehow in a discussion with the Lt. about getting Jeff evacuated, it was mentioned there would be a supply chopper in the area, and if Jeff was stable he could catch a ride back with them, saving a medevac and crew from having to make a special trip. The only problem was we didn't know how long it would be before they would get to us.

It made sense to me if we could send Jeff out by supply chopper we would be saving a medevac crew from making an unnecessary trip. After talking to the Lt., I returned to Jeff, who was sitting up against a tree, and re-examined him, checking his vision and vitals. I asked him how he felt about waiting for the supply chopper instead of calling a medevac, and he said he was fine with that. Feeling comfortable with Jeff's condition, I informed the Lt. we could wait for the supply chopper.

Unfortunately, what I hoped might take a half hour or forty-five minutes turned into what seemed like eternity. I don't remember exactly how long we waited, but it was much longer than I had wanted or expected, and I became quite agitated about it, concerned the longer it took the greater the possibility Jeff would experience complications from his wound. Though he did not seem to be coughing up any blood, I could not be sure what kind of internal bleeding there might be, or if it could affect his vision or if a blood clot might go to the brain.

Eventually the chopper arrived, and Jeff was able to walk to it under his own power. We later learned he recovered and eventually he even returned to the field, but in the meantime, my battalion surgeon was not happy with me. Dr. Dial sent a very pointed note to me a few days later letting me know I was never to let that happen again. If I had anyone with an injury of any significance, I was to call a medevac and get him out as soon as possible.

Of course, he was right. Looking back on it now I think, "how stupid of me!" That is what the medevacs were for. Why would any medic in a combat situation ask a wounded soldier if he wanted him to call a medevac? Requesting a dust-off was the right thing to do. We had a rating system for the seriousness of the injuries from Code 1 to Code 3, with 1 being the most serious. In his case, I probably would have given him a Code 2. meaning it was serious but not life threatening. Instead I treated it like it was a minor laceration, which presented no real threat.

I realize now how I handled that situation came out of my nature as a peacemaker, not wanting to make waves or tax the medevac crews. It was this tendency toward peace-making that made me an unlikely warrior. At the same time, it enabled me to be compassionate, to care about my men and even risk my life to save them. No, I was not a warrior in the same sense of the word as Rags, Lumpy, Jeff Haggedorn, or any of the other guys in my platoon. But I was a warrior, however unlikely and imperfect I may have been.

After evacuating Jeff, our platoon continued on its way, eventually making it back to the DDP for resupply. This was day nine of our fourteen-day mission in Cambodia. Just five more days, and we would be back on Vietnamese soil.

The next two days and nights passed without incident for Delta Company. On the morning of the 15th, we learned we would be pulled out that day and returned to Firebase Currahee. Apparently we had become a little sloppy in our military hygiene, which called for a shave at least every three days while in the field, because we were all told to shave that morning in preparation for our reunion with the rest of the battalion. I guess they wanted us to look good for LTC Jaggers, the battalion commander, in case he happened to show up. Who cared about the fact we had just spent ten days sweating in the hot humid jungles of Cambodia without the benefit of a shower or even a stream to bathe in? We might be able to wash our faces and shave our beards, but only a nice hot shower would get rid of the stench we must have carried with us.

We were glad to finally be leaving the NVA sanctuaries. Not many G.I.s who served in Vietnam could say they actually walked the infamous Ho Chi Minh trail, but we could. Not only had we walked it, but the 3/506 had spearheaded the biggest single air assault in the Vietnam War and was the only battalion to successfully get on the ground on D-Day. We were "The Stand Alone Battalion," and we had proven it.

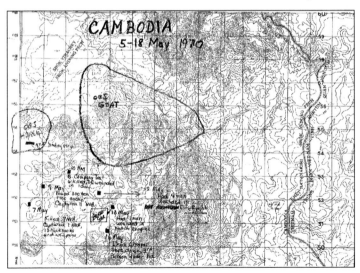

A map of our Area of Operation in Cambodia with notations of significant events and locations. The two circled areas were objectives we were unable to reach due to the significant activity we encountered and the limited time of the operation. Map and notations courtesy of Richard Greig.

CHAPTER TWENTY-SIX

BAN ME THUOT

"You turned my wailing into dancing;
you removed my sackcloth and clothed me with joy,
that my heart may sing to you and not be silent.
O LORD my God, I will give you thanks forever."
Psalm 30:11-12

On Friday, May 15th, we were lifted back to Firebase Currahee, where the battalion chaplain held services for us. The next day we were air assaulted out of Cambodia back to South Vietnam, where we were to assist the 4th Infantry Division in Operation Wayne Jump. Lt Greig, my platoon leader, wrote home to his wife on the 15th:

> *This place really did a job on my platoon. I came here with 27 men and am down to 18 right now. Only six had to be medevaced, but that's still a pretty high percentage. I guess I shouldn't complain, though; we didn't get anyone killed, for which I'm very thankful . . . I'm just so glad to get out of this stinking Cambodia. I thought I'd had it the other day; bullets were hitting so darn close I still can't believe I wasn't hit. I know beyond the shadow of a doubt that the Lord is truly protecting me, and my men. Tell everyone to keep praying back there, it does help.*

Because I can only account for five wounded from our platoon being evacuated from Cambodia, I can only assume the others were related to illness. Lt. Greig seems to recall at least one man being sent out due to malaria. Lee Van

206

Tho being sent home on leave would account for one more. Perhaps there were a couple who left for R&R or because their tours were up.

On May 18th Operation Wayne Jump was halted, and we were motor marched to the Ban Me Thuot area in Darlac Province, approximately 100 miles south of Pleiku City, where we were OPCON to the IFFV (First Field Force Vietnam). There we were to provide road security and perform clearance operations.

On Wednesday, May 27th I wrote home to my mother.

...we left Cambodia the 16th and came to Ban Me Thuot around the19th. The last few days we humped pretty hard checking out an area off the road we were on. We'd hump like mad 'till noon to cover our days' 4,000 meters and then break for the day. Four Thousand meters may not sound like much, especially when you make it before noon, but with a 50 to 75 pound ruck on your back and nothing but uncut jungle ahead, it's a long hard hump. You sweat like mad, your heart aches and your stomach upsets as you drive to make each 1,000 meters before a break. But when you're finally there and you plop down with that heavy ruck it sure does feel good! You rest a minute, take off your boots to dry your feet, check yourself for leeches you might have picked up in the swamps, make sure you're not sitting in a pile of ants, lean back in the shade (you're now resting on your ruck and not the ruck on you) and take an afternoon siesta. Boy does that feel good! But after all that humping we didn't find a single thing, thank goodness! About all we came across of interest was one giant spider the size of my hand and lots of fresh signs of that huge animal, the elephant; unfortunately no elephants themselves.

I have forgotten many things from Vietnam over the years, but I never have forgotten that spider. It was in a huge web at about face level just to the left of the trail we were on. We all just stared at it as we cautiously walked by, not wanting to disturb it.

That morning, we were picked up by trucks and taken back to the airbase to pull security for the next three to five days. On the way we saw a large elephant about 75 meters off the road. This was Montagnard country, and elephants were used as work animals.

Being at the airbase was amazing, because we had access to the Air Force facilities, including the PX Club whenever we had free time. We went as often as we could. Our job at the airbase was simply to provide perimeter security, which was pretty easy, leaving us lots of spare time. As the medic I had little to do.

With my letter I enclosed copies of Orders for my Award from the action on Hill 474 and wrote

> *I was put in for the Silver Star which is just one higher, but, as usual, they downgraded it one. All the same, to be put in for any medal at all was something I hadn't expected as I had only done what I could which was my job anyway and even that wasn't enough. The men who deserve all of the glory are those who died and I'll always wonder if I could have done more to save their lives. It is of them that I will think whenever I wear the ribbon or see the medal and it is for them that I must strive to live up to the standards of a good soldier, both in the eyes of God and of men. For they are the ones who died, not I, and if this war is ever won it is to the dead that the credit must be given, not the living. It is by the words of the living that the dead will be remembered and thus in the hearts and lives of the living that the dead will be loved. The medal is for them.*

I was awarded the Bronze Star with a "V" Device for Valor, but there was no formal presentation, and I did not even see it until it was handed to me by a clerk along with other medals and papers as I went through a processing line for my return to the States, as I mentioned earlier.

On Saturday the 30th, Bravo Co. took over security at the airbase, and we moved to another area, where we were put up in tents. Saturday and Sunday we were taken by truck to an ARVN Basic Training Camp. They had a tower on which we learned to repel. We got to take turns repelling as if we were going down a rock face cliff, and then as if we were stepping off of the skid of a Huey to repel into an area with no LZ. We also learned how to repel face forward with our rifles in hand, ready to fire in case we had to repel into an area under fire. The training was easy, and we actually spent more time sitting around than training. One of the guys found a bake shop on the base and bought some warm loaves of bread to share. What a treat! This was definitely different from what I had experienced my first four months in the field!

I wrote another letter home on June 1st telling them we were supposed to be moving out to guard a bridge soon and would be there until the 7th. After that we were supposed to go back up to An Khe for more training. I was thrilled to be enjoying some easy duty after four grueling months of living in the jungles and mountains of South Vietnam and Cambodia. By my count I had just fifty days left in the field as long as there were enough medics to replace me. *"I think I'll like it in the rear,"* I wrote.

On the morning of June 2nd, we were trucked out to a bridge near a firebase. I wrote a couple more pages to include with the letter I had written the previous day.

Well, here we are on a bridge. We got here this morning and it's real nice. We've got a nice sized pond on one side so we can go swimming all we want. Also, we get a hot meal every day and will probably get mail and a cold pack of sodas without too much trouble.

We're right next to a Montagnard village and a lot of young kids hang around. They'll wash our clothes and other things for us and we just give them some C rations, candy, cigarettes, or even Viet money, if we've got it.

The village was actually on the other side of the pond a couple of hundred yards away or so.

I became particularly close to several boys who I would guess were 10 to 12 years old. I let them do what little work I could find for them rewarding them with goodies from my C-rations. They also joined us in our daily swims in the pond.

One day they brought me a gift of corn on the cob. Not wanting to be rude, I accepted it and that afternoon asked Lee how I should cook it. He suggested I build a fire and let it burn down to the coals, then insert the corn, still in the husks, into the embers and let them roast. Having never cooked corn this way before I thought it was worth a try. I don't remember if anyone else joined me in eating the corn, but I can't imagine having eaten it all by myself. That night I got as sick as a dog and found myself in the wee hours of the morning puking up everything I had eaten. I was truly miserable.

The next day the boys brought me another gift of corn. Wanting to be polite I accepted it, but insisted the boys stay and help me eat it this time. I figured if I was going to get sick from eating this corn, then they were going to share in it as well. Instead of roasting it, I shucked the corn, filled my steel pot (helmet) with water, and put it on the fire to boil the corn like we did back home. The boys and I ate the corn, and that night I didn't get sick. My only assumption is roasting the corn had not been effective in killing all of the bacteria, or maybe there were other contaminants on the corn that made me sick, since the corn was not washed before cooking. In any event, it was a memorable experience I have laughed about it many times over the years.

Our time at the bridge was glorious, and though it only lasted a week, it seemed much longer. We were able to swim two or three times a day, received a hot meal from the mess hall every day at noon, and relaxed without any real fear of being attacked. One day I even took a bamboo pole, attached a piece of string to it, fashioned a hook out of a safety pin, cast the line into the water, and sat down to read a book with my soft cap and some sun glasses on. I knew there probably weren't any fish in the pond, but it was just something to do that reminded me of home.

Every morning the Armored Personnel Carriers came rolling down the road and across the bridge on their daily missions returning later before dusk. The Montagnard villagers also made their way across the bridge and down the road, driving some of their cattle as they went. They came back later in the afternoon with bundles of sticks for firewood and who knows what else. Through our scout I offered my medical services to the villagers, but only one elderly woman stopped by who had a sore on her foot, which I treated.

There were some beautiful sunrises, sunsets, and some amazing rainbows I captured in pictures. There was also a young soldier who drove a water truck. He had a pet monkey, and one day I rode with him to the water tower from which he filled his truck. I asked him if the monkey liked bananas, and he said "no." I happened to have a banana that had been sent down to us from the mess hall with our lunch, and so I peeled it and handed a piece to the monkey, which I was holding. To my surprise and the truck driver's, the monkey took it and ate it. So much for a monkey that didn't like bananas!

On June 8th we were transported back to An Khe for eight days of training, according to *The Stand Alone Battalion*. I don't remember doing any training, but it may be during this time some of us were put on a refuse burning detail. I remember spending several days out behind the barracks pouring jet fuel into 50-gallon barrels that had been cut in half and placed in the outhouses to catch human waste. Trucks brought the half-barrels to us, and we spent the day burning the waste, after which the barrels were picked back up and redistributed.

Maybe the 4th Infantry Division just didn't have anything they really needed us to do at the time, which is why some of us wound up on refuse burning detail. That came to an end however on June 16th, when we were sent out to yet another area of operation.

Me giving aid to a woman with a sore on her foot.

Me cooking corn on the cob in my helmet (i.e., "steel pot")
with the four village boys who had given them to me as a gift.

CHAPTER TWENTY-SEVEN

THE SONG MAO MOUNTAINS AND PHAN THIET

*"No one whose hope is in you
will ever be put to shame,
but they will be put to shame
who are treacherous without excuse."*

Psalm 25:3

On June 16th we were moved about 200 miles south on C-140 transport planes to the Binh Thuan Province and Combat Assaulted from an airstrip into the Song Mao Mountains for what was called Operation Hancock Mace. I wrote home on the 21st letting them know where I was.

We're at Song Mao in the mountains and it's not too bad here so far. It rains every day, but usually in the evening when we're already set up and able to keep dry under our ponchos. I am just getting over a miserable head cold so you know I ain't even gonna get wet if I can help it. So far I've done ok!

There aren't any fresh signs of VC here, though we've crossed some pretty well worn trails; also a lot of big rocks, but no caves. We found about 15 bunkers but they were pretty old and not recently used. So, anyway, things have been ok so far and they'll probably stay that way. This is a fourteen to twenty-one day mission and then we are headed once again for the unknown, to us anyway. But it don't mean nothing!

213

This was a phrase we used a lot in Vietnam because there was just so much that didn't make sense to us, and we were powerless to do anything about it. We were just cogs caught in the great war-machine moved here and there, doing what we were told. None of it was personal, and to us it really didn't mean anything. Our goal was simply to survive and hopefully go home in one piece. It didn't have to make sense. It was what it was. *It don't mean nothin'!*

On the 23rd we were extracted and taken back to the airbase. I took time to write another letter and explained, *"Tomorrow we are going back out to a new area about 10,000 meters to the north of here. Ranger teams have been hitting it with the VC there, so we'll go in to ambush. Sure hope it is just another 'Ranger trick.' No VC for us, that is."*

Either the VC decided to avoid us, which was often the case, or we just happened to be in the right place at the right time as far as we were concerned, because none of us really wanted to run into the enemy. We spent a week out in the bush and didn't find anything significant. On July 1st we were pulled out of the field and transported down to Phan Thiet, the old stomping grounds of the 3/506 where I had begun my journey with the Currahees some six months earlier.

It was great to be back at Phan Thiet, which overlooked the South China Sea and had a beautiful beach we could walk to for a swim. We had tents to sleep in, and there were NCO Clubs, a PX, and even movies. But it wasn't all fun and games. I wrote home about it on July 4th. We were supposed to have gone out to the field that morning, but the AO was socked in by bad weather, so the choppers couldn't fly. We were to go out the next day instead, weather permitting. I went on to write

> *Last night was kind of a bad night all the way around. Some guys got caught smoking pot which means a Court-Martial with one in our Platoon; and somebody else threw a grenade into a room where a group of guys were playing cards. Several*

guys were hurt, but they're all ok. I hope that whoever it was gets caught and gets the max put on him. It's bad enough over here without GIs killing GIs. I don't care what the reason was. He needs his ass put in jail for about fifteen years to straighten him out. Maybe then he'll value life a little more.

Fragging, as it was called, was not an uncommon problem in Vietnam, but this was my first and only experience with it. I can still remember hearing the explosion and wondering what was going on. It didn't take long for the word to spread about what had happened. I don't know if the culprit was ever caught, but I was certainly infuriated by it. What a terrible thing it would have been to have survived five months in the bush including Hill 474 and the Cambodian Invasion only to be killed by one of your own in the rear because of a grudge of some sort.

I didn't mention anything about the fact it was Independence Day. I don't know we even thought about it. For us, it was just another day in Vietnam.

On July 8th I wrote another letter home letting them know where we were. *"We're out in the field again, though it took them a couple of days to do it. The weather kept forcing the choppers to delay, so, after two days they finally chose a new area and managed to get us out. It's real nice country here so I can see why the VC chose to live here. So far it's been nice and quiet and will hopefully stay that way. We're traveling in a company size element so we've at least got the power."*

It may have been here, since we were traveling as a company-sized element, something rather humorous happened. As part of the CP I was often around the Lt. and Cpt. when we were at our DDP or NDP. Cpt. Ohl and Lt. Greg were both Rangers, and they took a lot of pride in it. On one occasion the two of them were sitting talking about their Ranger School experiences, and I must have been right there listening. In an effort to add some humor to the conversation, I made some wisecrack. I can't even remember what I said.

But Cpt. Ohl looked at me very seriously and in a calm, yet firm voice said, "Son, when you use the word 'Ranger' you had better bow down to the east seven times." I knew at that point I had crossed the line, and if I wanted to remain in the captain's favor I had better watch my step. I have always greatly respected Captain Ohl for his gentle yet firm leadership.

Many years later at a reunion, Cpt. Ohl's RTO, Ronnie Pierce, shared with me an experience that even further boosted my already high respect for him. On one occasion when they were traveling with another platoon, they had humped quite a ways from the previous night's NDP to a new NDP. When they got there, Ronnie went to reset the radio frequency for the night. Frequency settings were changed on a nightly basis to keep the enemy from picking up on our transmissions; frequencies for each day were kept in a code book. When Ronnie looked in his ruck for the code book, he couldn't find it. He began to think about the last place he had seen it, and it had been that morning at the previous NDP. He remembered setting it on the ground, and he figured he must have left it there. When he told Cpt. Ohl about it, the Cpt. looked at him and said, "Ronnie. If we don't go get that code book the Army will have to change the codes for all of Vietnam. Get your rifle, you and I are going to go get it." By this time it was already getting dark, but that didn't stop Cpt. Ohl. He went to the platoon leader and said, "Ronnie and I are going out for a little while, and we will be back in an hour or two." He didn't tell the platoon leader why they were going, and he didn't berate Ronnie in front of anyone else. They simply went back all the way in the dark, found the code book, and returned. Nothing more was said about it. I am sure Cpt. Ohl already knew how bad Ronnie felt.

I continued my letter:

> *Yesterday we found some bunkers and partially built hutches just worked on in the last few days. We destroyed them*

today and also found a marker our Scout says indicates the direction the VC went. It seems pretty much that they heard us coming in on the choppers and either made tracks then or after they observed us coming their way. Anyway, they'll probably stay out of our way as is often the case.

The first day we were here a squad found a fresh grave. In checking it out it turned out to be a Vietnamese male approximately 22 years old killed by artillery. He had been buried only about three days before. So, anyway, we know that they're here or at least were, but at present the danger is minimal under the circumstances.

I really owe a lot to the Lord for the care He's given me and my continued praise, prayers, and service done in His respect are the least I can do. It's strange, but in the light of all that God has done and continually does do for us it's the least we can do to give our ALL to Him in return and the most we can do is to love Him with our ALL as He loves us.

I just had thirteen days left to hit my six-month mark in the field. However, the battalion was severely short of medics, and it wasn't looking good for me to be replaced anytime soon. In fact, Charlie Company only had one medic for the whole Company, so instead of putting them in the field, they had three platoons on a firebase and one in the rear on standby as a reactionary force.

Even though I had been thinking about extending in Vietnam in order to get out of the military early, I was thinking less and less of it. Even though we weren't seeing any action right now, I was getting pretty weary spending two weeks in the jungle here and another two weeks there humping through the boonies. Even though I would be in the rear by that time, I think I had decided I just didn't want to spend any more time in Vietnam than I had to.

On July 19th Delta Company was pulled out of the field and taken back to Phan Thiet, where we were put on standby with one hour notice. The 1st of the 50th Infantry was supposed to be checking out a suspected enemy meeting place, and we were their back up in case they got into trouble. One third of our platoon could go to the beach for one hour at a time, while the other two thirds remained in the tent area in case we were called on to react.

On the 20th we were to head back to An Khe, but we had no idea what we would do after that. I think that is one of the reasons we felt like peons much of the time. We were rarely told what was going on or where we would be going next. I realize this was essential to keep the enemy from discovering our movements and planned operations. Lots of Vietnamese civilians worked on the bases as barbers, doing laundry, and a host of other menial jobs, and many were known to be VC informants. So, the best way to keep operations secret was to tell as few people as possible beforehand.

I ended the letter with, *"Well, that's about it for now. I think I'll close and maybe nap or get up a game of hearts. Take care, thanks for everything and remember . . . Love Always, Mike."*

Extraction by Chinook Helicopter (CH-46) after a brief operation in what was known as Cat Valley. We didn't encounter any live enemy, but we did come across some bloated bodies of enemy soldiers apparently killed by artillery bombardment.

The platoon waiting at the helo-pad for the weather to lift so we can make another combat assault into a new area. Photo courtesy of Tom Landers.

CHAPTER TWENTY-EIGHT

QUI NHON

"As a father has compassion on his children,
so the LORD had compassion on those who fear him;
for he knows how we are formed,
he remembers that we are dust."

Psalm 103:13-14

On July 21st the 3/506 was moved back to An Khe and put on a six-day stand-down before beginning our next operation. It may have been during this time we heard rumors one of our sister battalions up north had been overrun by an NVA unit, and for some reason it hit me particularly hard. One of the guys from my platoon had gotten his hands on a bottle of vodka and was sitting on the grass outside of the barracks with two more of my men, passing the bottle from one to another. I stopped to talk to them, and one of them asked me if I wanted a drink. Being somewhat depressed, I let my guard down and said, "Yes," sat down, and took a couple of swigs. Not being a drinker, it didn't take much before I was feeling lightheaded and then sick. The last thing I remember was crawling off into some bushes next to the barracks to throw up. In the morning I woke up on a cot outside the barracks next to another soldier also on a cot. When I asked someone what had happened, he said we were both drunk and so noisy they decided to put us outside to sleep. Then one of them asked me if I knew anybody who had been killed in the unit that had been overrun. I said, "No. Why?" He then explained I had been going on and on about the tragedy, and he thought maybe it was because I knew someone who had been killed.

Why this incident hit me so hard I am not sure, except for the sheer magnitude of the reported losses. Having lost men of my own, and seen the casualties Bravo Co. experienced in Cambodia, I was deeply saddened by yet another one of our units having suffered such devastating losses. I didn't have to know them to experience their pain. They were my brothers in arms, and I knew what it was like to be trapped in a hopeless situation with men wounded and dying. Their grief was my grief, and their pain my pain.

On July 28th we were taken by truck convoy to an area just outside of Qui Nhon near the coast. On August 1st I wrote a letter home and told them about the move.

> *Well, things here are fine. The operation at Phan Thiet went real well. We found MR-6 but the "Dicks" were gone. We destroyed a lot of bunkers and stuff during the fourteen days but it stayed quiet. The 21st we came back up to An Khe and spent six days on stand-down. That was great. The 28th we moved to our present local by convoy. We're just east of An Khe out of Qui Nhon on the coast. The area is pacified and we ain't even got any problems or worries. The weather is hot though and we do all we can to get ice and sodas out to us. So far, we've done alright. We get it expensively through the Vietnamese or reasonably through our rear; whichever is easier. Money don't mean much out here anyway.*

Instead of being in the jungle, we were in an area of fishing villages, and it was extremely hot. Vietnamese women came to us with cases of Cokes and some blocks of ice from the city, and we bought Cokes for $1.00 each (a lot of money back then, especially since I only drew $25 each month), and we pitched in to buy a block of ice for $5.00 which we shared. We took the warm can of Coke, laid it on its side on the block of ice, and rolled it with our hands, wearing a groove in the ice. Before long the Coke was ice cold, and we could drink it with a great deal of satisfaction.

On August 2nd I received my first letter from Barb. The next day I wrote back, expressing appreciation for her decision to write and to put our differences behind us. It had been over five months since I had asked her to write back and tell me one way or another whether she wanted me to keep writing or not. Years later, she told me the only reason she finally wrote to me was because she woke up one night with a horrible thought: If something happened to me and I were killed in Vietnam, she would feel guilty the rest of her life for having not written me. After thanking her for writing I continued, *"...the 21st through the 27th we were in the rear at An Khe and so, relatively safe. Still, as always it proved to be full of trials and temptations, good and bad experiences, and the Lord graciously pulled me through. Sometime I'll tell you about it. In the meantime, thanks for praying!"*

In another part of the letter I continued,

> *I really owe God a lot of thanks for taking care of me over here. He has always helped me in all places and at all times. Bong Son, An Khe, Cambodia, Ban Me Thuot, Song Mao, Phan Thiet, and now, Qui Nhon. In each of the first three I saw men killed and wounded. Through the last four it has been quiet. But through all seven I have been kept safe both physically and spiritually. Whether it be by grace or divine intervention makes little difference: It is of God and I praise Him for it. That is all that matters.*

Apparently in her letter she asked me about how I felt about being a medic, so I continued,

> *As far as being a medic goes, I'll have to say that I really enjoy it, even though it carries a lot of responsibility, for it is no easy thing to be in charge of 30 men's lives actively engaged in war. Still I am glad to be what I am. I don't think at all that I am the best medic in the world, or even as good as I should be. But I believe I am as good as most. I believe that under the*

circumstances I have done a good job. I'm proud to be a medic and always will strive to do my best. I thank God for His mercy.

My letter writing must have been interrupted as I later continued,

I am writing this letter on guard outside of an old three room school house. I wrote the first part of this letter this afternoon from outside a small fishing village. We're working right now about five to ten miles outside of Qui Nhon, with the Vietnamese Regional and Popular Forces. At night we set up ambushes together and during the day they check out villages while we secure them. It's really nice as it's a well pacified area and we don't even expect any trouble. We have close contact with the people and can learn about and from them. Yesterday, believe it or not, I ate a 100% Vietnamese meal using chop sticks, a small rice bowl and sitting on the floor. It was really good and lots of fun.

Regarding the above, as I recall, the village chief invited Lt. Greig to be his guest for dinner, and he invited his RTO, the platoon sergeant, and me to accompany him. It was my one and only experience of authentic Vietnamese life and cuisine during my time there.

I continued, *"Tomorrow will be my platoon's last day and then we're being CAed across the bay here onto a peninsula to check it out. Supposedly what few local VC there are here hide over there. I don't really expect much to happen."*

August 4th I received another card from Barb, so I sat down to write her again. I expressed how glad I was she was finally writing to me, and I included an article from the Army Newspaper *Stars and Stripes* about two teenage boys who had set a world seesaw record in Castro Valley, California, where Barb lived. I then wrote, *"We left the village at 4 PM and hurried back for cold sodas, milk and mail. It was only about a twenty to thirty minute walk at a fast pace but the sun made it hot. Anyway, your card was the only mail I got. But even if I had gotten a dozen letters, yours would have still made the day for me as it did this morning. Thanks again for writing!"*

I went on to respond to a comment she had made about how wonderful God is. In part I wrote,

> *Yes, Barbs, our God is so very wonderful! . . . Look into the sky and see how vast the universe is. That's how big our God is, how strong His love is, how mighty his Spirit is, how wonderful our Lord is! "He's big enough to rule the mighty universe, yet small enough to live within your heart!" I've seen it over here, Barbs! I've walked "through the valley of the shadow of death" more than once. I have eaten "in the presence of mine enemies. My cup runneth over!" I've seen men cast into eternity, yet I live. I've forsaken my God yet He has not forsaken me. I owe so very much to God, so very, very much!*

My reference to having forsaken God was probably an allusion to having gotten drunk back at An Khe.

On August 6th I wrote another letter to Barb. *"I just thought I'd jot out a few lines in hopes of having some peace of mind, but I don't think it's going to work. Today was resupply and there are a hundred little kids running around trying to beg borrow or steal whatever they can get. All the hustle and bustle of breaking down chow and stuff, people hollering and all drives you nuts!"*

I then shared with her what had happened on our ambush on the peninsula where we had been CAed at about 4:30 PM the day before. As was common practice, gunships prepped the LZ with rocket fire before we landed, and as a result the dry grass caught fire. Immediately after landing, we moved to a safe location across some sand into a clump of trees upwind of the fire. We sat there resting in the shade until after sunset and at 8 PM moved out to find our ambush site. We moved 3,000 meters or so mostly through clear open terrain, across some sand dunes, then through some ten-foot tall elephant grass and finally through some knee-deep paddie water. It was a clear night with a bright moon that illuminated the countryside making it easy to move. It was 11:15 PM by the time we were finally settled in to our ambush site and I got to sleep. Forty-five minutes later it was my turn to pull guard duty. I later wrote, *"It took me thirty minutes to wake up, and the last thirty I admired the stars. We slept in until 9:00 AM and then moved to some trees back in the sand dunes where we slept all day until 4:00 PM. At 4:45 PM we were picked up again and brought back, another platoon inserted in our place for the night. Tonight I should really sleep well."* I continued,

> *It's hard to believe there are VC over there as the area has very little cover to hide. The mountains have some rocks though, so they could hide in caves. There is supposed to be a UDT (Underwater Demolitions Team) of 25 or so, a sapper team, and a local group. Believe it or not two Caucasians (G.I. type) are supposed to be helping them, living with them. It's hard to believe, but it's not the first time it's been reported. Americans fighting for the communists . . . how could they do it?*

On August 7th I wrote a letter to my mother detailing much of what I also wrote to Barb. I also mentioned I might not get my R&R until October, and that there still weren't enough replacement medics. I wrote, *"...if the other guys can spend their whole tour on line, then I can too. I'm no better or more special than they are. I'm just one more G.I."*

We were no longer working with the Regional Forces, just pulling the ambushes with platoons rotating to the peninsula, and it would be our turn again "tomorrow night." I explained, *"We're just still ambushing, and I don't even have to go on many of those. We just sit around all day and do nothing.... The weather here is still hot and dry, but we have cold sodas every day and a hot noon meal. We even barbecued last night (I was the cook) and they had steaks the night we were on the peninsula."*

On August 12th I wrote home again. My R&R had come through for September, but I didn't know the exact date. Also, my promotion to Spec. 4 had finally come through. I mentioned we were still in Qui Nhon and it was still really hot, but we had plenty of sodas and ice every day. *"It may not sound like much of a war, but believe me I've seen mine, many are still seeing theirs, and I've still got at least three and a half months to go. So, believe me there's a war, it's just that we're (my battalion) out of it for right now (and hopefully 'till I get out of 'Nam)."* I mentioned we were the Reactionary Platoon that day, another rotating responsibility, in case we were needed somewhere quickly. *"Tomorrow we'll hump back to our company and to the regular routine, which isn't much, ambush at night, relax during the day."*

Our time at Qui Nhon was easy duty, much like it was in Ban Me Thuot, apart from the heat, occasional humping, and ambushing.

I remember one day when we were pulling security for the Regional Forces at a village, we came across a small bullet-riddled abandoned Catholic church, the scene of a previous battle at some point. Some of us went in, and I found on the floor a broken cast metal statue of Jesus, about a foot in length. It was broken into three pieces, the two legs severed from the body and the feet severed just above the ankles. The hands were extended out and upward, holes in the palms where they would have been attached to the cross. I picked the pieces up and, after examining them, put them in my back pack. I later sent them home and still have them in a box, a reminder of the ravages of war and of the price Jesus paid on the cross for our sins. I have often thought about how God must be grieved by the senselessness of war even as He was grieved by the death of His Son. And yet it is God who has given the power of the sword to governments, and it is God who determined before the creation of the world to send His Son to die for us. These are great paradoxes, yet both are true. I am so thankful for God's infinite wisdom and grace, even though I cannot understand the depths of them.

CHAPTER TWENTY-NINE

BACK IN THE BUSH

"I wait for the LORD, *my soul waits,*
and in his word I put my hope.
My soul waits for the LORD
more than watchmen wait for the morning,
more than watchmen wait for the morning."
Psalm 130:5-6

The easy duty of Quin Nhon did not last. On August 17th we were pulled out of the field and moved by truck back to An Khe. I wrote a letter home and enclosed my orders for my Combat Medical Badge and my promotion. I mentioned I had learned my R&R had been scheduled for Sept. 26th– Oct. 3rd. I also mentioned some new medics had come in and Tony Foster, the 2nd Platoon medic, had been replaced. Next it would be my turn, and I hoped it would be soon.

In Vietnam, when it came to how much time you had left in your tour, you were a three-digit wonder or a two-digit midget, a "short timer" as they were also called, and I was close to being the latter at this point. All G.I.s, especially those in the field, knew exactly how many days they had left before they caught the Freedom Bird back to the "real world." The closer you got to going home, the more anxious you became about getting out of the field to a safer environment. I wrote home:

I really can't tell you what our next operation will be. They haven't told us yet for security reasons. But I do know this much; we're finished with being swing battalion for II Corp. We're moving back with the Division up North. We'll be landing in Phu Bai and move from there to the base we'll be working out of. None of us really likes the idea of going up North, but who can prevent it. Anyway, it could turn out alright. The monsoons are starting up there in September and last into January. Fighting is greatly reduced at this time because of the conditions. No U.S. troops can operate in the A Shau at all and it's the same in other places, I'm sure. So, it's rumored that we'll just be securing some base throughout the monsoon season. I don't know. I guess we'll find out when we get up there. Anyway, all I need to do is last 'till either my replacement comes in or I come out for R&R and after that I'll have less than 50 days before I can come home. I just hope it goes by fast. But I don't imagine it will.

The weather here at An Khe is wet. It rained all last night, but it is just cloudy and cold right now. Thank goodness we're in a barracks, even if they don't have doors and just have screens for windows. At least the roof doesn't leak and it does block out some of the wind. The cots are comfortable too.

On the 24th I wrote a letter to Barb from a service club. In it I explained we had been pulled from the field on the 17th and were back at An Khe waiting to go north to Phu Bai. We were supposed to have left on the 20th or 21st, but they had problems getting clearance for us to leave II Corps. Whatever the snafu, it had been cleared up, and half the battalion had left that day. The rest of us were to leave the next.

Rumor was we would likely be guarding a base during the monsoon season, but like most rumors, it proved untrue, dashing my hopes of being in a relatively safe situation. I wrote to Barb asking for extra prayer:

Within five days we should be in the field and I pray to God that the area we work in will be quiet. The next two to three weeks should prove to be real trying ones, a time in which

*extra prayer and strength may well be needed. Pray for my
testimony before the men, that I may live as well as preach
and teach the things of God to them. Pray for me that I may
be diligent in my own prayer life, and that I might be faithful
in holding Sunday worship services when our Chaplain is
absent, always speaking with wisdom and truth. Pray that I
may be more careful for others['] lives and souls than I am
for my own. Pray that I may abide in Christ and him in me.*

The very next day, Sept. 25th, the rest of the battalion
was moved to Phu Bai, and Camp Eagle became our new
base of operation. It didn't take long, however, before Delta
Company was back out in the boonies. On August 30th at
12:20 PM, apparently during a lunch break, I sat down and
penned another letter to Barb.

*Here we are out in the boonies and I'm sittin' in a shady spot,
so I thought I'd write a few lines. It may get a little sloppy as
I'm writing on my lap and the bugs are driving me batty so
that I have to swat every few seconds, but I think we'll make
it, or at least I hope so.*

*Things here are, at least for the moment, pretty fair. We were
chopper inserted into this area about 8:00 A.M. yesterday
and went right to work checking the area out. Sometimes I
wonder though if perhaps the enemy isn't better at checking
us out. Three times yesterday enemy (VC or NVA) soldiers
were spotted just outside our platoon's perimeter where we
had set up. Each time we cleared the area with frags (grenades) and small arms fire, but each time they got away. It's
odd that they never shot at us, didn't return with their buddies
after escaping, or didn't try to mortar us last night. I really
owe God a lot of thanks. We all do.*

*This morning we took two squads out and moved about four
hundred meters, checking out trails and looking for a good
spot to set up tonight. Boy, the trails are sure well used! It
would be so easy for the enemy to ambush us or at least set*

booby traps for our point man to hit. Oh, how badly I need God's protection!

And God does deliver! Listen to this! Today another of our platoons checked out a trail which we ourselves had come down just yesterday morning. And behold, they found an enemy planted anti-personnel mine which had already been stepped on, triggered, tripped, or whatever else you want to call it, but it hadn't gone off. Imagine it! One of us, several of us, or perhaps even most of us stepped on that one little mine, at least all of us passed by it, not seeing it, and at least one of us and probably more could have been ruthlessly killed or maimed for life, BUT GOD, by His grace delivered us! Today our other platoon found it, examined it and destroyed it. Praise God for His deliverance!

You know Barb; I was really scared last night on guard. Perhaps I shouldn't burden you with this, perhaps, as a man, I should bear up and play the hero, but I'm going to be honest with you. I was scared. Any man who says he isn't over here is either in a relatively safe job, sitting back taking it easy, or else he's a liar or a fool! Nobody is scared all of the time, but everybody is scared some of the time! I'm scared whenever we move down enemy trails and might meet the enemy or his traps. It's happened before. I'm scared when we're chopper lifted to make a combat assault (our choppers have been shot at before); I'm scared at night on guard, in the dark silence, waiting, listening, afraid that the enemy will hit any time, afraid that his mortar tube might pop on us anytime! Afraid to live, afraid to die!

But Barbara, this one thing I know to be true; when we are in perfect union with Christ we are in perfect union with peace! When we love Him, serve Him, come to know Him better, we realize that we have no need to fear. I do not say we will not fear. I do say that we will realize that our fear is without foundation, that in Christ we have all hope, and that God is all in all and cares for us. Knowing this we can overcome our fear, put it aside and reach out to accomplish our task, seek to meet our match, and prove to be faithful in our service to

Christ. 'Perfect love casts out fear!' (1 John 4:18) Oh, how we ought to be so aware of this truth, how we ought to give thanks to him for it!

Barbara, after nine months over here a guy kind of runs out of things to say; but if I can keep my eyes on Jesus, if I can 'fix my eyes upon Him,' then everything is great and there is much to say. Without Christ I'd truly be lost for eternity! I'd never have made it to 'Nam, let alone through it.

With just 96 days to go I'd covet your prayers. I know you're praying for me and I believe you'll continue. The mail is slow right now but when it comes I will look for your letters. Keep writing and remember this . . . Yours in Christ, with love, Michael. John 15:5.

We were short men at this point, so instead of pulling radio watch at the CP, I was pulling guard duty on the perimeter in a foxhole along with the rest of the guys. Because of the triple canopy jungle we were operating in, and the fact the stars and moon were more often than not hidden by clouds, the darkness was quite thick. It was impossible to even see your hand in front of your face. Before going to sleep, every man had to know exactly where the man replacing him was sleeping, so he could find him in the dark and lead him by the arm back to the foxhole.

Once in the foxhole in the dead of night, I knew if an enemy soldier tried to sneak up on me and tripped one of the flares, I would have to hit the clickers and blow him away. Should he be able to bypass our trip fares, it was possible he could kill me even before I ever saw him. On the other hand, if I couldn't see him, then hopefully he couldn't see me either. Such were the thoughts that went through my mind as I waited anxiously for my watch to end.

On one of these nights, when it was so dark I couldn't see anything beyond the nose on my face, I reached out in front of me to feel for something I had set on the ledge of the foxhole and accidentally hit the clicker for one of the claymore mines. "Ka-boom!" The earth shook violently as the claymore's blast rocked the terrain in front of it, sending shrapnel, dirt, rocks, and whatever else lay in its path flying through the air and into the jungle beyond. Because I didn't have a radio at this position, there was no way for me to let anyone know what had happened. I could hear some whispering from some of the other positions, but then it died down. Undoubtedly everyone had been awakened and waited to see what would happen next. When nothing did, everyone, except those on guard, went back to sleep.

The next day, August 31st, I wrote another letter home letting them know I was back out in the field and was doing okay.

Today was our third day here in the field up North. It's been quieter than the last two. The first day we spotted six NVA, but missed them. The second day our 2nd Platoon killed two and two escaped. The two escaping passed by us and nearly got a couple of our men, but after our exchange of fire they duffed. Today there was no enemy contact, but one of my men got shot in the foot accidentally. It wasn't too serious, but bad enough to send him in.

The first night on guard I was really scared. Cambodia was the last place we'd seen any action and that's been three and a half months ago, so you can see why. But like David of old, I managed to encourage myself in the Lord, realizing His love and power to save, and I made it! I won't say I'm not still scared on guard, but I can say that in Christ I feel less afraid, or at least better able to cope with my fear.

It became too dark for me to finish my letter, so I continued it the next evening.

Here it is 7:00 PM again, and I'll try to finish tonight. Last night it got too dark. Today was resupply day and it was good to get mail again. Today was quiet but scary. We've got some NVA on our same radio frequency and they keep talking about an attack. At noon today we thought we were going to get mortared but it didn't come. Now they've mentioned a night attack to start at 8:00 PM. We doubt that it is us, but I'm scared anyway. Naturally, if I get this letter mailed (which won't be for another three days, next resupply) everything is ok! I'm really praying for protection for all of us!

Last night it sprinkled just enough to be nice. The weather is hot and humid up here. But I kind of hope it doesn't rain tonight. Every other night would be sufficient I think.

Well, there really isn't much to say. I guess I've really said too much, talking about the war and all. I guess I could prevent it, but then there wouldn't be anything to write about at all. Remember, 93 days and, Lord willing, I'll be coming home. Just twenty days and I go in for R&R. After that I sure don't plan on returning to the boonies. Now, take care, and don't forget, Love Always, Mike.

On Sept. 2nd at 9:30 AM I began another letter to Barb thanking her for a package she sent.

...I know my handwriting is mighty sloppy, but we're sitting right in the middle of this trail, undoubtedly NVA, and I'm trying to write on my knee using my steel pot as a seat.

I really appreciate your extra prayer for me as we're surely operating in "no man's land." The enemy trails are numerous and well used and we can even pick up NVA transmission on our own radio. Our Scout, who was NVA once himself, listens and translates them for us. I'm always in prayer with our Lord and I continually strive like David of old to encourage myself in Him and to have faith that all is and will remain well. But perhaps you can imagine how difficult it can be under these circumstances and after nine months without real Christian fellowship. Please pray, not only for me, but also for my Lieutenant, Richard Greig, who is also a Christian, and my whole platoon, both saved and unsaved, for their

*safety and spiritual destiny. Pray that the hand of God may
really be upon this individual platoon, that it might become a
special testimony to the very power of God Himself. Pray for
me that I might be used instrumentally of God in showing the
power of God to save and to keep, to those here with whom
I labor.*

I went on to talk about the fact I had just twenty days
left in the field before R&R, and I would try to write at least
once every three days. I also talked about hopes I would be
assigned to the west coast when I returned to the States. *"It's
impossible to say, but I know that if the Lord can take me
home from a place like this, safe and sound, then surely I'll
have far less trouble surviving any assignment in the good
old U.S.A.; just so long as I do get back ok."*

My letter writing was interrupted by rain and the need
to go out on patrols, so I finished it later that afternoon.
*"Here it is 3:40 PM and once again I'll try and finish this
letter. Between the rain and going on patrols it's been an
impossible task. I'm really thankful though, that things have
remained quiet. We've been following well worn trails all
day, but haven't found anything. Just a large well dug hole
which they can use for hiding themselves or their supplies.
It wasn't camouflaged though, so apparently they never got
to finish it."*

We had a couple of new scouts working with us during
this time, one by the name of Tran Van Nhi, who had been an
NVA officer with a tank division, and the other, Nguyen Van
Hung, a common soldier whom I mentioned earlier. Hung
did not speak very much English and did not fit in well with
the platoon. On the second day he was with us, he wrote a
poem and showed it to me. I asked Nhi to translate it for me,
and I used his rough translation to rearrange it in English. It
reminded me that in this "no man's land," we Americans were
not the only ones who felt alone and discouraged at times.

One Among Many
It was yesterday I came to where I am,
And I feel both funny and sad,
For I am one among so many
And their language I don't understand.

Their language is different, this we all know,
It's sad, so sad around me.
But then there's a change as the rain comes down,
And together we stand by the trees.

The rain, it does fall for at least two hours,
And I decide it is time to cook chow.
I say to myself, "Just why am I sad?"
And I pray for better days than right now.

His poem reminds me of another poem written over 2,500 years ago by another warrior, perhaps King David, at a time when he, too, was going through a difficult time in his life. In Psalm 42:3-5, the Psalmist wrote,

My tears have been my food day and night,
while men say to me all day long,
"Where is your God?"
These things I remember,
as I pour out my soul;
how I used to go with the multitude,
leading the procession to the house of God
with shouts of joy and thanksgiving
among the festive throng.
Why are you downcast, O my soul?
Why so disturbed within me?
Put your hope in God
for I will yet praise him,
my Savior and my God.

I finished my letter to Barb. *"Boy, I really don't seem to be saying much, but I guess it's because there really isn't that much to say about Vietnam. The Lord has been good to me and I should be thankful for it. I know that in many ways I have failed Him, but He has never failed me. How anxious I am to return to the States and my brethren so that I can fellowship in Him, rejoicing in His care."*

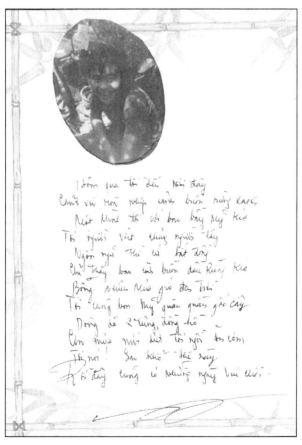

Kit Carson Scout Hung and his poem written in Vietnamese.

237

CHAPTER THIRTY

COUNTDOWN

"I sought the LORD, and he answered me;
he delivered me from all my fears.
Those who look to him are radiant;
their faces are never covered with shame.
This poor man called and the LORD heard him;
he saved him out of all his troubles."

Psalm 34:4-6

With less than twenty days left in the field, I spent what little free time I had writing letters home to Barb and my family with most of them going to Barb. Perhaps it was the only way to keep my sanity as I struggled with "short-timer fever."

On Sept. 4th I began to write a letter to Barb in response to a card and letter I had received from her that morning, a letter I added to over the next three days. I was so thankful to finally be receiving regular communication from her. *"It was great to hear from you as your cards and letters are always so encouraging no matter what they say. There's a touch about everything you do, whether it's the cards you send, the way you wrap a package, or the way you sing or smile. Everything to me is so perfect."* Cleary the correspondence was drawing our hearts back together, though I knew there was still a measure of apprehension on her part because of how deeply I had hurt her when we had broken up.

Barb asked me in her letter to tell her about the medals I had been awarded, so I tried.

First of all I was put in for a Silver Star which is fairly high. That was for action on January 25th during which time I tried to save the lives of four men while under intense enemy fire and during which time I treated two other wounded men under the same circumstances. In short, what happened was that we were pinned down for over 18 hours after walking into the mouth of an NVA Regimental Headquarters. Eighteen of us escaped on our bellies after evacuating the two wounded men and one deaf man by medevac in the early hours of the 26th and being forced to leave four dead, whose bodies were recovered later. That was the worst I've ever been through and I never want to see it again. My medal was granted after being reduced one grade to a Bronze Star with "V" device for valor.

Other than that, the rest is minor. I'll receive an Air Medal with probably two or three clusters. This is awarded for making a combat assault by helicopter while under fire, getting extracted by helicopter while under enemy fire, and for making over 25 combat assaults by helicopter. Each cluster represents another medal of the same equivalency as the one it follows.

My comments about the Air Medal awards were based on the fact others in the platoon had either already received their Air Medal award orders or were told they had earned them. Since I had been on every combat assault they had been on since coming into the field January 20th, I assumed I would receive the same awards. However, for some reason the other medics and I never received them until Captain Ohl, who retired as a colonel, went to bat for us some 42 years later, and I was awarded an Air Medal for my participation in the Cambodia operation.

I went on to explain I had also been awarded the Army Commendation Medal for meritorious service, and in

October I should receive another Bronze Star for Meritorious Service. I continued, *"Last but not least I proudly wear the Combat Medical Badge which signifies that I, as a Combat Medic, have performed my duties while under enemy fire. … Well, that's about it, and I assure you, it's not the way some people might think. I've only done my job and no more (sometimes I think less). I'm just plain me, I'm in the Army, I'm in Vietnam, and I'm waiting to come home. That's it; no more."*

After answering a question about whether or not I had done any creative writing since being in Vietnam I continued,

> *Things here are well as far as the war goes. There was no action the day before yesterday and none today. Yesterday one of our squads on ambush fired up an NVA soldier who had come pretty close. They thought sure they'd killed him but upon checking it out they found nothing at all; no body, no blood. He got away clean. I've seen it so many times; a G.I. or one of the enemy come <u>SO CLOSE</u> but get away clean. I have to believe there's been Divine grace shown to many of both forces; perhaps an extra day, or even their whole life to get right with God as He decrees right, when instead they should have died.*

Another medic, Norman Mah from San Francisco, California, probably the Company Medic at this time, was traveling with us. The ambush was a daytime ambush, and, because things had been relatively quiet, there was not much expectation anything would happen, so the Lt. decided it wasn't necessary to send a medic along. "If something happens I can have a fire team escort you to the ambush site," he said.

The ambush was set on a well-worn trail, and a lone NVA soldier came down the trail walking into the ambush. Apparently the squad sprung the ambush prematurely missing the NVA soldier and allowing him to escape. However, thinking they had injured or killed him, they called for me in case the enemy soldier needed aid. I remember when the shots were fired and the call came in "short-time fever" kicked in, and I was momentarily overwhelmed with fear at the thought of finding myself in another dangerous situation. Doc Mah must have sensed my apprehension and offered to go in my place. As tempting as it was, I knew I couldn't let that happen. What would my men think of me if they thought I was afraid to go? These were my guys, and it was my responsibility. "No, thank you," I replied. "I'll go. It's my job."

The fire team and I quickly saddled up in light battle gear, and with adrenalin flowing we headed down to the ambush sight. When we got there, the ambush squad was still in their original position. Only after I arrived did they move out to search for the enemy soldier. Perhaps they wanted me there not only to give aid to the enemy soldier but also in case any of them got injured in their search for him.

The next morning, Sept. 5th, I added a few more lines explaining the battalion commander had called that morning and wanted to see our captain, *"so we sent him and two squads down to the landing zone to meet him. I thought perhaps I should go with them, but the Lieutenant said that he didn't think it would be necessary as the area we are in now is real bushy with no trails. So, naturally, we don't expect any trouble. Still, I'll worry some until they get back safely. Being the only medic for thirty people sometimes presents a problem. So, that is it for this morning."*

On Sept. 6th I continued my letter and mentioned it had rained that afternoon but otherwise was hot and sunny. *"I think I prefer the rain as it's so much more comfortable. But by October the monsoons will be in full swing and that'll be miserable too."* I went on to explain even though we had moved to an area where there weren't any trails, we still had to put two squads out on ambush because *"higher command said we had to."* The battalion commander wasn't very happy with us because we hadn't been moving around enough, even using the same NDP two nights in a row. He told our captain we needed to move at least 300 meters each day. *"So, this morning we moved a little ways and this evening around 6:00 P.M. we'll move a little farther. It's ridiculous because there aren't any signs of enemy activity around and we're just moving further away from our landing zone where we'll take resupply tomorrow. In the morning we'll have to hump that extra distance to please the lifers."*

The next day I finished writing the letter so it could go out on the resupply ship.

The sky's clear and it's going to be hot today. There's a stream nearby so we may get to bathe if we get time. The resupply and chopper lift will crowd us for time. I guess I forgot to mention we're being lifted to another area today. At least we're supposed to be. One never can tell whether there's been a change or not.

Yesterday evening we had Platoon worship services and it was really great. I spoke from Philippians 3:1-4:1 and opened with the poem, "If We Could See Beyond Today," which Mr. M. sent me. Perhaps you've read it before. Keep it for me. OK?

I finished the letter: *"Well, Barbara, I'm going to have to quit and get this in an envelope or I'll never get it mailed today. I have to make a write up on a man I am sending in for possible internal bleeding of the gastro-intestinal tract. It may be ulcers. In the meantime, take care always. Yours in Christ, Mike."*

Though we did get resupplied that day and I was able to send in the soldier I had written about on the supply bird, the combat assault didn't happen. It was supposed to take place at 4:00 P.M., but due to low cloud cover and a rain storm that moved in the CA had to be called off. We moved off the LZ back into the jungle to spend the night at another NDP, and then we were back at the pickup zone the next morning at 9:00 A.M. for another try. In another letter to Barb written that evening (Sept. 9th), I told her about it and how the rest of our day had gone. Inspired by her inquiry about whether I had done any creative writing since being in Vietnam I decided to take a stab at it.

...with clear blue skies the birds came in and we went for a ride. Within five to ten minutes we were back on the ground and in our new A.O. (area of operation) high in the mountains. Within another five to ten minutes we had our seventy-five pound rucksacks on and were moving through the jungle to another objective.

Well, not much happened. We went down a hill and up another, then down again. We went under the vines, through the vines, over the logs and around the impossible spots. We slipped and jolted and fell and got up and tried again. We swatted the mosquitoes, killed the leeches, and watched out for ticks, spiders and other such creatures. In essence, it was another routine day in Vietnam.

But frankly, it's not as bad as it sometimes seems to us or sounds to you. After the humping is over (and sometime, or perhaps I should say, "most of the time," it's only a couple of hours in the A.M. and a couple in the P.M.) we can throw those rucks off our backs, take the ammo from around our waists, wipe the sweat from off our drenched bodies and breath with great relief and release. Maybe a couple of squads will go out in light battle gear and check the area to see that it's secure, but the worst is over.

The scene now becomes relaxed. A defensive perimeter is set up and men at guard positions stay alert but calm and at ease. Letters come out to be read a second or third time; tablets and pens go to work in response to the thoughts about home. A G.I. pulls out a canteen of Kool-Aid or a can of pudding received in a package last resupply from someone dear.

A deck of cards is shuffled as four go into a game of Spades or Hearts, or maybe its Poker or Twenty-One. G.I.s may set to work sharpening a knife or cleaning their weapon. Some may close their eyes to take a nap.

Everybody is occupied with something their own, each man's actions his own. But the thoughts are the same for all. His mind is drifting someplace else, someplace far, far away, but to his heart very close. He thinks about the girl he left behind, her hair so soft and eyes so clear, the girl he loves so dear. He thinks about his dear sweet mom, and dad that works so hard; his brothers, sisters and friends of old; so many thoughts he thinks, so bold. But most of all his thoughts are these; "The day I'll return! My plane will land and out I'll walk and there I'll see them stand. At first I'll look and then I'll smile, and next I'll run that one last mile to meet their outstretched arms. A thousand persons it will seem, pushing, tugging, laughing, hugging, smiling, crying, together sighing. And then on out we'll walk, and by some quiet shady street there will stand a lonely church; no one near, or so it seems; quite alone this night. But as we look inside its doors, we see its secret held. Two figures there will kneel in peace; their heads will bow in prayer. And each will softly, with great love, their hearts beholding Him above, give thanks for one's return. And on in life they'll walk, two lives made one in Christ and love. Praise God for one's return!"

Well Barbara, I'm going to have to stop this nonsense (excuse the term) or I'll run on forever. Either that or I'll get so homesick I'll die. I guess that's why I haven't done any creative writing over here; my position and the lack of someone to inspire me.

Well, I'll close for now and if anything more comes up I'll add it before resupply tomorrow. Remember, Love Always in Christ, Michael. Jn. 15:5.

On Sept. 11th I wrote my next letter to Barb. At the top of each letter I was now putting how many days I had to go until DEROS from Vietnam. On this day it was 89. I also mentioned I had just 11 more days before R&R. I thanked her for a special edition magazine she had sent to me and then went on to talk about what my day had been like.

I had to stop writing as we had to hump to a new hill top. Boy was it wild! Parts were as good as straight down and there wasn't much to hang on to. Coming down the first hill I made it all the way without falling . . . until the last ten feet, that is. But at least I didn't have far to fall and I slid on my bottom that little ways. Then it was down a little stream with fish in it and back up, straight up another hill! Wow, that three day ruck sure didn't help much! But here I am again, with a big bees nest hanging in a tree about twenty-five meters away, and with that in mind I'll finish this letter.

Yesterday afternoon it rained, and after that it rained some more. In fact, it rained half way through the night too. Guess what? You're right! I got wet! But today it's just right; warm with a haze in the sky to keep it from getting too hot. Hopefully it won't rain tonight.

Though I always tried to remain upbeat in my letters to Barb, the reality was I was getting tired. The terrain we were operating in was extremely rugged, and the weather was becoming horrendous. The cold rain soaked through our clothes, and there were times when we could hardly stay dry. To sleep in the rain, we tried to find a small piece of high ground in the hopes the rain would drain away from us. We would lie down and wrap our ponchos around us with our weapons by our sides at the ready. I was used to sleeping with my steel pot on, not so much for protection as for warmth and comfort. The leather headband in the helmet liner held my head away from the hard outer shell, so in some respects it felt as if I were sleeping on a firm pillow.

As the days wore on and I became more and more weary, my language began to change, and I began to sound more like the soldiers I had tried so hard to witness to than the Christian I professed to be. I was so cold I even began smoking in the hopes it would somehow warm me up or at least take my mind off the miserable weather. The elements and terrain had become our enemy along with the VC and NVA. My days in the field may have been coming to a close, but they were anything but easy. They were downright miserable.

A tired Doc after a long, hot, hard hump in the bush!

CHAPTER THIRTY-ONE

HUMPING MADNESS

"Let us not grow weary in doing good,
For at the proper time we will reap
a harvest if we do not give up."

Galatians 6:9

On the morning of the 13th I borrowed some stationary and wrote a short letter to Barb. In it I told her it was going to be a very long day. We had received a call from Battalion telling us we had been moving in the wrong direction the past two days, and we were going to have to change direction to reach an old abandoned firebase by that afternoon for resupply. What made it worse was we had been going the direction Captain Shaw (our current company commander) had told us to go in, but he had gone in to the rear the day before for a two-day conference. Now we were going to have to make up three days of humping in less than one, a virtual impossibility under the conditions.

The distance we needed to travel was only 1,600 meters as the crow flies, but with the steep mountains and rugged terrain, it was much further in reality. Because we were traveling in largely uncut jungle, we had to cut our way through with machetes. Up to this point we had only been making about 500 meters as the crow flies per day. *"Well, what more can we say than, 'Yes Sir,' get it on and drive on or at least try,"* I wrote.

We were supposed to have moved out that morning at 7:15 A.M., but by now it was almost 9:00 A.M. We sent a squad out to start cutting a trail, but they had gone only about 150 meters in an hour and forty five minutes. *"To put it short, once again, 'it could be a long day!' I just hope I can get my mail out including this letter. It just all depends on our getting to the firebase and how they handle resupply."* With that I ended the letter saying I needed to get some things squared away.

I didn't get to write again until Sept. 15th at 6:45 P.M. At the top of the letter I wrote, *"79 days and a wake up!"* I was still counting. The 16th was another resupply, and I wanted to get the letter written before it got dark. I spent the first page and a half talking about a Scripture passage I had been reading, and then it got too dark to write. I finished the letter the next morning.

As it turned out we had been unable to reach our resupply point on the 13th. We spent the entire day and into the night cutting our way through the jungle. At one point we found a stream and were able to walk up the stream several hundred meters. Another platoon, which was supposed to meet us at the resupply point, secured our supplies and sent a squad to start cutting a trail in our direction. Needless to say, the unlucky squad was not happy about it.

At 7:30 P.M. their squad reached us, but we were still over 1,000 meters from our destination and most of it was uphill! We continued to walk into the night until around 9:00 P.M. Exhausted and hungry, we stopped on the trail by a small stream to sleep for the night. Few of us had eaten anything since that morning, having run completely out of food. Some men may have had a can of crackers or jelly but not much else. One of the men managed to catch and kill a catfish from the stream using a machete. Building a small fire, he cooked and ate it, though, as I recall, it wasn't all that appetizing. As I told Barb in my letter on the 13th, it was indeed a *very* long day!

(Again, I am very thankful for these letters, which have helped refresh my memory. All of these years I had in my mind someone had caught a turtle, and he tried to make turtle soup out of it in his steel pot. However, if that had been the case, I'm sure I would have told Barb about it. Instead, it was a catfish. Go figure.)

I continued to write to Barb.

The fourteenth, 6:15 A.M. we awoke, the sun yet to rise above the hills. At 6:45 A.M. we moved out determined to beat it to the top! It took us one hour and fifteen minutes to climb to old Fire Support Base Pistol, now deserted. Only two men had fallen out. Twice we all had to take a break. But we made it! 8:00 A.M. we started breaking down our resupply – mail call holding first priority. I got a package from home and a hometown newspaper. We all felt good, sodas in hand. Still, in one hour we'd have to be finished, rucks packed, ready for a ball game – Combat Assault – a chopper ride into a new area of operation! What would be waiting for us, we didn't know.

It all went smooth. By 10:00 A.M. we were all on the ground again. It was quiet and peaceful. We took a break; relaxed for several hours. That evening we moved four hundred meters to a night locale. This time the forest was clear, easy traveling. The hills moderate. We were glad.

The fifteenth: A quiet day. A few clover-leafs, and that's it. At night we move 25 to 50 meters to change night locale. It was nice.

The sixteenth: Today – a letter to someone special – in twenty five minutes we'll move to the LZ and take resupply. I'll look forward to mail call – I get to break it down. I'll send mine out. Today should be quiet and refreshing; a little hassle with the resupply.

*In the future: Tomorrow another ball game, another chopper
ride, another Combat Assault. Hopefully nothing will be
there to shoot at or get shot by. Seven days in the rear to
prepare for R&R–the 26th through Oct. 3rd – Tokyo, Japan –
fellowship; after that sixty more days in 'Nam. Then—–I need
not say! Lord willing, I'll be home! Take care and remember
I love you. In Christ, Michael (Jn. 15:5).*

On Sept. 15th I wrote a letter home thanking them for a
package I received on the 14th and venting about the events
of the last few days.

*Things have been mighty quiet lately as far as the war goes
and I'm glad. Just seven more days out here and off to the
rear I go. We've had our share of humping though and that
hasn't been easy. The terrain is mountainous and the jungle
impenetrable and the Army telling us from up above, "Go
here, go there, this way, that way, hurry, hurry. NO! Stop
here! You did it wrong! It's all soooo easy! What's wrong with
you?" To hell with the Army! That's what we say! Thank God
I can look forward to more out of life than this! Praise God
that even over here I can be thankful! It's a long story and
maybe I'll tell it someday.*

With just seven days left in the field, all of this humping
in difficult terrain, the changing weather from hot and humid
to wet and cold, and making Combat Assaults, were wearing
on my nerves. I was truly getting worn out by this time, and
my nerves were frazzled. Every time we got into those choppers and headed for a new AO, there was no telling what
we would run into. The adrenalin flowed through our bodies
and a pit formed in our stomachs as we contemplated the
possibility of a hot LZ and a nasty firefight. We hadn't seen
any serious action since Cambodia, and I had to wonder how
long it would last.

A resupply chopper being unloaded in a very rough
Landing Zone in the rugged mountains.

One of our machine gunners enjoying a cold
(or maybe not so cold) soda after resupply.

CHAPTER THIRTY-TWO

FINAL ASSAULT

"As the deer pants for streams of water,
so my soul pants for you, O God."

Psalm 42:1

A t 2:50 PM on Sept. 16th after resupply and the mailing of the letters, I wrote to Barb. *"Today I received your letter and package both of Sept. 8th. Right now I am eating some of the sun-flower seeds, using the paper and the new pen. Everything else I have packed away or distributed among the men. There were only a couple of things I can't use; the Tide, toothpaste and large gauze pads. Everything else is well taken care of. Thank you so very much."* The weather was sunny when I started writing, but it started to rain before I could finish, so I told her I would write more the next day.

The next morning I continued my letter to Barb. I told her it had rained the night before, but I had been able to build a shelter using my poncho and so was able to stay pretty dry. That evening I had enjoyed eating some Vienna sausage and canned tamales my mom had sent in a package. I went on to say I had been writing to the director at the children's home in Hollywood where I had worked at the end of the year I was at bible school, and they were interested in my coming to work for them after I got out of the Army. I also explained I was concerned about how any future plans I might have would affect our future relationship. I then went on to talk about what was on the schedule for the day.

Today comes another Combat Assault! It seems they sure keep us hopping from one place to another. I'm just so thankful that the Lord has kept us safe in the many places we've been.

The new area we're going to today is about ten to twelve kilometers from where we are now. They're re-establishing Fire Support Base Pistol where we took resupply on the 14th, and we'll get our gun support from there. The jungle is triple canopy which means the trees and overhead cover is extremely thick, impossible to see through from the air. How thick it is underneath I don't know. We'll have to wait and see.

Enemy activity is questionable. Trail networks and an enemy command post are suspected, according to agent reports. We hope they're wrong.

Terrain doesn't look too bad. Mostly we'll be traveling down-hill. Sounds nice.

Future resupplies may be a hassle; because of the thick forest we'll have to blow landing zones with high explosives; could create problems in extractions too. Next resupply we have one man to go in for R&R and the 22nd it's my turn. The Lieutenant wanted to go ahead and send me in today, but the Captain wouldn't go for it. So, the Lt. promises us, "Where there's a will, there's a way. We'll blow the whole forest down if we have to." Every man is humping two to three sticks of explosives (C-4).

Well Barbs, that's about it for now. You're right again. The Lord Jesus and our great God is so wonderful! To think that He should die for such a one as I! Praise God and keep rejoicing! Yours always, Michael.

The combat assault most likely took place sometime that afternoon as I wrote that letter in the morning starting at 9:20 AM. If all went well, this would be my last combat assault before going on R&R and, hopefully, the last assault of my brief military career. There was always a degree of apprehension and fear on combat assaults, but due to the fact I was so close to leaving the field, and because of the intelligence reports regarding NVA activity, I was especially nervous. What would this CA be like? Would the enemy be waiting for us as they had been in Cambodia? Would the LZ be laced with bamboo stakes as it had been at another LZ? Would the chopper I was riding in be shot down? Every CA we made was another opportunity for disaster. I had been so fortunate up to this point! Would my good fortune last one more day, or three?

Because of the suspected enemy activity, this assault, like many others I had been on, was accompanied by gunships that prepared the LZ for our insertion. As we lifted off and flew high above the jungle, I was struck again by the beauty of Vietnam, the lush, green forests and the rugged mountains. As we drew nearer to the LZ, the slicks began to make their decent to just above the tree tops. The Cobra and Huey gunships ahead of us opened up with their rockets and cannons, blasting the LZ's perimeter with their fiery volleys of explosives. I could hear the rockets' swishing sound as they were released ahead of us and then their massive explosions! "Boom! Boom! Boom!" Suddenly, the door gunners on each side of the slicks, one of them right next to me as I sat in the doorway, opened up with their M-60 machineguns, red hot lead flying from their barrels and shell casings dropping into the jungle below. As we flew over the treetops in the midst of this chaos, I looked down into the jungle and saw something I had never seen from the air before: a long, thin waterfall flowing over a flat rock slick cliff down into a beautiful long rock bed stream below. Even more amazing at the base of the water fall stood a deer-like creature looking up as if to say, "What are you guys doing here?" The scene was so serene and beautiful it stood out in stark contrast to the chaotic events of which we were a part at that very moment. In spite of the adrenalin flowing through my body, the pit in my stomach, and the sense of fear as we approached the LZ with the sounds of war all around us, for that one brief moment in time I was filled with a sense of awe and overwhelming peace. It was as if God were saying to me, "It's all right! You're going to be okay. I'm right here."

As our choppers came into the LZ, each of us made our way out quickly and fanned out in a circle, hitting the dirt in the prone position. There was no enemy fire, just the loud "WHOOP, WHOOP, WHOOP" of the Huey's rotors as each chopper came in, then left, lifting off again into the sky until they could be seen no more. Once they were gone, there was silence, the silence of the jungle around and below us as we had landed on a ridge line in the mountains, silence broken only by the rustle of an infantry platoon preparing to move out once again in search of the elusive enemy.

The afternoon of the 18th I wrote a letter to Barb describing the amazing scene I had witnessed the day before. For some reason I did not mention the deer-like creature, making me wonder if I had somehow imagined it afterward, and yet to this day I have a clear recollection of having seen it.

Things are good here. The C.A. went well yesterday. It looked like it was going to be a bit hairy from the air, but it went real well. We flew over some beautiful sites; a long thin waterfall over a flat rock slick cliff, falling into a beautiful long flowing rock bed stream. It was really beautiful. . . . The forest here is nice; all trees and clear forest underneath. We were lifted to a ridge line. Now it's easy walking as it's all downhill. We've moved around one thousand meters today, probably more.

Yesterday it rained for about fifteen minutes, but then stopped. It hasn't rained anymore since. It was pretty nice last night and has been today. Can't see much now, but looks a little cloudy. Hope a storm doesn't blow in.

I might go in tomorrow. I don't know for sure. It depends on how big of an LZ we can blow. Also, on what the Captain says. If not, it's just three more days anyway. I don't care too much, just so long as I'm in on time. Sure don't want to mess up my R&R.

On Sept. 19th I wrote my last letter to Barb from the field.
September 19, 1970

Republic of Vietnam
8:10 AM – Sunny
Dearest Barbara:

Hi there again!

Well, it rained yesterday after I stopped writing. It rained pretty hard for about an hour or more; by dusk though it was pretty well stopped. The Platoon Sgt. (Vance – a soul brother) and I put up a poncho hutch, plenty of leaves on the ground, another poncho on the ground and then we slept in our poncho liners. It was real comfortable and soft. We had it camouflaged so well that when Sgt. Marine, from one of the squads, came to wake Vance for guard he walked right past us on up the trail and finally wound up calling out "Mac? Mac?" I woke up and woke up Mac (Vance McMillan) and off he went. We all laughed about it this morning.

My feet got wet though and felt like ice this morning. Even now they're cold, but will dry out today. I'll have to get my boots off for a while today.

Don't think I'll get out today. The LZ is just big enough for the bird to hover above and kick out our supplies. We're going to stick around here though for the next three days and make it big enough to land. So, I guess I'll get out for sure the 22nd.

Saw a bunch of monkeys this morning; pretty big ones too, just a swinging through the trees. It's only the second time

*I've seen them in the wild over here, if that means anything.
I guess it don't.*

*If we get a kick out this morning (after 10:30) we won't be
able to send mail out. But I'll keep writing and send them
out as soon as I can. Are you getting my letters now? Let me
know, ok?*

I do not recall with any certainty whether I left the field
on the 19th or the 22nd. However, my strong suspicion is it
was on the 19th, because I recall being surprised when Lt.
Greig told me to get on the chopper saying, "Hurry up Doc.
You're going in for R&R!" I quickly grabbed all of my gear
and got on the bird. I didn't even have time to say goodbye
to the guys. The chopper lifted into the air and took off down
through a valley between two steep mountains, swinging
wildly back and forth from side to side in a zigzagging
pattern to avoid enemy fire. I was somewhat surprised by
the maneuver, as it was a new experience for me and we
hadn't had any enemy contact, so I was not expecting such
an evasive tactic.

I was full of mixed emotions. I had just spent eight
months in the field sharing good and bad times with a bunch
of guys I might never see again. I was thrilled to finally be
going on R&R and hoped I would not have to return to the
field, but at the same time I knew these guys whom I had
come to respect and love would continue to face the many
dangers and discomforts of life in the jungles of Vietnam. I
was free, at least for now, but they were not. For me there
was excitement and joy, but I was also conflicted with sorrow
and guilt from having to leave my guys behind.

CHAPTER THIRTY-THREE

LIFE IN THE REAR

*"Peace I leave with you; my peace I give you.
I do not give to you as the world gives.
Do not let your hearts be troubled
and do not be afraid."*

John 14:27

Back at Camp Eagle, I stored my gear in the Battalion Aid Station storage bunker and checked my weapon in at Delta Company Headquarters. Beyond that I have no recollection of what I did there in the days before catching a flight to Da Nang.

On Sept. 24th I sent a card to Barb from the R&R Center in Da Nang. I told her I had hoped to visit a buddy in the hospital there while I was passing through, but when I called the hospital they said he wasn't there. *"I saw this card and thought I would send it to you."* (The card has a very large Great Dane on the front of it looking happily at a Chihuahua and says, "I Go For You ... in a BIG way!") *"It's not often I get to purchase something like this over here, let alone purchase anything at all. Things are pretty nice here at the R&R Center; a big USO, a small PX, barber shop, snack bar and so on. But it's still not home and it's still Army. So I guess that's that, if you know what I mean."*

At the R&R center I was told I had to wear civilian clothes on my flight, a little fact I had somehow not even thought of. I guess I assumed I would buy some civvies once I got to

Japan. However, we were not allowed to leave the country in our uniforms. I was told the only place to get civilian clothes was from one of the Vietnamese tailor shops nearby. When I went looking, none of them seemed to have anything that fit me. Finally I found one pair of pants that were a hideous bright blue and a white shirt. Why I had not thought to ask my folks to mail me some civvies I have no idea, and why the PX didn't carry clothes at an R&R center defies logic. But I didn't care, as long as I got to go on my R&R.

My time in Japan was wonderful. The first thing I did was to call home and talk to my family, letting them know where I was. I spent one night in Tokyo at a Hilton Hotel, as I recall, and then took the bullet train to Osaka to meet my friend Dorothy Powell from church and her Literature Crusades team, with whom I stayed. On at least a couple of occasions I went out with them and helped distribute literature on the sidewalk. Of course, I couldn't speak Japanese, so they just taught me to say "Good Morning" or "Good Afternoon" in Japanese, and I held out a piece of literature. One day Dorothy and I took a train to Kyoto, where we toured a large Buddhist temple and petted the sacred deer in the park. One evening the team took me out to a Japanese restaurant for an authentic Japanese meal sitting on the floor in true Japanese style.

When I returned to Tokyo on the bullet train at the end of my stay, a very kind Japanese fellow sitting next to me, who spoke English, struck up a conversation and invited me to the dining car for some saki. He asked me if I had a place to stay in Tokyo, and when I said I planned to call a hotel once I got there, he expressed concern I might have difficulty finding a room. So, when we arrived in Tokyo he called around and found a room for me at the Princess Hotel, a very upscale establishment. They had just one room left. He then hailed a cab for me and gave the driver instructions. When I arrived at the hotel and checked in, there was a woman in the lobby desperate to find a room for the night, as all the hotels were full. As I recall, she may have had a child with her. I felt terrible about having gotten the last room and considered giving her mine, but as this was my last night of R&R and I had no idea where else I could stay, I bit my tongue.

Back at the R&R Center I bought a three-strand cultured pearl necklace for my mother and a couple of Seiko watches as gifts for my dad and step-dad before heading back to Vietnam. I seem to recall having spent a day or two at a Christian Servicemen's Center as well at the nearby Navy base, but not much else.

Once I arrived back at Camp Eagle in Phu Bai on October 5th, one of the first things I did was pick up my mail. I had four letters from different people back home and twelve letters from Barb. I had not written her all the time I was in Japan and felt terrible. I wrote back to her, *"I know I am hard on you for not writing while on R&R and yet I pray that you will forgive . . . Though I didn't write I did think of you often."* After talking about a number of things she had written about, including my coming to visit her when I returned to the States, I continued,

> *Guess what? . . . I'm out of the field, finny boonies, a full time REMP (Rear Echelon Military Personnel) AND HAPPY! Believe it or not, after eight months on line my replacement has finally come in. It's really great. But, you know? I am going to miss the guys in the platoon. I feel so responsible to keep a Christian witness before them. Pray that the Lord will allow me to keep in close contact with them and pray for their souls as well as physical safety.*

> *Tomorrow I start work at 7:30 AM in the Aid Station pulling sick call. There won't be much for me to do, but I'll at least be able to observe and maybe learn from those in charge. I sure hope so. Out in the field there isn't much we can do. Everything is either minor or else serious and beyond our*

knowledge requiring evacuation. Here in the rear I hope to learn more about my job.

Working in the rear was such a relief after having been in the field for eight months. On October 8th I wrote a letter home to Barb telling her about the peace I had.

It's about 8:00 PM and I am sitting outside of the medic's hutch under a clear starlit sky, and in the warmth of a nearby fire. It's beautiful and I'm at peace in the safety of our Lord's care. It's so good and almost indescribable. You know the feeling. It's the same peace that one experiences in the silent night only in the presence of God. It's the peace one knows when alone over the mild roar of his auto engine he sings hymns of thanksgiving to Christ. It's the peace of safety in the eternal bonds of Calvary; the peace of hearts and minds in Christ Jesus; the peace of God almighty only as God can give.

I went on to explain I was enjoying my work at the aid station, and I was *"going to get to stick with treatment in the morning working on my own and getting help from the doctor and clinical specialist when I need it."*

After getting off work that afternoon, I visited my old platoon, since the whole battalion was in the rear on stand-down. I didn't have much time to visit, and, to tell the truth, it was a bit uncomfortable. I think they had just come in that day, and they were all stuffed into a small barracks without any cots. They looked horrible. After just three weeks of being out of the field, I stood there in my clean uniform in stark contrast to a bunch of guys who were tired, ragged, filthy, and wet from living in the jungle during monsoon season. Though they seemed in fair condition, several of them had also been sick. I don't think I knew what to say to them, and they certainly didn't have much to say to me either. In fact, they didn't seem to have much to say to each other. They just seemed completely exhausted. I left feeling somewhat guilty I no longer had to face the prospect of going back out to the field as these men did.

On October 12th I wrote another letter to Barb telling her the weather had now turned *"wet, wet, wet"* and looked like it was going to stay that way for a while. I told her about the work I was doing in the aid station and things were pretty slow, so I was spending a lot of time writing letters. At the end of the letter I wrote, *"Well, Barbs, my mind seems to be blank right now and I wished it wasn't. I got a lot of sleep last night, but I don't know how much rest. I had several different dreams, but they were all nightmares. I just can't seem to win!"* Undoubtedly I was already experiencing the effects of PTSD without even knowing what it was at that point, because it had not yet been recognized by the medical community.

On October 15th I wrote another letter to her saying, *"Just a note to let you know that I'm ok and to assure you that I haven't forgotten you. In fact, last night you were in my dreams. So, I guess I can call you 'the girl of my dreams.'"*

On October 16th I wrote a letter home.

> *I really enjoy it back here, especially amongst all the comfort. You know, like a roof over your head (it's raining and windy right now), hot chow to eat, a cot to sleep on and so on. I hate to think of all the guys that still have to live out in this horrid weather, but I spent my eight months and was here twelve months, available, so there is no more they can ask. That's all they ask of any of them, just be willing to go twelve and do what you're asked. After twelve it's back to the World for all of us, so they'll be ok. We all have our part to do.*

Needless to say, while I was enjoying being in the rear I was also feeling guilty about it and needed to find a way to justify myself.

I continued,

It sure seems that the good Lord has really been looking out for me the past few months, (not to mention the whole year). My R&R was so really great, as I got to see those whom I hoped to and it was odd that I squeezed in just before the center was closed, even though others had priority over me. I even got one of the longest, if not THE longest R&R ever given. Also, the timing for being gone was pretty right. After I left, the rains increased and came down steady for several days; contact with the enemy increased and the battalion had several men wounded as well as two killed; the resupply choppers couldn't fly and they went four days without food; they had illnesses and immersion foot was overwhelming. Things just seemed to get bad. I'm almost ashamed to think that during this time I was in Japan living it up.

Now I'm in the rear and hardly have a complaint. Like I said, the Lord has sure been good to me. What else can I say? The Scripture tells me that "Every good gift and every perfect gift cometh down from heaven and is from the Father!" That's sure good to know. Somebody cares!

I went on to explain I was supposed to go out to a firebase on the 21st until the 29th. However, that never happened. I assume another medic was sent instead.

On October 24th I wrote a letter to Barb in which I told her I would be getting a twenty-four day drop, due to the drawdown of troops in Vietnam. I would be going through Fort Lewis, Washington, where I would also be assigned after my leave as part of the Transportation Dept. at Madigan General Hospital. I told her not to tell anyone, because I wanted to surprise my family, who expected me home December 4th. October 30th was my 21st birthday, and on November 1st I wrote my last letter to Barb from Vietnam, telling her I was just three days from beginning to process out. *"I'm floating on air!"* I wrote. *"I know it's going to be a hassle getting through, but it'll be worth it. Just like in the Christian life, we must keep our eyes on the Lord, I just need to keep my eyes on the ultimate objective (home) and stay calm. I really won't even know how to feel once I get there!"*

The next day, November 2nd, was a day of tragedy. Delta Company's 3rd Platoon was ambushed by a sniper that popped up out of a "spider hole" and opened up on them. Their medic, Jerry Rouse, from Coleman, Wisconsin, was hit and killed immediately, and their Platoon Leader Sgt. Douglas "Lumpy" Hunter was hit nine times. Doug had served with 1st Platoon as a squad leader when I first went to the field. He had completed his tour of duty, spent some time with an Army Unit in Germany, and then volunteered to go back to Vietnam as long as he could go back to the same unit he had served with before. (Apparently he had not adjusted well to Army life in Germany.) Lt. Greig, former 1st Platoon Leader who had recently been promoted to Company Commander, was glad to have him back and gave him leadership of 3nd Platoon because they were short of lieutenants.

When I got word of the tragedy, I struggled with whether or not I should go to the hospital to visit Lumpy, whom I knew was in critical condition. I am ashamed to say I didn't have the courage to go. I was afraid he might die, and I just didn't have the courage to face the prospect of losing another one of my men. I knew he would receive the best care available, and I prayed for his recovery.

Even though I did not know Jerry Rouse well, I volunteered to escort his body home for the funeral. I was so short with a new DEROS date of November 9th I thought the Army should have no problem granting my request. It was not uncommon for a soldier to accompany a body home from Vietnam, especially if they had been friends. The fact Jerry was a fellow medic was significant enough to make me want to show this respect to him and his family. It would simply be a detour on my way home.

My request was put through, but unfortunately, due to the poor health of his aged parents, and their devastation, the family thought it best not to delay the funeral in order for me to get orders to accompany the body home. I received a very nice letter written November 12th thanking me.

Dear Mr. Dingman,

In behalf of Mr. and Mrs. Albert Rouse, I want to express the deep sorrow they felt in not being able to request your presence at the burial of their son, Jerry, also your accompanying the remains to his home here. When the telegram was received for your request, a call was made to Capt. Spohn at West De Pere, Wisconsin. The Capt. called army headquarters, and was informed that the burial could possibly be delayed, if the request was granted. Due to Mr. and Mrs. Rouse being in deep sorrow, shock, and also in questionably poor health, they were advised that the least delay would be unadvisable.

Jerry was killed November 2nd and Mrs. Rouse suffered a stroke November 6th. She was not able to view the body or attend the funeral, but as of today her condition has improved. She knows her family and friends and is able to talk and sit up. Everybody is very thankful for her progress so far. The rest of the family and Mr. Rouse are holding up as well as can be expected.

The body was almost in perfect condition and was able to be viewed, what a blessing that was! Jerry was very much loved in this community and had a very large funeral. Enclosed for you, find a write up from our local paper.

Your writing to the Albert Rouse family would be greatly appreciated. Please write anything you knew about him. The family wanted so much to see you; they knew you could have given them some news of Jerry. They will write to you soon. We'll all pray for you!

Sincerely,
Mrs. Ed. Beaudoin, A Relative.

Needless to say, I was disappointed, but I understood the family's need to move forward with a quick funeral. Though I no longer recall, I am sure I wrote to them in response to their request, telling them what little I could.

A week before my new DEROS date I began the process of checking out, which meant I had to account for the equipment I had been issued when I first arrived. (Remember the guys tossing some of my equipment back onto the helicopter I had just gotten off of when I first arrived in the field?) I went to the Battalion Aid Station storage bunker to retrieve my back pack and my other equipment that had been stored there since the day I left the field. To my surprise, none of it was there. It had all somehow mysteriously disappeared. This presented a bit of a problem, in that the Army takes very seriously the responsibility of accounting for the equipment it issues to its soldiers. When I went to my Medical Platoon Sgt. he assured me he would take care of me. I have no idea whether my equipment had been scavenged up by other medics, taken and sold on the black market, or turned in as abandoned equipment, but the Platoon Sgt. went with me to supply and got them to sign off on my papers, arguing he had turned in all kinds of equipment to them that nobody could account for. Of course, I also had to account for my weapon, which I had turned in to Delta Company Headquarters. Unfortunately, it too was missing. However, when the company clerk checked with the platoons getting an update of serial numbers from weapons in the field, they found it had been issued to another soldier. One by one the hurdles were crossed, including going through a long processing line to get all of my orders and awards before heading to Cam Rohn Bay down south.

The last thing I remember from Vietnam is sitting on the tarmac at the airbase waiting to board the Freedom Bird for the Real World, as we called it. Once again I am sure I was filled with mixed emotions about all I had been through and about seeing my family once again, but most of all I was just anxious to get on the plane and leave Vietnam behind me.

In many ways, I left home just a boy who used to play in the woods pretending to be a soldier. Now I was coming home a man who had gone face-to-face with the realities of war and survived. I had been forced to choose between my decision not to carry a weapon and my responsibility as a medic to care for and protect those who might not be able to protect themselves. I had faced my fears and overcome them, relying on my faith in Christ and His promise to be with me always. I returned home a different person and in some ways a better person because of the things I had experienced. No matter how much I may have wanted to leave Vietnam behind, it was impossible, because it was part of who I had become. The joys, the sorrows, the sounds, and the smells of war may fade with the passing of time, but they never really go away. The stench of war remains with those who have lived it.

Epilogue

"I love you, O LORD, my strength.
The Lord is my rock, my fortress and my deliverer;
my God is my rock, in whom I take refuge.
He is the shield and the horn of my salvation, my stronghold.
I call to the LORD who is worthy of praise,
and I am saved from my enemies."

Psalm 18:1-3

I remember nothing of the long flight home. The plane landed at McCord Air Force Base near Tacoma, Washington, and we were transported by bus to nearby Fort Lewis, where we spent all night going through more processing, being issued new uniforms, receiving a month's supply of anti-malaria pills, signing documents, including a pledge to take the pills we had just been issued, getting paid, and finally being released in the wee hours of the morning to go on leave. Dressed in my Class As, duffle bag in hand, I went to the bus station on base to catch a bus south to Portland, Oregon, a four- to five-hour ride with stops. The date was November 10th, 1970.

Arriving in Portland in the wee hours of the morning, I decided to sit in the coffee shop and wait until a more reasonable hour before taking a cab home. However, while sitting in the coffee shop, I met a fellow who offered to give me a ride. It was still fairly early when I got there. I don't remember the exact time, but my mom, step-dad, and step-sister were either just getting up or I woke them up. They were indeed surprised, so much so I don't think they knew what to say.

I kept my promise to visit Barbara, staying at her family's upstairs apartment above a doctor's office in Castro Valley. I slept on the couch in the living room.

There one morning, as I was washing up in the bathroom, I took the anti-malaria pills I had been given and tossed them into the garbage can. There can be no reasonable explanation as to why I would do something like that, especially when I had spent eight months as a line medic making sure my guys took theirs. I can only suggest it was an emotional attempt to put the Vietnam experience behind me. After all, in those days there was no counseling to help a person transition back into a normal life upon his return back home, no time to decompress or talk about what you had experienced. You could be on the battlefield one day, bullets flying all around you, and a week or two later be back home on leave. Even though I had gone on R&R and spent my last month in the rear in Vietnam, there was still no real decompression there. The realities of war were still all around me. It is no wonder so many Vietnam vets buried much of what they experienced never to talk about it again. After all, no one else could really understand.

The mixed emotions one has after returning from a combat zone are difficult to explain. Sometime after my return I wrote the following, though I have no idea exactly when, to whom, or why. I recently found it in a collection of my papers, a picture of a young South Vietnamese soldier photocopied in the upper right hand corner of the page.

Vietnam is a land filled with fear and despair. A country torn by war, its ground saturated with blood and its air filled with the sickening stench of death. As you walk through the streets of its villages, towns and cities you see its people in rags, their bodies covered with the scars of poverty, ignorance and the battle they have had to fight to stay alive. Very small children take care of the still smaller children. Many tend to the sacred family water buffalo and the cows they work in the rice paddies, and they beg the G.I.s continually for food. At fourteen years of age and sometimes younger many find themselves in the very midst of the battlefield, rifles in their hands and men in their sights; red, white, yellow, black. Now that I am safe at home I must wonder why I should care and even yearn to go back. Could it be that they need help and that once I gave it to them?

One day while on leave, my older brother and I went to visit our old high school. Walking back to the car parked on the curb, a car backfired and instantly I hit the ground. My brother just laughed, but to me it wasn't funny at all.

I finished my military commitment at Fort Lewis driving an ambulance on emergency calls, transporting patients, and even making morgue runs on occasion. We drove sedans to pick up officers coming in at the airport. On one occasion, I got to take a group of wounded warriors out to a very nice restaurant on Lake Union in downtown Seattle. The owner hosted a group from the hospital once a month after closing hours. The soldiers could order anything they wanted from the menu, and as their driver I reaped the benefits as well.

I bought a '66 Monterey Mercury sedan with red vinyl interior using the money I had saved during my year in Vietnam and used it to make the three-hour drive home every chance I got.

I spent a couple of weeks in the hospital being treated for malaria, the symptoms of which I began to experience while still on leave. There were two types of malaria contracted in Vietnam, one that was recurring and another that wasn't. They were unable to diagnose which type I had, so they treated me for both, but only after putting me in isolation and doing a myriad of tests for all kinds of mysterious tropical diseases. Fortunately it was the non-recurring type, as I have never had a relapse all these years.

Even though I was supposed to attend a company inspection at least once a month in my Class As, I never did. I even got called into the company office by the 1st Sgt. and was firmly informed of the policy. Yet it seemed I was either working or had gone home whenever they had those inspections, so I never showed up, and I never heard another word about it. In fact, I was awarded the Good Conduct Medal in orders cut on May 5th, 1971 for "exemplary behavior, efficiency, and fidelity during the period indicated."

On May 28th, 1971, I received an early discharge so I could go to work at the children's home in Hollywood. I believe the Lord rewarded me for my obedience to Him the first time I was offered the opportunity to work and live there.

Several months later, Barbara also came to work at the children's home as their secretary. We were married on June 24th, 1972, in Hayward, California. My cheek muscles literally ached that night from smiling so much throughout the day. It was one of the happiest days of my life.

In 1973, we moved back to my hometown in Oregon to invest ourselves in my home church. On November 1st, 1978, I entered full-time ministry, just two days after our first daughter, Amy, was born. (She was born on my birthday.) We were blessed with a second daughter, April, four years later on January 24th, just 14 days after Barb's birthday.

Barb and I spent over thirty years in ministry and raising our two wonderful daughters, who are now married and have children of their own. Early in our marriage she woke me from many a nightmare as I continued to process my experiences in Vietnam. Whenever a helicopter flew overhead I became distracted, and if it hung around very long I became agitated, so I took up helicopter modeling as therapy and Barb bought me models for my birthday and Christmas. Over time all of those symptoms dissipated, in part, I am convinced, because I have been able to talk about my experiences in the context of ministry, sharing the lessons God taught me on the battlefield.

After about 25 years, I began looking for the guys from my platoon to see what had happened to them. I did so by purchasing a CD of the White Pages for the entire U.S. and began searching for the names of guys based upon where they had come from. When I found someone with the same name or close to it, I sent them a postcard explaining I was looking for such and such a person who had served with me in Vietnam in 1st Platoon, Delta Co., 3/506, 101st Airborne Division in 1970. I asked if they were that person or knew where he was, would they please contact me.

The first person to call me was Mike Kosky, who had lost his leg to one of our automatic claymores. About a year later when I was on a family trip to his home state, he and I met at a truck stop for breakfast. He then told me this amazing story about what happened after he was evacuated. He was first taken to an emergency medical facility where he was stabilized. Then he was taken to a hospital for treatment. At the hospital, the doctors were apparently overwhelmed with casualties and were doing triage. They took one look at Mike and told the orderlies to set him aside in the hallway. Mike was conscious for this and realized they weren't going to treat him. Shortly thereafter he lost consciousness.

Sometime later Mike came to, and he was in a large room filled with stretchers. He could see the back of an officer going from stretcher to stretcher stopping at each one. Sitting up a little Mike said to the officer in his typical fashion, "Hey, man! What's up?" The officer turned around white as a sheet and went running out of the room screaming. Mike was in the morgue, and the officer was a chaplain giving last rights.

Now the doctors had to treat him. Rushing him to the operating room, the doctor looked at Mike just before putting the anesthesia mask over his face and said, "You know we're going to have to amputate both of your legs."

Mike told me he looked right back at the doctor and said, "If you're going to take off both of my legs you might as well put me right back in that morgue!"

The doctor relented and said, "Okay. We'll try to save one of them." Needless to say, they were successful, and Mike gets along today with an artificial leg and a cane on a little ranch in Tucson, Arizona. He also married and has a daughter.

Eventually I found 15 to 20 more of the guys I served with in 1st Platoon, including Lt. Greig, who has been a great help and encouragement to me in writing this book. Rudy Boykins, who lost an arm as a result of his injury on Hill 474, has seen his share of tragedy in life but has raised a family and is still married to the same woman he was married to before he went to Vietnam. He and his wife both love the Lord and are thankful for His many blessings in their lives. Lumpy survived his injuries and eventually married and adopted a son, as he could not have children due to his injuries. He worked many years for the Veterans Administration, helping injured Vietnam vets get their full disability benefits. He also came to put his faith in Christ and is one of the most loving Christian men I know. Rags, wounded in the Tiger Team operations, went on to become a lawyer in California. Don Meyer, who was shot in the foot in Cambodia, went on to become a successful businessman in Northern California and wrote his own book about his Vietnam experiences titled *The Protected Will Never Know*. Jeff Haggedorn, who was wounded in Cambodia, retired as a state trooper and now paints houses. A number of us have gotten together a few times for reunions and hope to do so again. Others showed no interest in connecting, preferring to leave Vietnam in the past.

In June 2006, after serving in a variety of ministries, Barbara and I started a ministry to the military. On November 28th, 2009, Barbara went to her heavenly home, joining her dear mother, after a seven-year battle with an incurable cancer. Never did she waiver in her faith, and throughout her illness she continued to be a blessing and encouragement to me and many others.

Today I continue to serve in ministry reaching out to the military, sharing my story whenever I can, demonstrating once again God can use anyone, even an unlikely warrior like me. To learn more about my ministry, or to arrange a speaking engagement, you can contact me at unlikelywarrior@cox.net.

Glossary

AK-47	Soviet-made rifles most commonly used by the NVA and VC
Ambl.	Airmobile
Article 15	A form of administrative discipline handed down by a commanding officer
ARVN	Army of the Republic of Vietnam
AO	Area of Operation
Blocking Force	A unit or units strategically placed to prevent enemy escape
Boonie-Rat	A term used to refer to the soldier living in the jungles, rice paddies, and mountains of Vietnam, the boonies. I am sure we probably smelled like rats at times when we went long periods without a bath or shower.
CA	Combat Assault
CC	Command and Control
Charlie	1. In military speak the letter "C" in the alphabet, as in "Charlie Company." 2. A term used to refer primarily to the Viet Cong but sometimes used in a more generic sense to refer to the enemy in general.
Cherry	A soldier who had not yet experienced combat and therefore was still regarded as a "virgin" in that respect
Chicom	Made in Communist China

Chinook	A large two-rotor helicopter used to transport troops and equipment
CP	Command Post
Cobra	A fast attack helicopter gunship
Currahee	A Cherokee word meaning "Stand Alone"
DDP	Daytime Defensive Position
DD214	Discharge papers given to a serviceman upon his release from service
DEROS	Date of Expected Return from Over Seas
Dust-off	Another term used for a medevac helicopter or the evacuation of a soldier by medevac
Dicks	A term used to refer both to Viet Cong and NVA soldiers, also sometimes called "dinks"
Fire-team	Usually a team of two or three riflemen assigned to a task, as opposed to a squad which consisted of five or six men
FO	Forward Observer, a soldier who would coordinate mortar and artillery strikes
Gook	A derogatory term used to refer to the VC and NVA
GI	Government Issue, a term used from WWII to refer to U.S. troops, primarily soldiers
Grunt	A field solider or Marine, so called because of the heavy backpacks they carry causing them to make a grunting sound when they get up off of the ground wearing all of their gear.
HHC	Headquarters and Headquarters Company.
Hogg	A Huey helicopter equipped with rocket launchers, small cannons and

	machine guns for prepping landing zones or giving air support to troops on the ground.
Hootch	A hut or hutch usually constructed of bamboo poles and a thatched roof, some were very simple, while others were much more complex
Hump	To hike, usually with your heavy gear on, but can also refer to hiking with light battle equipment only. Humping implies carrying a load, whereas hiking sounds too much like a stroll in the woods. Thus, the soldier does not hike but humps.
KIA	Killed in Action
Kill Zone	The area in an ambush designed for maximum effectiveness in killing the enemy using claymore mines, grenades, machinegun, and small arms fire. This is the area you want the enemy to walk into to be killed.
KP	Kitchen Patrol
LBE	Light Battle Equipment
LRRP	Long Range Reconnaissance Patrol, usually six men who would go out for a couple of weeks at a time to reconnoiter enemy positions. Because of their small size, their purpose was not to engage the enemy so much as it was to gather intelligence. These teams were part of our Echo Company.
LOcH	A small, light observation helicopter, usually an OH-6A Cayuse
LTC	Lieutenant Colonel, one rank above a Major

LZ	Landing Zone
Lt.	Lieutenant, also seen as LT
M-16	Automatic and semi-automatic rifle carried by most U.S. troops in Vietnam
M-79	A short barreled grenade launcher that looked similar to a sawed-off shotgun
Medevac	A helicopter used to evacuate the sick and wounded from the field. For the Army these were usually Hueys. Also called "slicks."
NCO	Non-Commissioned Officer
NDP	Night Defensive Position
NVA	North Vietnamese Army
PX	Post Exchange
PZ	Pickup Zone
OPCON	Operational Control
Platoon	A small unit of 25 to 35 soldiers. Each line company was made up of three platoons for a total of 80 to 100 men. Platoons would sometimes have as few as 17 or 18 men if they had suffered a lot of losses or had a lot of men out sick or on R&R. In Vietnam the numbers constantly fluctuated with tours being completed and attrition from sickness and injuries. As new recruits came in the numbers would build back up.
SEARTS	Screaming Eagles Army Replacement Training Station
RPG	Rocket Propelled Grenades
R&R	Rest and Recuperation, a two-week leave given to soldiers during their Vietnam Tour
RTO	Radio Telephone Operator
SITREP	Situation Report

Slicks	Huey helicopters used to transport troops
Spec.	Specialist, the rank used for medics higher than Private, as in Spec. 4, Spec 5, Spec. 6, *etc*. Also, Spc.
SVN	South Vietnam
TET	"Tết, or Vietnamese New Year, is the most important celebration of Vietnamese culture. The word is a shortened form of Tết Nguyên Đán. It features aspects of the western Thanksgiving, New Year's Day, Halloween, and Birthday. It is the Vietnamese New Year marking the arrival of spring based on the Chinese calendar, a lunisolar calendar" (Wikipedia). Though a cease fire was usually negotiated during this time, it was also a favorite time for the VC and NVA to launch major offensive operations, such as the TET offensive of 1968.
Tunnel Rat	A reference to a soldier who went into caves to search for the enemy and his supplies. Because the cave entrances were often quite small, it sometimes fell to smaller men in a platoon to undertake this job.
USO	United Service Organizations
VC	Viet Cong
WIA	Wounded in Action

BIBLIOGRAPHY

As a memoir, this book is first and foremost a recollection of my own experiences in Vietnam supported by the many letters I wrote to loved ones. I am extremely grateful to my mother and my departed wife, Barbara, for saving all of those letters, along with articles, documents, and orders I sent home. However, I also found the following sources invaluable in providing information beyond my own knowledge that helped flesh out the larger story.

BOOKS
Berry, Jerald W., and Joe R. Alexander. *The Stand Alone Battalion: A Pictorial Chronology of the 3-506 Vietnam Odyssey (1967-1971)*. Kalispell, MT: Scott, 2002. Print.

Berry, Jerald W. *Twelve Days in May, the Untold Story of the Northern Thrust into Cambodia by 4th Infantry Division (Operation Binh Tay) in May 1970*. Bloomington, IN: Xlibris, 2010. Print.

Family Encyclopedia of American History. Pleasantville, NY: Reader's Digest Association, 1975. Print.

Meyer, Donald P. *The Protected Will Never Know*. Lincoln, NE: IUniverse,, 2003. Print.

AN UNPUBLISHED STORY
Nauman, John B. "Rags,". Aka "Rags," *Tiger Team Operation*.

PUBLISHED AND UNPUBLISHED GOVERNMENT DOCUMENTS:
3 Battalion 506th Infantry
Operational Report – Lessons Learned of 3rd Battalion (ambl), 506th Abn Infantry for Period Ending 31 January 1970, RCS CSFOR-65 (R2). 1 February 1970.
Operational Report – Lessons Learned of 3rd Battalion (ambl), 506th Abn Infantry for Period Ending 30 April 1970, RCS CSFOR-65 (R2). 10 May 1970.
3rd Battalion (Airborne), 506th Infantry (CURRAHEES) 1st Brigade, 101st Airborne Division (Screaming Eagles), VIETNAM History 1 January 1970-31 December 1970, Published by S-3.

PERIODICALS
Firebase 173 newspaper, March 16th, 1970 ed. Published by the 173rd Airborne Division, U.S. Army.
The Screaming Eagle newspaper, March 30th ed. Published by the 101st Airborne Division, U.S. Army.

CPSIA information can be obtained at www.ICGtesting.com
Printed in the USA
LVOW08s0938180414

382281LV00001B/117/P